Facets of

Ancient Indian History and Culture

Reconstructing Indian History & Culture
(ISSN 0971-3824)

1. Society in Ancient India by Sures Chandra Banerji (ISBN 81-246-0000-7)
2. Political Thought in Ancient India by G.P. Singh (ISBN 81-246-0001-5)
3. Early Indian Historical Tradition and Archaeology by G.P. Singh (ISBN 81-246-0005-8)
4. Vasantotsava: The Spring Festivals of India by Leona M. Anderson (ISBN 81-246-0011-2)
5. Ecological Readings in the Veda by M. Vannucci (ISBN 81-246-0009-0)
6. Vr̥ndāvana in Vaiṣṇava Literature by Maura Corcoran (ISBN 81-246-0024-4)
7. Social History of the Tamils (1707-1947) by P. Subramanian (ISBN 81-246-0045-7)
8. Ancient Indian Coinage by Rekha Jain (ISBN 81-246-0051-1)
9. Buddhism and Socio-Economic Life of Eastern India by Bimal Chandra Mohapatra (ISBN 81-246-0055-4)
10. Chandragupta Maurya by P.L. Bhargava (ISBN 81-246-0056-2)
11. Mr̥tyu: Concept of Death in Indian Traditions by Gian Giuseppe Filippi (ISBN 81-246-0072-4)
12. Yama: The Glorious Lord of the Other World by Kusum P. Merh (ISBN 81-246-0066-X)
13. Sacred Complex of Ujjain by D.K Samanta (ISBN 81-246-0078-3)
14. Vedic View of the Earth by S.R.N. Murthy (ISBN 81-246-0091-0)
15. Society in the Atharvaveda by B.S. Kharade (ISBN 81-246-0093-7)
16. Orissan History, Culture and Archaeology by S. Pradhan (ISBN 81-246-0117-8)
17. Education in Ancient India by Mitali Chatterjee (ISBN 81-246-0113-5)
18. Surā: the Liquor and the Vedic Sacrifice by M.B. Kolhatkar (ISBN 81-246-0114-3)
19. Human Ecology in the Vedas by Marta Vannucci (ISBN 81-246-0115-1)
20. Governance in Ancient India by Anup Chandra Pandey (ISBN 81-246-0135-6)
21. The Cultural Glory of Ancient India: A Literary Overview by Sures Chandra Banerji (ISBN 81-246-0137-2)
22. Kauṭilya's Arthaśāstra in the light of Modern Science & Technology; by Sunil Sen Sarma (ISBN 81-246-0187-9)
23. History of Jainism — with Special Reference to Mathura by V.K. Sharma (ISBN 81-246-0195-X)
24. Cultural Tourism in India: Museums, Monuments & Arts — Theory and Practice; by S. P. Gupta; Krishna Lal; Mahua Bhattacharyya (ISBN 81-246-0215-8)
25. Ancient Indian Historiography — Sources and Interpretations by G.P. Singh (ISBN 81-246-0228-X)
26. Republics, Kingdoms, Towns and Cities in Ancient India by G.P. Singh (ISBN 81-246-0237-9)

Reconstructing Indian History & Culture, no. 27

Facets of Ancient Indian History and Culture

New Perception

by

G.P. Singh

D.K. Printworld (P) Ltd.
New Delhi

Cataloging in Publication Data — DK

Singh, G. P. (Girish Prasad), 1942 –
Facets of ancient Indian history and culture.
Includes bibliographical references (p.)
Includes index.

1. India — History — To 324 BC. 2. India — History — 324 BC - 1000 AD. 3. India — Civilization — To 1200. I. Title.

ISBN 81-246-0238-7

First published in India in 2003

D. K. Printworld (P) Ltd.
Regd. office : *'Sri Kunj'*, F-52, Bali Nagar
New Delhi - 110 015
Phones : (011) 2545-3975; 2546-6019
Fax : (011) 2546-5926
E-mail: dkprintworld@vsnl.net
Web: www.dkprint.com

Preface

THIS volume is an anthology of my writings on some aspects of ancient Indian history and culture, both published and unpublished, which are arranged thematically and divided into three parts. The writings are based on my researches of last one-and-a-half decade. A new theory has been propounded about the origin and expansion of the Āryans. The Cīnas very often mentioned along with the Kirātas in ancient Indian literature and inscriptions have not received the attention they deserve. They have been properly indentified on the basis of the data available to us. And fresh light has been thrown on their origin and antiquity. The essays appearing in part two form parts of social, economic and religious history of ancient India. In the first essay of part three, an attempt has been made to prove on the basis of the data discovered by me that north-western India came under foreign attack even before the Persians. In the second and last essay of this part, light has been thrown on the political status of Assam in the Gupta age. Both the essays form parts of political history of ancient India.

I selected only those areas of ancient Indian history for my study and research in which there was scope for contributing something new. It is for the readers to judge as to how far I have succeeded in my attempt. The author shall consider his labour amply rewarded if this volume is found useful by scholars interested in ancient Indian history and culture.

The author craves the readers' indulgence for all the errors that may have crept into the volume.

G.P. Singh

Acknowledgements

I ACKNOWLEDGE my deep sense of gratitude to Prof S.D. Laddu, editor, *Annals of the Bhandarkar Oriental Research Institute*, Poona, for granting me permission to include the paper : "Ancient Indian Religious System in the times of Manu and Patañjali" publised in it (LXXV, 1994) in the present volume. I am equally grateful to Dr Heramb Chaturvedi, the chief editor, *Adhyayan, Journal of the Bhāratīya Itihāsa Adhyayan Saṁsthān,* Allahabad, for permitting me to include the papers: "India from Ariana to the Gaṅgā Valley" and "The Origin, Antiquity and Identification of the Cīnas as Depicted in Ancient Indian Literature and Inscriptions" published in it (II, 2, 1992; V,1 & 2,1995 respectively) in this volume. The first of the latter two has been included in revised and enlarged form.

I would also like to express my sincere thanks to all those scholars whose works I have utilised in my writings.

Contents

Abbreviations

ABORI	*Annals of the Bhandarkar Oriental Resarch Institute,* Poona.
Agn.	*Agni Purāṇa.*
AICL	*Ancient India as Described in Classical Literature.*
AIHA	*Aspects of Indian History and Archaeology.*
AIHT	*Ancient Indian Historical Tradition.*
AIIC	*Ancient India and Indian Civilization,* by P. Masson-Oursel & C.
AIMA	*Ancient India as Described by Megasthenes and Arrian.*
AISH	*Ancient Indian Social History.*
Ait.Br.	*Aitareya Brāhmaṇa.*
Anab.	*Anabasis (History of Alexander's Expedition),* by Arrian.
Antiquity	*A Quarterly Review of Archaeology,* Cambridge, England.
Āp.Dh.S.	*Āpastamba Dharmasūtra.*
ARAB	*Ancient Records of Assyria and Babylon.*
Ar.Ant.	*Ariana Antiqua,* by H.H. Wilson.
ARNWI	*Archaeological Reconnaissances in North-Western India and South-Eastern Iran,* by M.A. Stein.
Arth.	*Arthaśāstra of Kauṭilya.*
ASB	Asiatic Society of Bengal, Calcutta.
A.S.Res.	*Asiatic Researches (Comprising History and Antiquities, the Arts, Sciences, Ethnology and Literature of Asia).*
AV	*Atharvaveda.*
Baudh.Dh.S.	*Baudhyāyana Dharmasūtra.*

BGP	Bhāratiya Jñānapīṭha, Kāśī.
Bhāg.	*Bhāgavata Purāṇa.*
Bh.Sāv. (or *Bh.Sv*)	*Bhārata Sāvitri* (*An in-depth historical study of the Mahābhārata*), by V.S. Agrawala.
Bhv.	*Bhaviṣya Purāṇa.*
BI	*Buddhist India.*
BIS	*Bibliotheca Indica Series* (a Collection of Oriental Works), Asiatic Society, Calcutta.
Bmd.	*Brahmāṇḍa Purāṇa.*
BORI	Bhandarkar Oriental Research Institute, Poona.
Br. (or *Brh*)	*Brahma Purāṇa.*
Br. Sam	*Brhat* (*Vārāhī*) *Saṁhitā.*
BSOAS	*Bulletin of the School of Oriental and African Studies,* London
CAGI	Cunningham's *Ancient Geography of India.*
CAH	*Cambridge Ancient History.*
CAI	Classical Accounts of India (a compilation of the English translations of the Early Greek and Roman Writers' accounts of India), by R.C. Majumdar.
CCIM	*Catalogue of the Coins in the Indian Museum,* Calcutta, *Coins of Ancient India*, vol. 1, by V.A. Smith.
CHI	*Cambridge History of India*, vol. I, *Ancient India.*
Chro.Anct.Ind.	*Chronology of Ancient India.*
CII (or *Corp. Ins. Ind.*)	*Corpus Inscriptionum Indicarum.*
CNES	*Commerce and Navigation of the Erythraean Sea*, by J.W. McCrindle.
Co.An.Ind.	*Coins of Ancient India from the Earliest times down to the Seventh Century* AD, by A. Cunningham.

Com.Hist.Ind.	*Comprehensive History of India.*
DPPN	*Dictionary of Pālī Proper Names*, by G.P. Malalasekera.
EAB	*Ethnology of Ancient Bhārata.*
EAI	*Ethnography of Ancient India.*
EB (or *En. Br.*)	*Encyclopaedia Britannica.*
EHI	*Early History of India*, by V.A. Smith, rev. by S.M. Edwards, 4th edn.
EHIDS	*Early Hindu India : A Dynastic Study.*
EIHTA	*Early Indian Historical Tradition and Archaeology.*
EIP	*Early India and Pakistan to Ashoka,* by M. Wheeler.
EP.Ind.	*Epigraphia Indica,* Delhi.
E'tude.	*E'tude Sur la Geographie Grecque et Latine de l' Inde* (Geography of India as Derived from the Greek and Latin Sources), by M.V. de St. Martin.
fn.	footnote.
Gau.Dh.S.	*Gautama Dharma Sūtra.*
GDAMI	*Geographical Dictionary of Ancient and Medieval India,* by N.L. Dey.
GDEP	*A Critical Study of the Geographical Data in the Early Pirāṇas*
GEB	*Geography of Early Buddhism*, by B.C. Law, Vārāṇasī, 1973.
GEM (or *GESM*)	*Geographical & Economic Studies in the Mahābhārata*, *Upāyana Parva*, by Motichandara.
Geographical Essays	*Geographical Essays Relating to Ancient Geography of India, by* B. C. Law.
Geog.Jour	*Geographical Journal,* London.
GSH	*Geographical System of Herodotus.*
HA	*History of Antiquity*, trans. from the German of Max Duncker by E. Abbott.

HAG	*History of Ancient Geography Among the Greeks and Romans from the Earliest Ages till the Fall of the Roman Empire*, by E.H. Bunbury.
HAI	*History of Ancient India.*
HASA	*Historical Atlas of South Asia.*
HASL	*History of Ancient Sanskrit Literature*, by F. Max Müller.
HCSL	*History of Classical Sanskrit Literature.*
HDAI	*Historical Disquisition Concerning Ancient India.*
HGAI	*Historical Geography of Ancient India,* by B.C. Law.
HHW	*Historians' History of the World* (A Comprehensive Narrative of the Rise and Development of Nations as Recorded by the Great Writers of All Ages).
HIL	*History of Indian Literature.*
Historical Researches	*Historical Researches into the Politics, Intercourse and Trade of the Principal Nations of Antiquity.*
HOS	Harvard Oriental Series.
HPL	*History of Pāli Literature*, by B.C. Law.
Hv.	*Harivaṁśa Purāṇa.*
IC	*Indian Culture — Journal of the Indian Resarch Institute*, Calcutta.
IETBJ	*India as Described in Early Texts of Buddhism and Jainism.*
IGI (or *Imp. Gaz. Ind*)	*Imperial Gazetteer of India.*
IHQ	*Indian Historical Quarterly*, Calcutta, new rpt., Delhi.
IHR	*Indian Historical Review.* Journal of the Indian Council of Historical Research, Delhi.
Ind.Alt.	*Indische Alterthumskunde* (A German work on the History and Antiquities of India), by C. Lassen.
Ind. Ant.	*Indian Antiquary* (*Journal of Oriental Research in Archaeology, History, Literature, Language, Folklore, etc.*), Bombay.

JA	*Journal Asiatique*, Paris.
JAOS	*Journal of the American Oriental Society.*
JARS	*Journal of the Assam Research Society*, Gauhati.
JASB	*Journal of the Asiatic Society of Bengal,* Calcutta.
Jāt.	*Jātaka.*
JBBRAS	*Journal of the Bombay Branch of the Royal Asiatic Society,* Bombay.
JBIAS	*Journal of the Bhāratīya Itihāsa Adhyayan Saṁsthān*, Allahabad.
JBORS	*Journal of the Bihar and Orissa Research Society*, Patna.
JDRI	*Journal of Deendayal Research Institute*, Delhi.
JGIS	*Journal of the Greater India Society,* Calcutta.
JGRI	*Journal of the Ganganath Jha Research Institute,* Allahabad.
JIH	*Journal of Indian History*, Trivandrum.
JISOA	*Journal of the Indian Society of Oriental Art*, Calcutta.
JOR	*Journal of Oriental Research*, Madras.
JPASB	*Journal and Proceedings of the Asiatic Society of Bengal,* Calcutta.
JRAI	*Journal of the Royal Anthropological Institute of Great Britain and Ireland,* London.
JRAS	*Journal of the Royal Asiatic Society of Great Britain and Ireland,* London.
JRASMB	*Journal of the Royal Asiatic Society, Malayan Branch,* Singapore.
JRGS	*Journal of the Royal Geographical Society*, London.
Km. (or *Krm*)	*Kūrma Purāṇa.*
LAIJC	*Life in Ancient India as Depicted in the Jaina Canon and Commentaries.*
Lg.	*Liṅga Purāna.*
Mahā.	*Mahāpurāṇa.*
MAICL	McCrindle's *Ancient India as Described in Classical Literature.*

MAIMA	McCrindle's *Ancient India as Described by Megasthenes and Arrian.*
MAIT	McCrindle's *Ancient India as Described by Ptolemy.*
Manu.	*Manu-Smṛti.*
MASI	*Memoirs of the Archaeological Survey of India,* Calcutta.
Mass.	Massachusetts, USA.
Mat (or *Mts.*)	*Matsya Purāṇa.*
Mbh.	*Mahābhārata.*
Mbh.Ko.	*Mahābhārata Kośa* (*A Descriptive Index to the Names and Subjects in the Mahābhārata*), by R.K. Rai.
MDJG	Manikchand Digambara Jaina Granthamālā Series, Bombay.
Mkd.	*Mārkaṇḍeya Purāṇa.*
Nat.Hist. (or *Hist. Nat.*)	*Naturalis Historia* (*Natural History*) *or Historia Naturalis* (*History Natural*), by Pliny.
OUP	Oxford University Press.
PAPDI	*Pre-Aryan and Pre-Dravidian in India* (Eng. trans. of Original French articles by Sylvain Levi, Przyluski & c), by P.C. Bagchi.
PASB	*Proceedings of the Asiatic Society of Bengal,* Calcutta.
Periplus	*Periplus of the Erythraean Sea*, trans from the Greek and annotated by W.H. Schoff.
PHAI	*Political History of Ancient India*, by H.C. Raychaudhuri, 6th edn.
PIOC	*Proceedings* (*or Transactions*) *of the International Oriental Congress.*
PK	*Paurāṇic Kośa*, by R.P. Sharma.
POC	*Proceedings of the All India Oriental Conference.*
PPIP	*Prehistory and Protohistory of India and Pakistan.*
PTS	Pāli Text Society, London.
Purāṇa	Half yearly Bulletin of the Purāṇa Department, All India Kāśīrāj Trust, Rāmnagar, Vārāṇasī.

QRHS	*Quarterly Review of Historical Studies*, Calcutta.
RANIT or *RENIT*	*Racial Affinities of Early North Indian Tribes.*
RPICO	*Report of the Proceedings of the Second International Congress of Orientalists.*
RTGEA	*Researches on Ptolemy's Geography of Eastern Asia.*
R̥V	*R̥gveda.*
Śat. Br.	*Śatapatha Brāhmaṇa.*
SBA	*Sacred Books of the Aryan Series,* Delhi.
SBB	*Secred Books of the Buddhists.*
SBE	*Secred Books of the East*, Oxford.
SGAMI	*Studies in the Geography of Ancient and Medieval India.*
SI	*Select Inscriptions Bearing on Indian History and Civilization.*
Tai. Aran.	*Taittirīya Āraṇyaka.*
Taitt. Br.	*Taittirīya Brāhmaṇa.*
Taitt. Saṁ	*Taittiriya Saṁhitā.*
v	Verse.
Vāj. Saṁ	*Vājasaneya Saṁhitā.*
Vāl. Rām.	*Vālmīki-Rāmāyaṇa.*
Vāl. Rām.Ko.	*Vālmīki-Rāmāyaṇa Kośa* (Descriptive Index to the Names and Subjects of *Rāmāyaṇa*), by R.K. Rai.
Vas. Dh. S.	*Vasiṣṭha Dharmasūtra.*
VE	Vikrama Era.
VI	*Vedic Index of Names and Subjects*, by A.A. Macdonell and A.B. Keith.
Vmn. or *Vām.*	*Vāmana Purāṇa.*
VS	Vikrama Samvat.

Vṣṇ	*Viṣṇu Purāṇa.*
vv.	verses.
Vy	*Vāyu Purāṇa.*
YCTI	*Yuan Chwang's Travels in India* (AD 629-45), by Thomas Watters.

Introduction

Introduction

THE construction and reconstruction of a subject are the two distinct phases of study and research and manifestations of a productive exercise and progressive knowledge.

It is undeniable that both Indian and foreign scholars have made substantial contributions in the past to the discovery of history and culture of ancient India. And researches are still being carried out by some of them on the subject. However, there is still an ample scope to throw fresh light on some of the phases and facets of ancient Indian history. There are still some broken chains in our existing knowledge about the subject which can be restored with the help of new findings and new discoveries. Historical perceptions are changing in the light of fresh study and research on the subject. Many new evidences have come to fore which need fresh interpretations. In recent past, many new facts have come to light which necessitates the historical reconstruction.

The origin and expansion of the Āryans have long been a controversial and debatable subject. Several scholars, both Indian and foreign, including philologists, ethnologists, historians, archaeologists and indologists have worked on it during the past two centuries. The results of the researches are both positive and negative.

Filippo Sassetti, a merchant of Florence (Italy), stayed in Goa for five years (1583-88), studied some of the principal languages of Asia and Europe and declared for the first time that there existed a close relation between Sanskrit and some European languages. The scholars have not taken any notice of it because of vagueness of expression.

The science of comparative philology, which had come into existence towards the close of the eighteenth century, actually contained the seeds of Āryan controversy. The seeds virtually sprouted in early nineteenth century and gradually developed into a tree with several stems and branches which have almost dried up now but its root still remains.

In 1786, Sir William Jones, the famous English orientalist, in his presidential address to the Asiatic Society of Bengal, Calcutta (founded by him in 1784 for the promotion of oriental learning), pointed out that the similarities between Sanskrit, German, Greek, Latin and Celtic could be established on the assumption that these languages had "a common parentage" or common origin. Hegel later called it "the discovery of a new world." However, this discovery, which was nothing more than a hypothesis, did not immediately ignite the spark of Āryan controversy. The term Indo-European which included the said languages was first used by Thomas Young in 1813. Franz Bopp, the famous German philologist, included the Zend, the language of ancient Persians, in 1816, and later the Slavonic, the language of Slavs, in the Indo-European family of languages. The Slavic was added to the languages of this family first by Rask of Denmark in 1818. Bopp after having made a comparative study of all the seven languages of the said family found that they were closely related to each other. The publication of his *Comparative Grammar* in 1835 placed comparative philology on a firmer ground or "scientific footing." In fact, he in his said work built the first superstructure of comparative philology on its foundations laid by William Jones. That is why he has been called the "real founder of the science of comparative philology."

The celebrated German grammarian, Adelung (who died in 1806), placed the cradle of mankind in the valley of Kashmir. He has traced back the antiquity of original common language to the time of earliest human habitation in Kashmir. His view, that the human race originated in the East, became widely prevalent. The famous Indian scholar, L.D. Kalla, also took Kashmir and the Himālayan region as the homeland of the Āryans.

The German scholar, Friedrich Schlegel, in his *Essays on Language and Wisdom of the Indians* (published in 1808) categorically stated that peoples' movement was from the East (northern India) to the West. By 1819-20 he was unequivocal in his statement about Asiatic origin of the Āryans. He, however, did not draw any positive conclusion.

The theory based on supposition that the human race originated in Asia in comparison to Europe at a much later period was accepted by V. Kennedy in 1828 as appears from his *Researches into the Origin and Affinity of the Principal Languages of Europe and Asia*, and later by other scholars.

The comparative linguistic evidence adduced by some European philologists of the nineteenth century in support of the foreign origin of the Āryans may be taken as the root cause of the whole Āryan problem. By establishing the similarities between the seven principal languages — Greek, Latin, German, Celtic, Slavonic, Sanskrit and Zend — of so-called Āryan or Indo-European family, and by placing the ancestors of the Indians, the Persians, the Greeks, the Romans, the Slaves, the Celts, and the Germans in a common home in Asia or Europe and by arguing that they had same forms of speech or were speakers of a primitive Āryan language and by showing their diffusion or dispersion from their original common home following their division and separation towards their respective countries sometime between *c.* 2500 BC and 1500 BC, they propounded the Āryan race and migration theory. But they failed to give satisfactory explanations about Āryan speech and the cradle of the Āryans. They are divided in their opinion regarding the exact location of said common home the reason for which is not far to discover. The speakers of Āryan languages have been clubbed together as an Āryan race which never existed as such. The philological and ethnological explanations regarding the identification of an Āryan language with an Āryan race are conflicting. The similarities of few words do not necessarily constitute a proof of common origin of their speakers, rather they indicate their commingling and socio-cultural contacts and fellowship. The theory of a common home of the members of so-called Āryan family whether in Asia or Europe cannot be accepted merely on the evidence of linguistic palaeontology.

The hypothesis, that Central Asia was the cradle of the Indo-European race, which for half a century was generally accepted, was first propounded in 1820 by J.G. Rhode. His argument was based on the geographical indications given in the first chapter of the *Vendidad* of the *Avesta*. Bākhdhī (Bactria), one of the sixteen place names described in the text, was taken by him as the earlier home of the Persians or Iranians. But the fact remains that in the contemporary geographical setting, Bāhlika (old Persian Bākhtri = Greek Bactria) was a part of north-western India and not of Central Asia. Some places of Central Asia are, of course, included in the said text, but they are not the places of original settlements of the ancestors of so-called Persian or Iranian Āryans but the places where one of their sections later migrated after living their original homeland in Hapta-Hindu (Sapta-Sindhu) region.

The Central Asian hypothesis was propounded also by W. von Schlegel, Pott, Lassen, Grimm, Schleicher, Spiegel, Max Müller and other scholars of Europe. They have advocated more or less the same theory so far as the Asiatic origin of the Āryans is concerned. All of them were of the view that it was Asia from where the Āryans wandered to the West. The highlands of Central Asia — the region of the sources of Oxus and Jaxartes — was generally held to be original home of the primeval Āryans. The noted German scholar, Pott, while expounding the Central Asian origin of the Āryans, asserted that the region watered by the Oxus and Jaxartes, north of the Himālaya and east of the Caspian Sea(-Europe-Asia), was the true cradle of the Indo-European (Āryan) race. It was his firm belief that "migration has always followed the sun's course, westward from the East." In 1847, Lassen supported the view of Pott on the ground that "the Sanskrit people must have penetrated into the Punjab from the north-west through Kabul, and that the traditions of the *Avesta* point to the slopes of the Belurtag and the Mustag as the place of their earlier sojourn." He further assumed that before their separation the Indo-Iranians inhabited the steppes between the Oxus and the Jaxartes. In 1848, Jacob Grimm declared that "all the nations of Europe migrated anciently from Asia. . . ."

Some of the propounders of the Central Asian origin of the Āryans surmised that the Āryan home must have been somewhere in the region of the Caspian Sea (i.e., the steppes of Lower Russia). Some scholars have opined that Bactria was the homeland of the Āryans as they had migrated from here eastward, westward and southward.

The Genevan philologist, Adolphe Pictet, in the first volume of his *Les Origines Indo-Europ'eennes Ousles Aryas Primitifs Essai de Paleontologie Linguistique* (published in 1859) constructed an elaborate theory of the successive migrations of so-called European Āryans from Central Asia. According to him, the Hellenes and Italians migrated "by a route south of the Caspian through Asia Minor to Greece and Italy, and the Celts south of the Caspian through the Caucasus to the north of the Black Sea, and then up the Danube to the extreme west of Europe; the Slaves and Teutons marching north of the Caspian through the Russian steppes." His arguments were based on philological speculations. However, his view was endorsed by Schleicher. In 1862, he also propounded the theory of the successive migrations of the so-called Āryan races from the east. He writes in his *Compendium* that "The home of the original Indo-Germanic race is to be sought in the central highlands of Asia." "The Slavo-Teutonic races first began their journeyings towards the west; then followed the Graeco-Italo-Celtic peoples; of the Āryans who remained behind, the Indians travelled south-eastward, and the Iranians spread in a south-westerly direction."

Another distinguished philologist, Professor A.H. Sayce, wrote in 1874: "When the Āryan languages first make their appearance it is in the highlands of Middle Asia, between the sources of the Oxus and Jaxartes," which is recorded in his *Principles of Comparative Philology*. This theory was approved by some of the eminent European scholars without making a thorough investigation into it. In 1880, when Benfey and Geiger expressed their reluctance to accept such hypothesis, Professor Sayce justified the reason of placing "the primeval Āryan community in Bactriana, on the western slopes of the Belurtag and the Mustag, and near the sources of the Oxus and Jaxartes," as we find in his *Introduction to the Science of Language* (vol. II, 1883). However, it appears to us a mere postulation. He argued that on the testimony of comparative philology the Asiatic origin of the Āryan languages can be established. His belief that the region occupied by the speakers of Sanskrit and Zend must have been the nearest to the primitive centre of dispersion was based on the tradition (of a legendary nature) recorded in the *Avesta* that the first creation of mankind by Ahura-Mazda took place in the Bactrian region. He, however, admitted that this legend is applicable only to the Zoroastrian Persians.

The statements of the learned author, Professor Sayce, "that Sanskrit and Zend are the most archaic of the Āryan languages, and that the cradle of the Indo-Iranians must also be the cradle of the Āryans," are nearer to the truth.

The noted Indian scholar, R.L. Mitra, also joined the debate on the original homeland of the Āryans in 1870s. In one of his essays bearing the title "The Primitive Āryans," which appeared in second volume of his *Indo-Āryans* (published in 1881), he has stated that ". . . if we admit a primitive language as the parent of the Greek, the Latin, and the Teutonic languages on the one hand, and of the Sanskrit, the Zend, and the Ostiak on the other, we must also admit that the different peoples who speak those languages are related to each other by blood, and descended from a common stock. A language could not spread over so vast a tract as the best portion of Europe and a good part of Asia, without the nation which spoke it spreading likewise. . . . The hypothesis, therefore, must at once be conceded that there was not only a primitive language from which Indo-European languages have descended, but also a primitive race which spread that language over different parts of the earth." This hypothesis of the European philologists is not worthy of our acceptance. In his further elucidation of the subject, particularly about the original home of the Āryans, he has asserted that ". . . the word Ārya is some form or other appears to have been the name of the race. And if the tribal name may be associated with the original home of the race, seeing that such was the case almost invariable in ancient times, that home must have been situated along the Hindu Kush, or the tract to the south of a line extending from Herat to Balkh and the western slopes of the Belurtag and Mustag, near the sources of the Oxus and the Jaxartes, where Greek writers trace the site of ancient Aria." Following the philological line of arguments he has also upheld the theory of successive migrations and dispersion of different Āryan groups from their original home. He has opined that the Āryans had occupied a great portion of Afghanistan before the time of Zoroaster, and made it an integral part of ancient Aria. They "confined themselves to the country north of the Hindu Kush (i.e., Bactria)." The present writer is not in agreement with him so far as the use of the word race or tribe for the Āryans, and extension of the territory of Āryan original home to the highlands of Central Asia are concerned.

E. Herzfeld in his *Iran in the Ancient East* (1941) has also propounded the hypothesis that from the third to the mid-second millennium BC the Indo-Europeans had inhabited as an undivided ethnical group the vast plains of the Oxus and the Jaxartes in Central Asia ("*Eranvej* of the two rivers Vahvi-Datiya and Ranha"), which was their original or common home. After their separation they were divided into two groups. The bigger group (called European Āryans) moved towards Europe and the smaller called Indo-Iranians after having lived together at some place for a considerable period of time became further divided into two branches, one entering Persia and the other India.

It is worthy of remark that those scholars who advocated the theory that the land between the two rivers — Oxus (Vaṁkṣu of the *Mahābhārata*) and Jaxartes (Sītā of the Purāṇas) — was the cradle of the Āryans included Bāhlika, a place of Vedic antiquity, in Central Asia without taking into account the contemporary geography and history of north-western India. Bāhlika on the Vaṁkṣu formed an integral part of greater north-western India in the Vedic age. It was not a part of Central Asia. It was the epicentre or original seat of the Vedic Āryans. Their ancestors in the valley of the Vaṁkṣu were originally Indians. The land on the other side or north of the river Vaṁkṣu (Oxus) generally called trans-Oxus region (part of Central Asia) was never the abode of their original settlements. They were originally confined to the basin of the Vaṁkṣu or Oxus lying north of the Himālaya or Hindu Kush in Afghanistan. Bāhlika (South of the Vaṁkṣu), which was for sometime original common home of the ancestors of the Vedic Āryans and so-called Persian or Iranian Āryans, was later called by the Persians Bākhtri or Bākhdhī and by the Greeks Bactria, identical with modern Balkh in north Afghanistan. It is perhaps because of this linguistic transformation that some Indian and foreign scholars falling into the grip of confusion about the exact geographical position or location of Sanskrit Bāhlika placed the Greek Bactria in Central Asia for showing it as the cradle of Āryans.

According to Herzfeld, a group of Indian and Iranian Āryans (Indo-Iranians), who had detached themselves from the main body, after leaving their common home (Central Asia) and before entering their respective countries moved westward and settled in Western Asia and set-up their principalities and spread their language and culture. Eduard Meyer has located the Āryan homeland in the region of the Pāmīr plateau which cannot be taken as worthy of credence. According to him, the migrations of the Indo-Iranians from the Pāmīr eastward and westward took place about the middle of the second millennium BC. They settled simultaneously in India and Iran and in different parts of Western Asia. The theory of westward migrations of the Indo-Iranians from their common home was accepted also by Oldenberg, Keith and J̆. Friedrich.

The Āryans, in fact, had migrated from their original cradle, Sapta-Sindhu region, to the west. India was connected with Western Asia by land in the direction of Kandāhār

Kabul and Bāhlika or Balkh. They actually settled in different parts of Western Asia (Mesopotamia including Mitanni = modern Iraq, Syria and Turkey) in the course of their expansion outside India. They profoundly influenced the religious system, cultural patterns and linguistic structures of West Asian countries through their commercial and cultural contacts with the people which can fairly be attested to by both historical and archaeological evidence including the inscriptional record of Asia Minor dating back to *circa* 1400 BC. The influence of Vedic culture in West Asia was admittedly more pervasive than that of Iranian culture. The view held by some scholars, that the Indo-Iranian speech-forms then current in Western Asia were older than the Vedic Sanskrit and the Avestan Zend, smacks of philological bias. It is also noteworthy that the Āryans had expanded from Sapta-Sindhu over greater parts of Central Asia, and Western Asia including Iran, and over some parts of Europe.

George Rawlinson's observation (made by him in one of his essays on Herodotus), that ". . . the great migration of the Āryan race westward from beyond the Indus, simultaneous probably with the movement of a kindred people, the progenitors of the modern Hindus, eastward and southward to the Ganges and the Vindhya mountain range, is an event of which the most sceptical criticism need not doubt; remote though it be, and obscurely seen through the long vista of intervening centuries," is worthy of our attention.

The theory of Āryan migrations from Central Asia to India, Persia, West Asia and Europe, originally propounded by some European philologists of the nineteenth century, is no longer tenable.

The famous oriental scholar of Germany, Max Müller, who belonged to the school of philologists of the nineteenth century, devoted special attention to the subject. He was one of the chief exponents of the theory of Central Asiatic home of the Āryans. According to him, the ancestors of the Greeks, the Romans, the Germans, the Celts, the Russians, the Indians (Vedic Āryans) and the Persians (or Iranians) were living together in their original home in Central Asia. They belonged to the "Āryan family" or "Āryan race." They were speakers of primitive Āryan language. After their first separation about *circa* 3000 BC they were divided into two branches, the north-western and south-eastern. The north-western group comprising the first five migrated towards Europe through different routes and south-eastern group comprising the Indians and the Persians crossed over the narrow passes of the Hindu Kush, entered Afghanistan in north-west India and settled in the land of the "Seven Rivers" (Indus or Sindhu and its five tributaries, the five rivers of the Punjab, and the Sarasvatī). They spoke the language common to Sanskrit and Zend. They remained undivided for sometime. After their second and final separation sometime between *c.* 2000 and 1500 BC, the Persians marched towards Persia and the Indians remained in their territories, and ever since India has been called their home.

The first statement regarding the Central Asian origin of the Āryans was made by Max Müller in 1847, and then he propounded his theory in 1859, which is contained in his book *A History of Ancient Sanskrit Literature* (published in the same year), and further expounded it in his popular *Lectures on the Science of Language* (1st series, 1861) and lecture on "The Veda and Zend-Avesta" delivered at the philosophical Institution, Leeds, in March 1865, which appeared originally in *Chips from a German Workshop* (vol. I, 1868).

As a sequel to revulsion of his opinion, Max Müller protested the unholy alliance of two sciences, comparative philology and ethnology. He himself stood against the mixing of both. After having realized his mistake, he himself denied the existence of an "Āryan race" and the uniform primitive language of the Āryan family. He did not hesitate to change some of his statements made earlier. He was honest enough to admit that the process and date of Āryan separation, and exact location of "the original home of the Āryan speech" and "the cradle of Āryan race" cannot be determined with much accuracy. The learned scholar gave a final pronouncement on the subject in 1887. He wrote: "If an answer must be given as to the place where our Āryan ancestors dwelt before their separation . . . I should still say, as I said forty years ago, 'somewhere in Asia', and no more" (*Good Words,* August 1887, rept. in his *Biographies of Words and the Home of the Aryas*, pub. in Nov. 1887), which is more vague, and perhaps more probable than Bactria, his earlier and more definite selection. He does not appear to have drawn any definite conclusion. He like Holc and Morris, the two American writers, and other scholars went on advocating various forms of the Asiatic hypothesis.

Adolf Kaegi, a German Vedic scholar, like some other European savants of the nineteenth century also propounded the theory that Central Asia was the common home of the speakers of Āryan language. After their separation, one group travelled west towards Europe and the other travelled East towards Persia and India. The Indians travelled south-eastward and the Iranians spread in south-westerly direction. The eastern branch of the Āryans (Indians) after their separation from Iranians entered India by crossing over the western passes of the Hindu Kush at the time of the composition of the hymns of the *Ṛgveda* (*c.* 2000-1500 BC) and settled in Afghanistan, the Punjab and Sindh in the north-west and then further moved towards east in the Gangetic plain. In the first half of the twentieth century too, the same hypothetical theory was propounded by other scholars. E.J. Rapson in his *Ancient India from the Earliest Times to the First Century* AD (pub. in 1914) has described the Āryans as invaders. He does not support the hypothesis of Max Müller that the term Āryan includes the whole family of Indo-European languages. He has restricted it only to the Persian and Indian groups of this family on the basis of some of their common characteristic features. He has postulated that ". . . there must have been a period in which the ancestors of the Persians of the *Avesta* and of the Indians of the *Rigveda* lived together as one people and spoke a common language. When a separation took place, the Persian Āryans occupied Bactria, the region of Balkh, i.e., Afghanistan north of the Hindu Kush, and Persia, while the Indian Āryans crossed over the passes of the Hindu Kush into the valley of the Kabul river in southern Afghanistan, and thence into the country of the Indus, i.e., the North-Western Frontier Province and the northern Punjab."

The old assumption of the philologists, that the relationship of language implies a relationship of race, was disproved and disposed of by some anthropologists. With the progress of the science of comparative ethnology the conflicts between philologists and ethnologists over the issue further sparked off the controversy about the Āryan origin. Many contradictory theories began to be propounded by them about the subject. Among the anthropologists, the French anthropologist, Paul Broca, was perhaps the first to question the validity of claims of the philologists. In 1862, he observed that ". . . races have frequently within the historic period changed their language without having apparently changed the race or the type . . . the ethnological value of comparative philology is extremely small. Indeed, it is apt to be misleading rather than otherwise. But philological facts and deductions are more striking than minute measurements of skulls, and therefore the conclusions of philologists have received undue attention." Topinard, a distinguished follower of Broca, remarked that ". . . if the Āryans came from Asia they could have brought with them nothing but their language, their civilization, and a knowledge of metals. Their blood has disappeared. In France, we are Āryans only by speech. By race we are mainly cymry in the north, and Celts in the central region."

E.B. Tylor, a cultural anthropologist from England, rightly pointed out in his book, *Anthropology — An Introduction to the Study of Man* . . . (1881) that "a man's language is no full and certain proof of his parentage." Sayce, a philologist, as noted before, correctly observed in his *Introduction to the Science of Language* (1883) that philology and ethnology are two different sciences. He further added that on the basis of relationship of language we can prove the socio-cultural contacts between the two groups but we can not identify the race or decide the racial ethnology. Language is more useful to a historian than to an ethnologist. The German anthropologist, Virchow, very rightly stated sometime before 1889 that no one can prove that the "primitive Āryans were dolichocephalous and had blue eyes, blond hair and a white complexion". A.H. Keane did not find either philological or ethnological data of any help to provide satisfactory explanations of the terms, "Āryan" and "Indo-European" (*Ethnology*, 1896). He wrote: "While German anthropologists are still . . . loyal to the traditional view that the first Āryans were best represented by the tall, long-headed tawney-breed, blue-eyed Teutonic barbarians of Tacitus — who, now tell us, have completely disappeared from sight of the present population. The Italian school, or at least its chief exponent, Sergi, was equally convinced that the picture was a myth, that such Āryans never existed, that the true primitive Āryans were not long, but round-headed not fair but dark, not tall but short and are in fact today best represented by the round-headed Kelts, Slavs and South Germans" (*Man: Past and Present*, 1920). The views expressed by W.Z. Ripley in 1900 in his *The Races of Europe*, and A.L. Kroeber in his *Anthropology* (1924), that one cannot arrive at any positive conclusion by correlating race, language and culture, are very much applicable in case of the Āryans.

J.J. Shaffer in one of his articles (in *The People of South Asia*, ed. by Lucaks, 1984) pointed out that the linguistic similarities in the West were established in the course of cultural contacts and interactions of the Vedic Āryans with the people in the post-second millennium BC and not before. Colin Renfrew (Professor of Archaeology at Cambridge University) has rejected the theory propounded by Max Müller and other scholars that the speakers of the languages of Indo-European family lived together in their original home for sometime but after their separation some wandered around Europe and Western Asia and some moved towards Persia and India. He in his *Archaeology and Language — The Puzzle of Indo-European Origins* (1987) has unequivocally stated that it is difficult to establish the linguistic similarities between Sanskrit and Western languages. According to him, an archaic from of Indo-European was spoken before *c.* 6500 BC and in India in particular before *c.* 1500 BC. According to his theory, eastern Anatolia was the original homeland of Indo-European ethnic group. He has traced back the antiquity of the place to the seventh millennium BC. The population growth caused by the development of farming resulted in the expansion of the Indo-Europeans westward and eastward. He also refers to the written record of the fifteenth century BC discovered at Boghaz-Koi in Cilitia (Asia Minor), the captital of the ancient Hittites. He has further stated that the Indo-Europeans were in northern Mesopotamia in the fifth or fourth millennium BC, and in southern Caucasus. He has propounded hypothesis after hypothesis. As a matter of fact, Western Asia was not their original home. The two different groups of Indian and Iranian Āryans had settled there in the course of their gradual expansion, as noted before.

The theory of Asiatic origin of the Āryans was rejected by some German and British scholars in the latter half of the nineteenth century, and they started looking for the Āryan home in Europe. There were some scholars who initially advocated the theory of Asiatic home of the Āryans but suddenly shifted to European home. Thus, they shifted from one hypothesis to the other. Their arguments were based chiefly on the evidence as to the antiquity and early history of man supplied by the new sciences of geology, anthropology, ethnology and prehistoric archaeology. The old traditional belief that the Central Asia was the cradle of the Āryans from where they migrated in succession to Europe and East was not upheld, and it was recognized that Europe had been continuously inhabited from remote ages. And, thus, the cradle of the so-called Āryan race was placed in Europe. A new controversy as to which part of Europe, western, eastern, central or northern, was the original home of the Āryans commenced. In the first half of the twentieth century, the European origin of the Āryans was further supported by some European scholars.

It is generally believed that it were the anthropologists, "the chief apostles of the new doctrine," who first raised the voice of protest against the old assumption of the philologists, but it must be acknowledged that such protest was first raised, before anthropology became a science, by a man who was himself a philologist. He was none other than Dr. Latham. As early as 1851, in his edition of the *Germania* of Tacitus, he asserted that "no valid argument whatever had been produced in favour of the Asiatic origin of the Āryans." He pleaded in favour of their European origin. According to his theory, the main body of the Āryans were in Europe, and a small detached body in Asia. But it is very difficult to answer whether the smaller body broke away from the larger, or the larger from the smaller? The Indo-Iranians in Asia, according to the theory, were more closely united with each other than the European Āryans. He has propounded two possible hypotheses. The Āryan languages must either have all originated in Europe; the Indo-Iranians after their separation from the rest migrated to their present position, or they must all have originated in Asia and have migrated to their respective positions; there would have been a single migration, or successive migrations, as to which there is no evidence whatever that they ever migrated at all, and whose tradition affirm that they were autochthons?

In 1868, Benfey, relying chiefly on the geological, archaeological and anthropological evidences than the philological one, contended that Europe has been the abode of man from time immemorial. He did not accept the arguments advanced in favour of the migration of the Āryans from Asia. He advocated the theory of migration of the Āryans from the region eastward of the Caspian.

In 1871, Geiger, another distinguished German scholar, placed the cradle of the Āryans in the region to the north of the Black Sea, but more to the north-west, in Central and Western Germany. He maintained that since no proof has ever been adduced of any Āryan migration from the East to the West, the cradle of Āryans may be placed in Europe than in Asia. Thus, he supported the European and not the Asiatic origin of the Āryans. In the same year, Cuno, who was also a German scholar, propounded another theory. According to him, ". . . the great plain of Northern Europe, stretching from the Ural Mountains over Northern Germany and the north of France as far as the Atlantic" was the original home of the "Āryan race." At the beginning of the historic period, this region was in occupation of the Celtic, Teutonic, Lithuanic, and Slavonic races, whom he regards as autochthonous. He maintains that at some earlier time the Italic and Hellenic races had extended themselves to the south across the mountain chain of Central Europe, and the Indo-Iranians had wandered further to the East, subduing and absorbing non-Āryan tribes.

The old theory that the "Āryan race" had inhabited the steppes of Central Asia, extending eastward of the Caspian for more than a thousand miles beyond Lake Balkash, before their separation was totally discarded, and the new theory of European origin of the Āryans was generally accepted. Taking into account the conditions of climate, of soil, of greater geographical extension, and of proximity to the regions now occupied by the Āryans, the European rather than the Asiatic plain was selected as the probable cradle of the "Āryan race."

The whole theory of the successive migrations of so-called Āryan tribes from the East to the West was swept away in 1872 by J. Schmidt. The migrations of the European Āryans in successive waves from their parent hive in Central Asia to find new homes in Europe was doubted.

In 1873, Friedrich Müller supporting the agruments adduced earlier by Benfey and Geiger also suggested the European origin of the Āryans. He agrees with Cuno's selection of Central Europe. About the same time, Spiegel changing his earlier opinion placed the cradle of the Āryans in "Europe between the 45th and 60th parallels of latitude. He maintained that this region was well suited for the development of the "primitive Āryan race." And here there was room for their expansion both to the East and to the West.

In, 1878, Pösche maintained that anthropology and archaeology must supplement and correct the conclusions of philology. Basing his arguments on anthropological and archaeological findings he declared that "... there is only one race, the tall, blue-eyed, fair-skinned German race with abundant beard and dolichocephalic skull, which can claim to be genuine Āryans by blood as well as by language. He identified this race with that whose skeletons have been found in the Alemannic 'row-graves' of Southern Germany, and contended that it has existed in Europe since the Neolithic period."

Some German scholars have strongly pleaded in favour of German homeland of the Āryans. Their arguments are based mainly on anthropological, archaeological and philological findings. The arguments put forward by them in support of their contention may be summed up as follows: The Indo-European form of speech first came into existence on Germanic soil; the Germans have been speaking language of Indo-European family since time immemorial which is supported by a discovery of copper-plates in their language; there has been some physical and racial similarity between the Germans and Āryans; the pottery of the prehistoric period discovered in Central Germany bear geometrical and conventional designs of the Āryans.

Only on the slender thread of evidence it will not be reasonable to consider Germany the original homeland of the Āryans. Sigmund Feist has already proved that the Germans did not belong to the Indo-European stock.

K. Penka (more a anthropologist than a philologist) in his remarkable work *Origines Ariacae* (1883) stated that "the pure Āryans are represented only by the North Germans and Scandinavians (the people of Norway and Sweden). His contention, that Scandinavia was the "cradle of the whole Āryan race," cannot be approved in view of the fact that the forest-clad valleys of Norway and Sweden were not the places for the habitation of the "primitive Āryans." It is believed that Celtic races of Central Europe, rather than the Teutonic race of Scandinavia, are the lineal descendants of the "primitive Āryans."

O. Schrader, a well-known German scholar, has discussed exhaustively the question of the origin of the Āryans (whether subjectively or objectively) in his treatise, *Sprachvergleichung and Urgeschichte* (1883). Relying on the testimony of history, tradition, ethnology and linguistic archaeology he held that the earliest known seat of the European Āryans was in Northern Europe and that of the Asiatic Āryans on the Jaxartes. The results obtained by him from his investigation into the subject are somewhat different from those of the others. First he did not treat the Āryans as one undivided group as others did. He rather divided them into two groups. His belief in the unbroken geographical continuity of the European Āryans anterior to the linguistic separation is based on philological doctrine. He has placed them in Northern Europe, "the Slavo-Lithuanians in European Russia, and the Celts, Latins, Hellenes, and Teutons farther to the West." His contention, that no evidence has been adduced in favour of any migration of the European Āryans from the East, received wide support from his contemporaries. The Asiatic Āryans (Indo-Iranians) have been placed by him on the Jaxartes. The Indians and Iranians according to him, "formed a united people" somewhere to the north of the Himālaya. After their separation they were divided into two branches. The Sanskrit-speaking "race" entered India from the north-west. "In the Vedic period, they lived on the banks of the Indus, and had only an indirect knowledge of the Ganges." While discussing the question whether the European Āryans came from Asia or the Asiatic Āryans from Europe he changed his earlier view. He did not draw any sharp line of division between the European and the Asiatic branches of the Āryan family. He asserted that certain races and languages of Europe are closely connected with those of Asia. He has referred to the close relations between the Indo-Iranians and the Greeks. He did not approve the old assumption that since the Indo-Iranian speech (Sanskrit and Zend) is more archaic than the European, the cradle of the Āryans must have been somewhere towards the East. He was of the view that the results yielded by linguistic palaeontology are not decisive. On the basis of his fresh evidence he concluded that the cradle of the undivided Āryans was in Europe. He further stated that if the earliest historical notices and traditions are taken credible, the movement of the "Āryan races" were in a southward and to some extent in an eastward direction. If early tradition is given credence to, "a portion of Western Asia must have received from Europe its Āryan population of Phrygians and Armenians. This tradition, according to him is supported by the near relationship of Armenian to the European languages. Here we are reminded of what George Rawlinson said: ". . . in the silence of authentic history, Armenia (in erstwhile USSR, north-west of Persia) may be regarded as the most probable centre from which the Indo-European nations spread" (*Herodotus*, vol. I). This hypothesis is, however, in direct conflict with the ancient Indian and Persian traditions, and is opposed to the opinion of the Max Müller, Wilson, Martin Haug and other scholars.

After delving deep into the subject, O. Schrader himself admitted that the question as to whether the earliest home of the Āryan "race" was in Europe or in Asia has no positive answer. Nevertheless, he by withdrawing his earlier opinion that the Āryans had originated in Asia supported the European hypothesis, that is, the cradle of the Āryan "race" was in the West and not in the East. He contended that there is no indisputable evidence to prove the migrations of the Āryans from the East to the West.

The Asiatic hypothesis was abandoned by several scholars, including Professor Sayce, who, like Dr. Schrader, had supported it in former years. After their conversion to the new view they all stood in favour of European home of the Āryans.

The English philologist and ethnologist, Isaac Taylor, in his *The Origin of the Āryans* (1889) has also advocated the theory of European origin of the Āryans. He has enough substantiated his arguments advanced in favour of the new view. He says: "The southern and eastern extensions of Āryan speech may be due to Āryan conquest, or to the gradual expansion of Āryan civilization over contiguous tribes, and there is, therefore, no difficulty in regarding the great plain of Northern Europe as the region in which the Āryan race originated."

The views of some German scholars (other than those noted before) also deserve our notice here. On the basis of the discovery of some artefacts (stone implements) of the prehistoric period in the region of the West Baltic coast, Dr. Much identified this region with the original home of the Āryans, which cannot be accepted by any stretch of imagination.

Nehring's view, that "the Indo-European's original home lay indeed also in south Russia, but extended far beyond to the West," does not deserve our assent. The view of Brandenstein, that the north-western Kirghiz steppes to the south of the Ural mountain was the original home of the undivided Indo-Europeans and from here the Indo-Iranian "tribes" moved eastward (the Central Asian hypothesis in a modified form), can be disposed of as hypothetical. The assumption of Fl'or, that the Ural region in Central Russia was the original zone of the Indo-European culture, is also untenable. Morgan's belief, that the cradle of the Indo-Europeans was in Western Siberia, is nothing but a far-fetched imagination.

In the early twentieth century too, some British scholars advocated the theory of European origin of the Āryans. P. Giles has postulated that the migrations of the Āryans from their orignal habitat — Hungary, Austria, and Bohemia — took place about *c.* 2500 BC. The Indo-Iranian branch moved towards east and reached India through Asia Minor, Mesopotamia, and Iran. The acceptance of this particular view will amount to vindication of the theory of migrations from the West to the East. But the fact remains that the process was reverse.

V.G. Childe in his *The Āryans* (1926) has examined the issue relating to the origin of the Āryans on the basis of linguistic and ethnological data. First he reviews the hypothesis of the Asiatic cradle of the Āryans. He does not find evidence to substantiate the arguments adduced in favour of successive migrations of the Āryans from the East to the West. He finally rejects the theory of Asiatic origin of the Āryans. Then he goes on to review the European hypothesis. First he accepts Central Europe and then the great plain of Northern and Eastern Europe as the cradle of the Āryans. He rejects North European cradle. Then he jumps over to South Russia and expresses his confidence that it may probably be accepted as Āryan home. But he finds that his confidence in this theory also is shaken. Thus, he shifted from one hypothesis to the other without drawing any positive conclusion. He has aptly remarked that "extension of the term Āryan to embrace all speakers of languages of Indo-European family is illegitimate." He has admitted that "the Āryan tribes scattered about the North-West from the Kabul and Kurram to the headwaters of the Ganges and the Jumna" are described in the hymns of the *Ṛgveda*.

The Russian scholars hold that south Russia was the original home of the Āryans. The view that has been current in erstwhile Soviet Russia since 1970 is that the ancestors of Indian (Vedic) Āryans had entered India after having migrated from their original habitat in the great plain around the Black Sea in South Russia (or South-Eastern Europe) through Central Asia about *c.* 2000 BC. The view is based on the belief that the socio-religious and cultural traditions of the Āryans are almost identical with those of the Slaves of Russia whose ancestors formed the part of so-called Indo-European family. L. Poliakov questions the origin of so-called Āryan race in Europe.

R.R. Chanda, an Indian anthropologist, in his *The Indo-Āryan Races: A Study of the Origin of Indo-Āryan People and Institutions* (1916) says that the early Āryan "invaders" belonged to the dolichocephalic brand and they occupied the greater portion of India. The later Āryan "invaders" belonged to the brachycephalic brand. He observes: "The Ārya immigrants from Mesopotamia (Western Asia) must have absorbed a good deal of semitic blood in their Syrian home and were probably dark like the Semites." He has gone to the extent of surmising that the Purus, Druhyus, Anus, Yadus and Turvaśas (mentioned in the *Ṛgveda* and the Purāṇas as five indigenous Āryan peoples) "may have come from the same quarters and probably of the same physical type." He further adds that in the prehistoric period the Pāmīr region was inhabited by a very brachycephalic population of Āryan or Indo-European speech. These are all fanciful notions.

The racial classifications of the anthropologists are great hurdles in the way of the historians from the point of view of historical research into ethnology of ancient India. The anthropological data provided by the anthropologists need further historical examination to confirm their authenticity. B.S. Guha (an anthropologist) in his two important works, *An Outline of the Racial Ethnology of India* (1937) and *Racial Elements in the Population* (1944), has divided the races into six main groups. He has placed the so-called Indo-Āryans under the Nordic group, characterized as leptorrhine dolichocephals.

S.K. Chatterji (a renowned Indian philologist, and an erudite scholar) in one of his articles, "Race Movements and Prehistoric Culture" (in *The Vedic Age*, ed. R.C. Majumdar, 1965), has also placed the Vedic Āryans under the same Nordic group, who are said to have entered India from the Eurasian steppe lands sometime during the second half of the second millennium BC. In his *Indo-Āryan and Hindi* (1960) he clearly states that the vast Eurasian plain to the south of the Ural mountains was the original homeland of the Indo-Europeans. The main body or the European body went westward, while one branch of the Indo-European people, the ancestors of the Indo-Iranians, probably stayed on. "Or it may be that the ancestors of the Indo-Āryans and of the 'Hittites' of Asia Minor left the primitive homeland in the North-Central Asian steppes first, trekking south-west through the Caucasus into Asia Minor and Mesopotamia and Iran during the second half of the third millennium BC."

B.K. Ghosh in his article, "The Āryan Problem" (in the *Vedic Age, supra*) has categorically stated that South Russia more than any other region can be regarded as "cradle-land" of the Āryans (= Indo-Europeans).

The term "Indo-Āryan" or "Indo-Āryans" has been used by the philologists, anthropologists and historians, both Indian and foreign (with few exceptions), to legitimize the theory of coming of one branch of Āryans into India after their migration from original common home (which we do not know till today) and separation from the Persians. The use of the said term amounts to falsification of the history of Vedic India.

We do not have any authentic evidence at our disposal to prove the existence of any Āryan race or Āryan tribe and their mighration into India from outside. The Āryan race theory — an invention of the nineteenth-century Europe — has been rejected by J. Huxley of England, L.B. Synder of America, Koenraad Elst of Belgium and some Indian Scholars. P. Choudhury in his marvellous work, *The Āryan Hoax* (1995), has outrightly rejected the Āryan race and migration theory.

The theories relating to whether European or Asiatic origin of the Āryans are purely based on hypothesis. The places described by the propounders of the two opposed theories as the cradle of undivided Āryans (noted before) include Central Asia, Bactria (northern part, on the other side of the river Oxus extending northward to Jaxartes = Central Asia), Eurasia, Armenia, Anatolia, South Russia, Austria, Hungary, Scandinavia (Norway and Sweden), and Germany. The fact remains that none of these places was the original homeland of the Āryans. In fact, the Āryans were autochthons of the land.

The philology, ethnology or prehistoric archaeology is not an aid to us to solve the tangled Āryan problem.

The theory of the Arctic Home of the Āryans propounded by Bal Gangadhar Tilak in his *The Arctic Home in the Vedas* on the evidence of literature and astronomy has already been rejected by A.C. Das, and G.B. Levin a Russian Indologist. According to Tilak, the Āryans had originally lived in the Arctic or North Polar Region. They abandoned this region on account of the intense cold about *c.* 8000 BC and gradually moved in different directions. They reached Central Asia about *c.* 6000 BC. Some of them further went to Iran and India and finally settled there. In the absence of description of the Arctic region in the *Ṛgveda* as the Āryan homeland, it will not be wise to accept this theory.

History cannot be reconstructed merely on the basis of theories, hypotheses and assumptions. Such reconstruction will be more or less a destruction. The observation made by Abinas Chandra Das in this regard is very striking : The Study of comparative philology, comparative culture, geology, archaeology, ethnology, ancient geography, the ancient histories of Āryana and Western Asia, and the "prehistoric picture of the European Races as outlined by competent scholars, should be brought to bear on the subject with a view to test the accuracy of the several results of investigation."

The evidence recorded in the *Avesta,* the literary record of the ancient Persians or Iranians, composed sometime between *c.* 660-583 BC, invalidates the theory of migrations of the ancestors of Vedic Āryans and Persian or Iranian Āryans (the eastern branch of so-called Indo-European stock) from their original or common home somewhere is Central Asia or Europe and their settlements in Afghanistan and Sapta-Sindhu region and the second separation of the latter from the former and their further march towards Persia. From this text (part I, *Vendidad*) it distinctly appears tht *Airyana-Vaejo* or *Arieno-Vaijo* (= Sanskrit *Āryānām-Vijam*), which comprised Herat and the adjoining regions watered by Haroyu (= old Persian Haraiva = Ṛgvedic Hariyūpiyā = modern Hariruda), Kabul, Kandāhāra, and the territories lying along the Indus and its tributaries, and Bākhdhī (= old Persian Bākhtri = Sanskrit Bāhlika = Greek Bactria = modern Balkh in Afghanistan), Harahvaiti (not Sarasvatī as misunderstood by some scholars, but the tract extending from Herat to Kandāhāra) and *Hapta-Hindu* (= Ṛgvedic *Sapta-Sindhu*) were the places of their original settlements. The *Airyana-Vaejo* of the *Avesta* is more or less identical with *Ārjika* (a territory of the Āryans in Afghanistan) of the *Ṛgveda*, *Ariana* of the classical (Greek and Roman) writers which comprised the whole of Afghanistan being bounded on the north by the Hindu Kush, on the east by the Indus and on the west by Persia or Iran, *Airyadagya* of the French as it occurs in the *Yacna,* Āryavartta of Manu, and Āryadeśa (land of the Āryans). R.L. Mitra's statement, that the name Ariana signifies the early extension of the Āryans to Afghanistan, "but it was not the *locale* of their original dwelling," can fairly be disputed. Mr. Pavgee's excellent work, *Āryāvartic Home*, contains valuable information about the original home of the Āryans in the Āryāvartta which included greater part of north-western India too.

The ancestors of the Persians (Parsis) lived together with the Ṛgvedic Āryans in Afghanistan, and in the vast tract lying along the Indus and its tributaries (a part of Sapta-Sindhu or Hapta-Hindu region) until their separation from the latter and dispersion towards the end of the Ṛgvedic age. After their separation they went to Persia through Afghanistan because of its geographical proximity to the former, and finally settled down there. One section of them probably moved in the direction of Central Asia. The details of the places provided in the *Avesta* bear testomony to their original settlements in Afghanistan and in some parts of Sapta-Sindhu region.

The Sanskrit Ārya corresponds to the Avestan Airya. Several words in the *Ṛgveda* are identical with those in the *Avesta* in meaning. The linguistic similarities between the Sanskrit, the language of the Ṛgvedic Āryans, and the Zend, the language of the Persian Āryans, are far more than those between other languages of the so-called Indo-European family. The historic relationship of the Persian Āryans or Parsis and the Ṛgvedic Āryans can fairly be attested to by the affinities in their languages, and their common religious beliefs and practices, customs and traditions. The Parsis worshipped the Vedic divinities and followed the Vedic religious system until they embraced a new religion popularly known as Zoroastrianism founded by Zarathushtra or Zoroaster. They came to India in the seventh century AD after Persia or Iran fell into the hands of the Arabs in AD 642. Re-membering their old history and culture, they still consider themselves the descendants of the Āryans. Martin Haug's work, *Essays on the Sacred Language, Writing and Religion of the Parsees*, is a very valuable document on the ancient history and culture of the Parsis.

It is striking to note that after the word *Ārya* extended to Persia (the land of the Parsis) it bore the name of Iran and ever since then it has been called by this name. Some classical writers included it in Ariana (land of the Āryans). The famous Persian king, Darius (*c.* 522-486 BC), calls himself, in one of his cuneiform inscriptions, "an Āryan and of Āryan descent;" and in the Behistun inscription, Ahura-Mazda, the great God of the Zoroastrians, is styled "the God of the Āryans." The Sassanian kings called themselves the kings of "Āryan and un-Āryan Races." The Persian literature and inscriptions show the Āryan connections of the Persians.

The present writer expresses his disagreement with N.M. Chapekar so far as her statement, that "The Indo-Europeans were the common ancestors of the Indians and the Iranians" (*Ancient India and Iran*, 1982, ch. 2), is concerned. Eduard Meyer states that the ancestors of the Vedic Indians and the Iranians belonged to the Āryan or Indo-Europeans family. ". . . their residence must have lain chiefly in the great steppe which stretches north of the Black Sea and the Caspian, through South Russia, to Turan (Turkestan) and the Oxus and Jaxartes. For here we continually discover traces of Iranian nationality. . . . From the region of the steppes the Āryans must have penetrated into the cultivable land of Eastern Iran; thence one part spread over the district of the Indus, then on again to the Ganges; another move westward. . . ." His hypothesis cannot be accepted in view of the fact that the region shown by him was never the cradle of the ancestors of Vedic Āryans or Persian Āryans (or so-called Indo-Iranians). Moreover, it conflicts with other hypotheses. However, it is a fact to reckon with that one section of the Persians moved to West Asia from their native land after leaving Sapta-Sindhu region and not directly from their so-called original home in Central Asia, South Russia or Russian Turkistan. The conventional view, that most of the places, which form part of *Airyana Vaejo* are situated in or about Central Asia, is no longer tenable. It is true that a few places of Central Asia figure in the *Avesta* which does not mean that the ancestors of Persian Āryans were of Central Asian origin. As already stated, one section of the Persians after leaving their original home in the north-western part of India and while passing through Afghanistan went to Central Asia. *Airyana Vaejo*, the birth-place of the ancestors of the Persians who are sometimes called the primitive Āryans, cannot be placed in Central Asia or to the south-eastern foot of the Caucasus. Its exact geographical location has already been indicated herebefore.

The theory of so-called Indo-Āryan or Āryan invasion of northern India (Afghanistan and the Punjab) was first propounded in 1919 by J. Kennedy, and was later supported by some Indian and foreign scholars. In 1928, J. Pathi, and in 1929, E.J. Thomas and C.V. Vaidya and further in 1940s some Indian and foreign scholars described the "Indo-Āryan" as invaders, conquerors and so on.

In 1946, Sir Mortimer Wheeler propounded a misleading theory of Āryan invasion and destruction of Indus Valley towns. Accroding to him, the Āryans entered north-western India from outside, and invaded and destroyed Indus Valley cities, Mohenjo-Dāro (in the district of Larkānā in Sindh) and Harappā (on the Rāvī in the Montgomery district of west Punjab) in or about *circa* 1700 BC or about the middle of the second millennium BC. His theory is the result of his misinterpretations of the details of the destruction of sons of Vṛcivāna at the hands of Indra at Hariyūpiyā narrated in the *Ṛgveda*. The root cause of his whole misunderstanding of the episode is that he mistook Hariyūpiyā (a place on the bank of the river of same name = modern Hariruda river near Herat in Afghanistan) for Harappā. He asserted that there was wholesale massacre of the inhabitants of Mohenjo-Dāro including women and children at the hands of Āryan invaders. Though he himself confessed that it was just a conjecture and not proven, some Indian and foreign scholars blindly supported his view. Even a scholar no less than A.L. Basham in his famous work, *The Wonder that was India*, wrote that the Indus cities fell to the "barbarians" who triumphed not only through greater military power but also through other means. L. Wolley in his *Beginnings of Civilization* (vol. I) writes that the Āryans had occupied north-western India considerably earlier than 1500 BC. They were "a non-urbanized people or semi-barbarians." The Harappan civilization was non-Āryan. The Āryan invaders completely destroyed the urban culture and civilization of the Indus Valley people around 1500 BC. They were wholly involved in massacre of the people. And Indra was destroyer of cities. He has himself contradicted his statements by stating that either the civilization of the Ṛgvedic Āryans was for a long time contemporary with the Harappan civilization or those Āryans instead of having destroyed the Harappan civilization were "actually its authors."

G.F. Dales, an eminent American archaeologist (of Philadelphia) rejected Wheeler's theory of destruction of Indus Valley towns and massacre of the inhabitants of Mohenjo-Dāro by the so-called Āryan invaders on the basis of his findings in the course of excavations at Mohenjo-Dāro conducted in 1964. He has called it a "mythical massacre." He did not find any evidence to substantiate the supposed invasion and destruction of Indus Valley towns. Neither the ruins of burned fortresses nor the skeletal remains of the invaders and defenders were found in the course of archaeological excavation at the site. Despite extensive excavations at the largest Harappan site not a single evidence was found to prove the Āryan invasion and destruction of the towns of the Indus Valley. "The myth of Āryan invasion of harappan towns" has also been exploded by an Indian scholar, K.M. Srivastava.

S. Piggott's view, that those Āryan-speaking people who established themselves in the Indus Valley in the second millennium BC after leaving their common home were conquerors, can unhesitatingly be disposed of.

The Āryan invasion of India is a myth and not the truth. The Āryans were neither invaders nor conquerors. They were not the destroyer of the Harappan civilization but one of its authors.

The Āryan migration and invasion theory has already been demolished by some Indian and foreign scholars, notably, N.R. Waradpande (*The Āryan Invasion: A Myth*, 1989), S.G. Talageri (*The Āryan Invasion Theory: A Reappraisal,* 1993; *Āryan Invasion Theory and Indian Nationalism,* 1993), N.S. Rajaram (*Āryan Invasion of India: The Myth and the Truth*, 1993; *The Politics of History: Āryan Invasion Theory and the Subversion of Scholarship,* 1995), David Frawley, the American Vedic scholar popularly known as Vamadeva Shastri (*The Myth of the Āryan Invasion of India*, 1994; *Vedic Āryans and the Origins of Civilization: A Literary and Scientific Perspective*, by him and Rajaram, 1997), and Michel Danino. They all have proved through their researches that the Vedic Āryans were of Indian origin. We do acknowledge their contributions to the enrichment of our knowledge about the subject. Rajaram and Frawley, the two noted scholars, devoted special attention to the subject during the closing decade of the last century. They have made memorable contributions in the field of discovery of the truth about the origin of the Āryans.

The theory of Āryan migration from Central Asia or Europe towards the East (India) sometime between *c.* 2000-1500 BC and that of Āryan invasion and destruction of Indus Valley towns about 1700 BC or the middle of the second millennium BC gave birth to false history and imperfect chronology as far as the origin and antiquity of the Āryans and the end of the Harappan civilization and the beginning of the Vedic one are concerned. It is on the basis of these two theories that some historians of ancient India have stated in their respective works that the Harappan civilization came to an end around 1750 or 1700 BC after its destruction by the Āryans and the Vedic age began with 1500 BC. The dates suggested by them are speculative and not conclusive. In the light of recent researches on the subject these dates can be set aside. However, we do admit that no date in ancient Indian history before 326 BC can be determined with absolute certainty. It can be fixed only tentatively.

On the basis of the evidence available in the *Ṛgveda*, the oldest record of the Āryans, it can conclusively be proved that they were the original inhabitants of India. There is not even a particle of evidence in it to show their immigration into India from outside. They were originally settled in different parts of Afghanistan, and in Sapta-Sindhu region or the land of seven rivers — the Sindhu or Indus, the five rivers of the Punjab, and the Sarasvatī. Kashmir also formed the part of Sapta-Sindhu region in the Vedic age. It is striking to note that the Ṛgvedic word *Ārya* stands for "honourable" or "noble" in contradistinction to the *Anārya* or the ignoble race. The word *Ārya* does not stand for any race or tribe but for indigenous people maintaining higher grade of culture in comparison to the culture of the non-Āryans.

Abinas Chandra Das was probably the first Indian scholar to strongly advocate that the Sapta-Sindhu region was the cradle of the Ṛgvedic Āryans. His work, *Ṛgvedic India: Cultural History of India as Depicted in the Ṛgveda* (1st published in 1920) is a masterpiece on the subject. Some other scholars, notably, Srikanta Śāstrī, Sampurnananda (*Āryoṁ Kā Ādi Deśa*, 4th edn., vs 2022), Rāhul Sāṁkṛtyāyana (*Rigvedic Āryas,* 1957), V.N. Reu (*Ṛgveda Para ek Aitihāsika Dṛṣti*, 1967) and P.L. Bhargave (*India in the Vedic Age — A History of Āryan Expansion in India*, 1956) have also upheld that the Sapta-Sindhu region was the original seat of the Ṛgvedic Āryans.

A.K. Raman in his *Āryataraṅgiṇī* (1969), a unique work, has correctly stated that the Āryans moved from their original habitat mainly in Afghanistan and the Indus Valley into the Indo-Gangetic plain. *Indian Ancestors of Vedic Āryans* (1994) is a monumental work of L.N. Renu. It is one of the most valuable works produced in recent times on the subject. The author of the said work has categorically stated that "the Vedic Āryans were originally Indians."

Here I cannot but quote what A.C. Das has said: ". . . in the Vedic literature we have a sure and easily accessible basis to go upon, and the materials furnished by it are all compact, which it only requires an adequate mental equipment to study for the discovery of historical truths. The task of reconstructing the history of the ancient Āryans on the basis of the researches made in Vedic literature should, therefore, prove far easier of accomplishment than that of writing the ancient history of any other people on the face of the Globe. . . . Such a history, if compiled, would moreover be a real history of the *Āryan people* — the people as they lived, moved, acted, struggled, hoped, thought and advanced step by step, towards progress and enlightenment, thousands of years ago. . . ."

On the basis of the testimony of the *Ṛgveda* itself it can irrefutably be proved that the Sārasvata region (the territories lying along the river Sarasvatī) was the sacred heartland of the Ṛgvedic Āryas. More than 35 hymns have been dedicated to this river in the text which show their nostalgic attachment to it. The Āryans were originally settled in the territories lying along the Sarasvatī and its seven streams or tributaries (called Sapta-Sarasvatī) which include Dṛṣadvatī (modern Citaṅga or Ghagghara) and Āpayā The river Dṛṣadvatī was one of its major tributaries. H.D. Sankalia, the renowned Indian archaeologist, has also proved that the Sarasvatī-Dṛṣadvatī doāb (the land between the two rivers *par excellence*) was inhabited by the Vedic Āryans at least by 2500 BC.

The *Mahābhārata* (*Āraṇyaka Parva* and *Śalya Parva*) also contains valuable description of the Sārasvata region — the land of the Āryans. The land between Sarasvatī and Dr̥ṣadvatī called Brahmāvartta was one of the important seats of their original settlements.

M.A. Stein was the first archaeologist to undertake an archaeological exploration to discover the dry beds of Sarasvatī. In 1941-42, he found one of its old bed in Bahāwalpur region (in erstwhile Punjab, now in Pakistan). The researches on the Sarasvatī were further carried out by various scholars, including archaeologists, geologists, scientists, geographers and historians, during the past two decades to find out its dried up course. The lost track of the river have so far been found in the Punjab, Haryana, Rajasthan Gujarat and in some parts of Pakistan. A research team of 18 scholars, including Sanskritists, archaeologists, historians, geographers and geologists led by V.S. Wakankar also discovered a number of lost Sarasvatī sites in Rajasthan and Haryana in 1985-86. The literary evidence of the Āryans' original settlements in the territories lying along the river Sarasvatī is now fully confirmed by the recent researches. It needs no further confirmation. B.B. Lal, an eminent archaeologist, has also recently made immense contributions in the field of discovery of the lost Sarasvatī sites in the Indian sub-continent.

The recent archaeological researches have also proved the continuity of the Sārasvata civilization from pre-Harappan times to its end. The settlements of the Vedic Āryans on the banks of the river Sarasvatī in pre-Harappan and Harappan period are well attested by their respective radio-carbon dates, *c.* 2500-2200 BC and *c.* 2200-1700 BC.

Of about 1200 sites of the Indus-Sarasvatī civilization explored so far, nearly 500 have been located in Rajasthan and Haryana on the Sarasvatī and its tributaries and only 173 sites of Harappan culture have been found on the Indus as informed by S.P. Gupta, an archaeologist of repute. He has been carrying out his research on this civilization for the past three decades. His new concept of Sindhu-Sarasvatī civilization has been widely acclaimed by the scholars in India and abroad.

A civilization that flourished on the Sindhu and Sarasvatī was predominantly Vedic in nature. It is believed that the Harappans in the Sarasvatī river basin were by and large Vedic peoples. Their religious motifs, deities and sacrificial altars bear the stamp of Āryan faith and culture. This has been proved by S.R. Rao on the basis of his archaeological findings.

The geological studies prove that the river Sarasvatī dried up early in the second millennium BC or about 1900 BC.

On the basis of new archaeological findings now it can be established that the Vedic civilization was older than the Harappan one. And the Harappan culture flourished not only in the valley of the Indus but also in the valley of the Sarasvatī where the Harappans were no other than the Vedic Āryans.

There is also Purāṇic evidence to confirm the indigenous origin of the Āryans. The five Āryan people — Purus, Anus, Druhyus, Yadus and Turvasas — originally mentioned in the *Ṛgveda* have been described in the Purāṇas in detail. Their dynastic genealogies are also given therein. It appears that their descendants spread over different parts of India and settled down there. The ancestors of the said five Āryan people were originally Indian. The reliability of Purāṇic genealogies are well tested. P.L. Bhargava also placing his reliance on the Vedic and Purāṇic tradition has proved the Indian origin of the Vedic Āryans. I have provided the detailed history of the five Āryan people in my work, *Early Indian Historical Tradition and Archaeology* (1994). F.E. Pargiter, an acknowledged authority on the Purāṇas, has pin-pointed in his *Ancient Indian Historical Tradition* (1922) that Indian traditions know nothing of any Āryan invasion of India from outside or any movement of the Āryans from the West to the East. The traditions rather confirm the Āryan overflow from India through the north-west into the countries outside (West Asia) where they founded various kingdoms and introduced their own language, religion and culture.

According to Pargiter, Pratiṣṭhāna on the confluence of the Gaṅgā and Yamunā in Prayāg (modern Jhūṅsī near Allahabad) in Madhyadeśa was one of the earliest seats of Āryans' original habitation from where they spread all over north and other parts of India which is supported by A.D. Pusalker and H.D. Sankalia.

On the combined testimony of the *Ṛgveda, Mahābhārata* and the Purāṇas it can indisputably be proved that the cradle of the ancestors of the Vedic Āryans was India and not Central Asia or Europe as assumed by some Indian and foreign scholars. The literary evidence of the Indian origin of the Āryans can be authenticated by recent archaeological findings and discoveries. Our disquisition into the subject gives us the result that India was the original Home of the Āryans. And there were several centres or seats of their original dwelling in India itself of which the Ariana region, the Sapta-Sindhu region, the Sārasvata region and the Gaṅgā-Yamuna doāb were the most important. It will not be reasonable to single out a particular place as their original homeland.

The original settlements of the Āryans in the valleys of the Gaṅgā and Yamunā during the Ṛgvedic period can be testified to by the evidence recorded in the *Ṛgveda* and some of the *Brāhmaṇas*. The recent geological and archaeological researches have also proved beyond doubt that after the desiccation of the river Sarasvatī around 1900 BC, the

Vedic Āryans moved towards the Gaṅgā-Yamunā doāb towards the end of the Ṛgvedic age. In the light of this finding, the veracity of the statement of some of the historians of ancient India that the Āryans moved from the Punjab to the said doāb in the later Vedic age can be questioned. It was the expansion of only the Kurus and not the Purus or Pauravas who had settled there earlier, i.e., in the early Vedic age. In the later Vedic age, there was further expansion of the Āryans. They moved to Kāśī, Kośala, Pañcāla, Videha, Aṅga, Magadha and other parts of eastern India. The groups of Vedic Āryans had gone also outside India. Their settlements in different parts of Western Asia and expansion of their culture are well-proven fact. The Āryan expansion was from the East to the West and not vice-versa.

Notwithstanding the new findings, some Indian and foreign scholars are still obsessed with the outdated view that the Vedic Āryans are of foreign origin which is really deplorable. They are still maintaining the conventional view regarding the antiquity of the Harappan and Vedic civilizations. In our research into such problems, we have to see that history should not turn into politics. Every possible efforts have been made to bring the work, "India from Ariana to the Gaṅgā Valley," which has appeared in the present volume in the from of an essay, up to date keeping in view its scope and limitations. It was not possible to accommodate all the available data on the subject within the small compass of this essay.

The present writer intends to bring out a separate book on the Āryans for throwing fresh light on their history and culture covering their origin, and expansion within and outside India. The book, it is hoped, will very soon see the light of the day.

The ethnology or ethnography of ancient India is another field of further historical study and research. The primitive tribes have their own place in the history of India. They have also contributed a lot to the making of history and culture of India. They are the subjects of not only ethnological or ethnographical study. They need also historical treatment. The ethnological and historical data are of equal importance in the context of the tribal study.

The Cīnas and the Kirātas figure prominently in the list of primitive tribes of ancient India. They have been mentioned conjointly in ancient Indian literature and inscriptions. In this volume, I have discussed only about the former in the essay, "The Origin, Antiquity and Identification of the Cīnas as depicted in Ancient Indian Literature and Inscriptions." A separate book on the latter under the title, *The Kirātas in Ancient India* has already been written by me.

In the said essay, light has been thrown on the origin and antiquity of the Cīnas, and an attempt has been made to solve the problem of their identification. On the basis of the results obtained from historical, archaeological and ethnological investigations into the subject, it has been proved that they were not the Chinese people of Mongolian origin as erroneously supposed by some anthropologists, philologists and historians but a non-Āryan race of Indian origin having settlements in north-eastern, and north-western parts of India in ancient times. Those who had settled in the mountainous regions of Tibet and Burma had no connection with the Chinese proper. They have been described in ancient Indian literature and inscriptions with the Kirātas of north-east India. Their antiquity can be traced back to the epic age. They were widely diffused non-Āryan tribe. In the literature, in particular, they have been associated with the Kāmbojas, Sindhu-Sauvīras, Śakas, Yavanas and Dardas of the north-west. They were outside the pale of Āryan culture.

No doubt, various works have been produced on ancient Indian society and economy. However, there is still a fair scope to throw fresh light on these two important aspects of ancient Indian history. The Buddhist and Jain literature contain abundant information about social and economic life of the people in ancient times. In the essay, "Ancient Indian Society and Economy in the Jain and Buddhist Traditions" light has been thrown on social transformation in the sixth and fifth centuries BC, the emergence of casteless society during the period, social changes that took place in post-Buddha and Mahāvīra period, the emergence of various professional and occupational groups, the formation of guild, the internal trade system, external trade relations with south-east Asian countries, East Asia (China), Central Asia and West Asia, etc. The expansion of Indian culture in both neighbouring and far-off Asian countries and establishment of the Hindu and Buddhist colonies especially in some parts of south-east Asia have also been dwelt upon.

There were various social and economic formations in the latter half of the first millennium BC which have been discussed separately in an essay on it. The formations of classes, castes and various social and economic associations and institutions during the period have been brought within the purview of the treatment of the subject. The importance and role of guilds in various spheres have also been highlighted.

Manu has provided a picturesque description of the the economic system that prevailed in his time. The details of agricultural practices, arts and crafts, indigenous industry, trade and commerce, taxation system, market economy, currency system, weights and measures, banking system, different occupational groups, guild formation, etc., available in the *Manu-Smṛti* have been brought to light. From the description of the subject it appears that a well-balanced economic system was maintained in India during his times. The availability of all economic facilities resulted in the Economic prosperity of the country. An attempt has been made to cover all the relevant aspects of the subject.

Ancient Indian religious system like social system underwent transformation time to time. In the times of Manu and Patañjali, the religious system was broadly based on the Vedic and Brāhmaṇical tradition in respect of the religious beliefs and practices. However, the introduction of idols-worship in the temples was a new religious development. Their times witnessed the growth of Śaiva and Bhāgavata cults of Hinduism. The co-existence of Brāhmaṇism, Buddhism and Jainism constitutes the distinguishing hallmark of the religious system that prevailed in their times. All these aspects of the subject have been focused upon in an essay, "Ancient Indian Religious system in the times of Manu and Patañjali".

Pre-Persian foreign expeditions of north-western India constitute a landmark in the political history of ancient India. The history of early foreign invasions of north-western India available to us does not deal with any invasion before the time of Persian king, Cyrus (*c.* 558-530 BC). However, there are some evidences in the classical sources and in some standard historical records to prove the two pre-Persian foreign expeditions of north-western India, one that was undertaken by Egyptian king Sesostris and the other by the Assyrian queen, Semiramis. After thorough investigation into the subject we find that there are some rooms for casting doubt on the Egyptian invasion, and, on the other hand, there are some concrete evidence to prove the Assyrian invasion a real one. The former is a myth, and the latter is the truth. The Assyrian invasion of India in the eighth century BC was no doubt an epoch-making event. In the course of invasion, some portions of north-western India were subjugated which formed parts of Assyrian empire which was later overthrown by the Persian king, Cyrus the great. The Persian empire in turn was overthrown by the Macedonians. The subject offers a scope for further study and research.

Assam known as Kāmarūpa in the Gupta age appeared on the political map of India for the first time during the reign of Samudragupta (*c.* AD 335-80). The political status of Assam underwent transformation during the days of imperial and later Gupta monarchs. From its subordinate status in the fourth century AD it attained an independent status in the latter half of the sixth century AD and then further reached the pinnacle of glory in the first half of the seventh century AD or during the rule of Bhāskaravarman. The vicissitudes in the political fortunes of Kāmarūpa kings were closely linked with those of the imperial and later Gupta kings. The subject has been discussed in ancient Indian historical perspective.

PART I

The Āryans and the Cīnas

1

India from Ariana to the Gaṅgā Valley
On the Original Homeland and Expansion of the Āryans*

THE picture which emerges from the researches carried out so far by the Indian and foreign scholars into the subject concerned is neither very graphic nor accurate. There are certain aspects of the subject like the geographical position and identification of *Ariana*, the exact location of the original home of the Āryans and their antiquity, settlement — patterns and expansion, the factors involved in inter-tribal warfare, the Āryan-non-Āryan contest for political and cultural supremacy, etc., which need further investigation. And, hence, we find a fair scope for recasting the subject in correct historical perspective. There is no denying the fact that the *Ṛgveda* being the earliest among the extant literary sources provides some valuable information about the subject of the contemporary period. But there are several missing links in the said text which can be traced with the help of some other ancient Indian literary texts of the Vedic and post-Vedic period, including epic — the *Mahābhārata* — and the Purāṇas, the classical (Greek & Roman) accounts of the pre and post-Christian era, the literary and epigraphic records of Persia (the ancient name of Iran), the Chinese, German and French sources and some other reliable historical records by connecting them together for presenting a cohesive picture of the subject. The information which the Persians and the classical geographers add historians obtained about the farthest limit of northern India to the west of the Indus, the extent of Ariana, the location of different territories which formed parts thereof and the settlements of different Āryan and non-Āryan populations in greater north-western India is comparatively more trustwortny than those of many ancient Indian writers and some modern scholars of the East and the West. However, the epic and Purāṇic accounts of north-west India are to a greater extent supplementary to the Persian and Greek accounts. Thus, it will be in the fitness of things to place our reliance on the combined testimony of all the Indian and foreign sources concerned. The aim of

---

* From *Adhyayan*, *JBIAS*, vol. II, no. 2, 1992, pp. 1-21. (The paper originally published in this journal has been revised and enlarged in the light of further study and research.)

the present paper is to prove *Ariana*, which embraced considerable portion of north-west India, a cradle or common home of the Vedic Āryans and the ancestors of Iranian Āryans before the separation of the latter from the former and to show five distinct phases of the formers' settlements and expansion within India itself extending from the Oxus (Sanskrit Vaṁkṣu) basin (constituting the nucleus of Ariana) to the Gangetic valley from the pre-Ṛgvedic period to the later Vedic period. An attempt has also been made to reject the theories propounded by several scholars relating to Āryan invasion of India and hypotheses advanced by them about the Āryan connection with the Indo-European family on the basis of the study of comparative philology and their migration from Europe or Central Asia between *c.* 2500 BC and 1500 BC, etc. Due to erroneous geographical conception of the boundaries of India, the original homeland of the Āryans has been placed outside India. The use of the name "Central Asia", which was not known as such until the dawn of the seventh century AD, will not be justified in the context of ancient India of the period preceding to that century. Hence, the region very often placed in Central Asia like Bāhlika, which formed the part of *Ariana* and was inhabited by the Āryans during the period concerned, belonged to India as testified by all the contemporary sources. The paper is primarily based on the results which I have obtained from the investigation of all the relevant sources, including some very very rare ones which have hitherto not been much explored.

Ariane or *Ariana* (Āryāṇā = Āryadeśa) to the west of the Indus or Sindhu comprised Bāhlika (old Persian Bākhtri = Bactria or Bactriana of the Greeks = modern Balkh in northern Afghanistan) situated on the south bank of the river Vaṁkṣu called Oxus by the Greek geographers, the southern and eastern sides of the mountain ranges of the Hindukush (Paropanisos or Paropamisus), south-eastern Afghanistan (Arachosia of the Greeks and Harahvaiti of the Persians) extending westward up to Kandahār, the Kabul valley (Paropanisadae), the Gāndhāra region on both sides of the Kabul river, the whole northern, western and southern Afghanistan, Herat (derived from the Sanskrit word Hari-Ruda — a river, the Aria or Areia of the Greeks and Haraiva of the Persians), Bluchistan (Gedrosia of the Greeks) and the surrounding regions, as evidenced by Megasthenes (*c.* 325-298 BC),[1] Eratosthenes (*c.* 278-196 BC),[2] Apollodorus of Artemis (before

1. *Indika*, Bk. I, Fragm. IV; Bk. IV, Fragm. LVI cf. *MAIMA*, 1st edn., pp. 48-49, 151-52, also pp. 10, 108, note; E.A. Schwanbeck, *Megasthenes' Indika*, pp. 29, 30, note 24; see also Fragments of "*Indica*" of Megasthenes collected by Schwanbeck and tr. by J.W. McCrindle in *Ind. Ant.*, ed. by J.A.S. Burgess, vol. VI (1877), pp. 127-28; R.C. Jain (ed.), *MAIMA*, App. 3; R.C. Jain, *Ethnology of Ancient Bhārata*, pp. 59-52.
2. *Geog.*, Bk. III quoted by Strabo in his *Geog.* (completed about AD 19), Bk. XV, I, 10-11; XV, 2, 8 cf. *MAICL*, pp. 15 and 86-88.

the time of Strabo),[3] Strabo (*c.* 64 BC - AD 21),[4] Pliny (*c.* AD 23-79),[5] the author (anonymous, first century AD) of *Periplus*,[6] Ptolemy (middle of the second century AD),[7] Arrian (*c.* AD 96-180),[8] Dionysios Periegetes (third century AD),[9] Ammianus Marcellinus (latter half of the fourth century AD or *c.* AD 380-400),[10] Nonnos (fifth century AD),[11] E.H. Bunbury,[12] Saint Martin,[13] M. Elphinstone,[14] Rawlinson,[15] Lassen,[16] V.A. Smith,[17] H.H. Wilson,[18] A.

---

3. *History of Parthia* quoted by Strabo in his *Geog.*, Bk. XV, 2, 8 cf. *MAICL*, p. 88, also p. 81, note 1; see also H.H. Wilson, *Ar. Ant.*, pp. 120-21.
4. *Geog.* Bk, XV, 2, 8 and 9 cf. *MAICL*, pp. 86-89; R.C. Majumdar, *CAI*, pp. 93-99, 101; also Eng. tr. of his *Geographica* by H.C. Hamilton and Falconer, III, pp. 77-78, fn. 3.
5. *Naturalis Historia*, VI, 23; also *MAICL*, p. 80, fn. 1; see also Eng. tr. of *Nat. Hist.*, by B. Riley.
6. *The Periplus of the Erythraean Sea*, tr. from the Greek and annotated by W.H. Schoff, pp. 163, 183 & 189; see also J.W. McCrindle, *The Commerce and Navigation of the Erythraean Sea, Periplus* Section, pp. 120-21, also p. 186, fn. 36.
7. *MAIT*, pp. 34, 269, 308, 310-13, 315-19, 328.
8. *Indica* pt. II, Ch.XXVI; *Anabasis* Bk. IV, Ch. XXII; Bk. VI, 24, 2; see Eng. tr. of both *Anabasis* and *Indica* by E.J. Chinnock; also J.W. McCrindle, *The invasion of India by Alexander the Great*, p. 58 and notes 2 & 4.
9. *Bassarika*, LI.1080-1165, *MAICL*, p. 188.
10. *Hist.* Bk. XXIII, Ch. IV, *MAICL*, p. 93.
11. *Dionysiaka* (a Greek epic poem in hexameter verse), *MAICL*, p. 199 and fn. 4.
12. *A History of Ancient Geography among Greeks and Romans from the earliest ages till the fall of the Roman Empire*, vol. I, pp. 425-29; vol. II, pp. 641-42.
13. *E'tude sur la Geographie Grecque et Latin de L' Inde*, pp. 9-14 quoted in *MAICL*, p. 15, fn. 3 and *MAIMA*, p. 108.
14. *The History of India*, 9th edn. (London, 1911), pp. 331-36; see also his, "The Greek accounts of India", rept. from above in M. Elphinstone, E.B. Cowell & Co., *Ancient India* (Varanasi, 1983), p. 12.
15. *Ind. Ant.*, vol. V, pp. 329-20; *JRGS*, vol. XII, pp. 113f.
16. *Indische Alterthumskunde*, vol. I, pp. 142, 290f; vol. II, pp. 631f.
17. *The Early History of India*, 4th rev. end., pp. 158-60.
18. *Op. cit.*, pp. 120-34.

Cunningham,[19] E.B. Cowell,[20] E.J. Rapson,[21] and Aurel Stein.[22] The Ariana region concerned (lying within the geographical limits of India intact till the dawn of the sixth century BC) was the land of the Āryans (designated as *Arians*, *Aria*, *Arianoi*, *Arianians*, etc.), who were of indigenous origin and bound together by the tie of a common language, Sanskrit. This can be confirmed by the statements of both oriental and occidental scholars.

M. Burnouf, a French scholar, identifies the appellation *Airyana* with *Airya-dagya*, which is said to be the "Sanskrit *Ārya-deśā*". *Ariana* and a variety of ancient denominatives of which *Aria* is a component element have been connected by him with the "Hindu term *Ārya*, excellent, honourable". This is fairly attested to by his own statements: " 'I' Arie dans sa plus grande étendue Cèst ā dire le pays habité pår la race des Arya ou des hommes nobles." His expression "less provinces non Ariennes" denotes Anairyya.[23] The accuracy of his statement can further be tested by the testimony afforded by H.H. Wilson. According to him, this is the region to which the "Hindus extended the designation of *Ārya*" and the Persians gave the name "*Airya* or *Airyana*," which for the first time was called *Ariana* by the classical geographers and historians of the pre- and post-Christian era. The *Ariana* of the ancients in the widest application of the term, according to him, was inhabited by both the Indians and Iranians, speakers of Sanskrit, which was very much akin to the Persian language, Zend. This linguistic affinity is a valid argument for regarding them as one people and the natives of one and the same country. "The traditions of the Hindus concur with those of the Persians in considering the tribes immediately west of the Indus, and even those towards the Oxus as their countrymen".[24] The *Ariana* is considered to be the concrete manifestation of the Sanskrit "Āryā-Vartta or Varṣa" (the Āryan territory). This is equated with the "Āryā-Varttahalf of the" ("the country of

---

19. *The Ancient Geog. of India*, p. 13; *Coins of Ancient India from the earliest time down to the seventh century AD*, p. 31.
20. 'The Brahmanical Tribes and Aborigines', in *Ancient India* (Varanasi, 1983), p. 63, fn. 2.
21. Ed., *The Cambridge History of India*, vol. I, *Ancient India*, Ch. XXII, pp. 487-89, 494 & 500; Ch. XXIII, p. 509; See also D.C. Sircar, *Studies in the Geog. of Ancient and Medieval India*, p. 66, fn. 1 (for general idea).
22. "The Indo-Iranian Borderlands : their prehistory in the light of geography and of recent explorations", *JRAI*, vol. LXIV (1934), pp. 179-202; also his *Archaeological Reconnaissances in North-Western India and South-Eastern Iran*, Ch. I, pp. 1-36. See also J.E. Schwartzberg (ed.), *A Historical Atlas of South Asia*, p. 17, pl. III, B.3-Map of Ariana.
23. *Commentaire Sur le yacna*, LXII, quoted in H.H. Wilson, *op. cit.*, pp. 121-22.
24. *Op. cit.* pp. 121-125.

excellent men") of Manu[25] which extends between the Himālaya and the Vindhya mountains or between the eastern and western sea.[26]

The Āryan settlements in the region concerned justifies the use of the classical denomination, i.e., Ariana. Like the ancient Indian writers of the post-Vedic period, the Greeks and Romans also applied the territorial designation to the Āryan population of northern India.

The *Ariana* as the earliest home of the Āryan population in the north-west is also corroborated by the evidences furnished by McCrindle in different translated Greek texts. He has clearly stated that the name of *Ariane*, *Ariana* or *Areia* is "connected with the well known Indian word *Ārya* — noble or excellent".[27] He has further observed that ". . . considerable tracts of the vast region so designated ('*Ariane*') have been from the earliest times down to the present day inhabited by tribes of Indian descent . . . various mountains, rivers, tribes and localities, that are situated in the west of the Indus including northern Afghanistan, were of Sanskrit origin . . . a fact attested both by historians and geographers and confirmed by the evidence of language . . . and that this region was at one time more or less fully occupied by Aryan settlers, who thence diffused themselves over the Punjab and other parts of India."[28] John Wilson also supports the view that the *Ariana* of the Greeks was an "ultimate extension of the name Ārya to the land of the Veda".[29]

N.L. Dey,[30] Masson-Oursel,[31] J. Talboys Wheeler,[32] Adolf Kaegi[33] and Max Duncker[34]

---

25. H.H. Wislon, *op. cit.*, pp. 121-22.
26. *Manu-Smṛti*, II, 22.
27. *MAIT*, p. 308; see also *MAICL*, p. 80, fn. 2.
28. *MAICL*, pp. 15, fn. 3, 80, fn. 1; see also Elphinstone, *op. cit*; pp. 331-36; Saint Martin, *E'tude*, pp. 9-14.
29. *India Three Thousand Years Ago*: *The Social state of the Aryas on the banks of the Indus in the times of the Vedas*, p. 18.
30. *The Geographical Dictionary of Ancient and Medieval India*, p. 11; *Civilisation in Ancient India*, pp. 1-3.
31. *Ancient India and Indian Civilisation*, p. 16.
32. *India from the Earliest Ages*, vol. III, pp. 8, 14-15.
33. *Life in Ancient India*: *Studies in Rigvedic India*, tr. from the German by R. Arrowsmith, p. 110, note 13.
34. *History of Greece from the Earliest times to the end of the Persian war*, tr. from the German by S.F. Alleyne, vol. I, p. 1.

(both German scholars) and Edward Thomas[35] have also admitted that *Ariana* (*Āryāṇāṁ*) was the original abode of the Vedic Āryans as well as the Iranians, but they refuse to accept their Indian origin probably because of vague geographical conceptions of north-western India. They have not established the geographical identity of the region in contemporary situation. That is why, some of them have connected the Vedic Āryans with Central Asia or Iran. In order to prove them as an immigrants, the Oxus region has been described as a gateway to India. But their findings have proved to be wrong precisely because of the partial examination of the problem by them.

The fact remains that the Āryans in remote antiquity were found scattered in different parts of Ariana to the west of the Indus as an indigenous people from where some sections of them gradually expanded over different parts of Sindh, Punjab and upper valleys of the Gaṅgā and Yamunā encountering the non-Vedic population for establishing their supremacy. D.D. Kosambi's[36] interpretaion of *Ariana* is not satisfactory at all. He has made only an incidental notice of the subject.

The land between the two rivers Cakṣu or Vaṁkṣu and Sītā mentioned in the Purāṇas[37] and the *Mahābhārata*[38] as two of the seven streams of the Gaṅgā (the former, Greek Oxus, Mongolian Bakshu, Tibetan Pakshu, Chinese Po-Chu or Arabic-Persian Vaksan and Amu Dariya, and the latter, Greek Jaxartes or Arabic Syr-Dyria, but not the Vedic Rasā[39]) to the north-west of the Hindukush originally known as Sugda (Sanskrit), Sughdha (Avestan), Suguda (old Persian), Sogdiana (Greek),[40] Suhak, Sugat or Samokan

---

35. *JRAS*, (The proceedings of the meeting held on 9 April 1866), New Series V, p. 420, fn; see also Z.A. Ragozin, *History of Vedic India*, pp. 49f. 51-56, 74-75.
36. *An introduction to the study of Indian history*, p. 82.
37. *Vāyu Purāṇa*, 47, 21; 47, 37-39, 44; also 43, 24; *Viṣṇu*, 2, 2, 34 & 37; *Matsya*, 114, 22; 121, 39-40; *Mārkaṇḍeya*, 53, 13; *Alberuni 's India*, Eng. tr. by E.C. Sachau, vol. I, Ch. XXV, p. 261; see also Wolford, *As. Res.*, vol. VIII, p. 330.
38. *Bhīṣma Parva*, 10, 15-35; see also V.S. Agrawala, *Bhārat Sāvitrī*, vol. I, p. 153; vol. II, p. 130; vol. III, pp. 60-63.
39. *Ṛgveda*, 1, 112, 12; 5, 53, 9; 10, 75, 6; 10, 108, 1-2; See also P. Gupta, *The Geographical names in Ancient Indian inscription up to 650 AD*, pp. 126f and A.D. Pusalker, 'Aryan settlements in India', in *The Vedic Age*, p. 247 — as a stream in the extreme north-west of the Vedic territory.
40. See *MAIT*, pp. 395-96, note.

(Chinese Su-hie and Sa-Mo-Kin)[41] and called Samarkand (now in Uzbekistan, formerly part of USSR) for the first time by an Arabian in AD 643[42] was not the original home of the Āryans as believed by some scholars. Bāhlika or so-called Bactriana constituting the principal part of *Ariana* or in the words of Apollodorus "the ornament of all *Ariana*"[43] and divided from Sogdiana by the river Oxus, of course, flourished as one of the earliest seats of Āryan culture. The so-called Sogdiana region is the Ramanaka-Varṣa of the Purāṇas[44] and the Oxus basin the Ketumala of the Purāṇas[45] and the *Mahābhārata*.[46] Sogdiana was divided from Bactriana by the river Oxus and extended northward from thence to the river Jaxartes. According to some scholars, this region in Central Asia was the common home of the Āryans which is far from the truth. It is said that "The region embracing the head-waters of the Oxos appears to have been the scene of the primaeval Aryan paradise. . . . The Oxos which rise in the Pamir lake at 300 miles south of Jaxartes . . . was one of very earliest seats of civilisation."[47] But the Āryan home cannot be extended to that region, E. Herzfeld's observation that "From time immemorial at least from the third millennium down to the middle of the second, the Āryans inhabited as an undivided ethnical group the vast plains of the Oxus and Jaxtartes, the land Eranvej of the two rivers — Vahvi-Datiya and Ranha"[48] can also be dismessed as unauthentic and vague. S.M. Ali has pointed out that both Bāhlika and Sughdha or Bactria and Sogdiana were the most ancient sites of human civilization because of all economic facilities.[49]

The absence of details of the Sughdha region or Sogdiana in the *Ṛgveda* confirms our doubt about the settlements of the Vedic Āryans there. But it can scarcely be doubted that the Rgvedic period saw the original settlements of the Āryans in *Ariana* region,

41. See T. Watters, *On Yuan Chwang's Travels in India, AD 625-645*, I, pp. 92-93.
42. *Ibid.*
43. Cf. Strabo, *Geog.*, XI, xi, 1, *MAICL*, pp. 100-1; According to H.G. Rawlinson (*Bactria*, p. 1, note 1), Bactria was the "most northerly of the four primitive Aryan settlements".
44. *Vāyu*, 45, 2; *Matsya*, 113, 60.
45. *Vāyu*, 34, 57; *Viṣṇu*, 2, 2, 24, 37 & 40; *Mārkaṇḍeya*, 53, 15; *Matsya*, 113, 44.
46. *Bhīṣma Parva*, 7, 11, 15.
47. *MAIT*, pp. 278-79.
48. *Iran in the Ancient East*, p. 190.
49. *The Geography of the Purāṇas*, p. 83.

including Bāhlika, though it does not figure in the text. It finds mention only in one of the later Vedic texts referred to here later.

It is said that the "Sugdha" region in Alexander's time was under the "Brahmin ascendency".[50] This may be because of the expansion of Indian culture and settlements of the brāhmaṇs there who were the speakers of the Sanskrit language.

The *Ariaca* of the *Periplus*[51] which is described as one of the strongholds of the Āryans by the translator and annotator of the text, and *Ariake* of Ptolemy (*Geog*., VII, I) called the land of the Āryas,[52] supported by John Wilson,[53] seem to be identical with *Ariana*. The land of the Arians of Herat (Afghanistan) or Aria is also identified with *Aryata-desa*.[54] Varāhamihira's *Āryaka* (*Bṛ. Saṁ*., ch. XIV), exactly corresponds with Ptolemy's *Ariake*. Kalhaṇa's *Āryānaka-deśa* mentioned in his *Rājataraṅgiṇī* is absolutely identical with *Ariana* of classical writers.

Before we proceed to cite the evidences from the *Ṛgveda Saṁhitā* in support of the Āryan settlements in some parts of *Ariana*, here it will quite profitable to answer one of the vital questions as to what extent Ariana formed the part of India or whether it was lying within the geographical boundary of ancient Bhāratavarṣa? This has not so far been answered satisfactorily.

Eratosthenes was the first classical geographer of the third century BC to affirm that *Ariana* was bounded on the east by the Indus and on the north by the Paropamisus (Hindukush) mountains or 'Baktra' (Bāhlika).[55] Pliny (*Nat. Hist*., VI. 23) has categorically stated that the Indus was not the western boundary of India because the Cophes (Kabul) river and four provinces — Arachosia (Kandahār), Gedrosia (Baluchistan), Paropanisadae (Kabul valley) and Aria (Herāt) — all parts of Arians — also belonged to India. This is supported by V.A. Smith,[56] H.H. Wilson[57] and McCrindle.[58] From the statements of A.H.L.

50. Arrian's *Anabasis*, VI, Ch. 16, quoted by B.N. Puri, *India as described by early Greek writers*, p. 57.
51. Schoff, *op. cit*., p. 70.
52. *MAIT*, pp. 39, 345, note.
53. *Op. cit*., p. 28.
54. Gerini, *Researches on Ptolemy's Geography of Eastern Asia*, p. 41; H.H. Wilson, *op. cit*., p. 129.
55. Quoted by Strabo, *Geog*; XV, 2, 8, *MAICL*, pp. 86-88.
56. See his *Early History of India*, pp. 32, 43, 50-54, 113, 132-34.
57. *Op. cit*., p. 121.
58. *MAICL*, p. 15, fn. 3.

Heeren,[59] B.C. Law,[60] H.H. Wilson[61] and Vasudeva Sharan Agrawala[62] it is quite evident that India before the Persian conquest of north-west India (sixth-fifth centuries BC) embraced within its boundaries not only the land lying immediately to the west of the Indus, but also Afghanistan, the Valleys of the Hindukush, Bactria and the north-eastern corner of the Iranian table land. This can also be indirectly supported to some extent by the statement of Mortimer Wheeler.[63] In the light of the evidences discovered so far, it can fairly be established that the Āryans of *Ariana* in the Ṛgvedic period were purely of Indian origin.

Ariana in all probability was the derivative of *Ārjika* (a territory of the Āryans in Afghanistan), as mentioned in the *Ṛgveda*,[64] and not *Ārjikiya* (a river). The Ṛgvedic references to the rivers to the west of the Indus, viz., Kubhā (modern Kabul river),[65] Suvāstu (Swāt in Afghanistan),[66] Gomatī (Gomal in Afghanistan),[67] Krumu (modern Kurram),[68] Rasā, Antibhā and Sarayū (Harayu of the Persians)[69] and Hariyupiyā (Hari-rūda in Herāt, Afghanistan)[70] and the place-names like Gāndhāra[71] testify to the Āryan settlements in different parts of Afghanistan, Kabul valley, Gāndhāra and Kandahāra. The references to Bāhlika region and Gāndhāra in *Atharvaveda*[72] also prove their constant association with these regions. The names of the rivers, viz, Śvetayāvari, Añjasī, Kuliṣī,

59. *Historical Researches into the Politics, Intercourse and Trade of the principal nations of Antiquity*, vol. I, *Asiatic Nations*, Persians, pp. 273 & 279.
60. *Historical geography of Ancient India*, pp. 10-11.
61. *Op. cit.*, p. 134.
62. *Bhārat Sāvitrī*, vol. 2, pp. 134-35.
63. *Early India and Pakistan*, p. 15.
64. IX, 65, 23; IX, 113, 2, see also A.A. Macdonell and A.B. Keith, *Vedic Index*, vol. I, pp. 62-63 and 179; J.E. Schwartzberg, *op. cit.*, p. 13, pl. III, A.1 — Map on Vedic India for Ārjika and Ārjikiya.
65. 5, 53, 9; 10, 75, 6.
66. 8, 19, 37.
67. 5, 61, 19; 10, 75, 6.
68. 5, 53, 9; 10, 75, 6.
69. 5. 53, 9; 10, 75, 6.
70. 6, 27, 5-6. See also Aurel Stein, 'On some River Names in the Ṛigveda', *JRAS* (1917), pp. 91-99; L. Renou, *Vedic India* (trans. from the French by Philip Spratt), p. 126.
71. *ṚV*, 1, 126. 7-8; *Atharvaveda*, 5, 22, 14.
72. 5, 22, 5, 7, 9, 14.

Vīrapatnī, Sarayū and Adinā as mentioned in the Ṛgvedic hymns[73] have been reasonably placed by A.C. Das[74] in Bactria (Bāhlika) region. Vedic allusions to the Pārthavas[75] and Pārśavas[76] show the continuity of contact between the Vedic Āryans and Persians during the period concerned.

The destruction of sons of Vṛcivāna or Varaśikha at the hands of Indra at Hariyupiyā (a place on the river of the same name), as narrated in the *Ṛgveda*,[77] has created a confusion in the minds of many scholars about its identification with Harappā. Actually, this event took place at the bank of Hari-rudā river or Herāt (Haritoya of *Vāyu Purāṇa*, 43, 26) in Afghanistan. That is why, some foreign Vedic scholars have placed it in "Arachosia".[78] Jamna Des Akhtar's interpretation of this event as the battle of Harappā[79] is not valid. This is the battle on the basis of which Mortimer Wheeler propounded a misleading theory of Āryan invasion of Harappā (which he re-excavated in 1946) about the middle of the second millennium BC, but this is merely a fanciful notion, as he has himself accepted that "these thoughts are mere conjectures and not proven".[80] The myth of Āryan invasion of Harappan towns has already been exploded.[81]

F. Max Müller also for sometime (from 1851 to 1871) held that the "Indo-Āryans" migrated from Central Asia — "the common home of the speakers of Āryan language" — and conquered India and finally made Sapta-Sindhu their home.[82] But later, after 1871 and specially in 1887 he changed his view and postulated that "somewhere in Asia" they had their earlier home. He did not accept the racial concept of Āryan, but went on

73. See 8, 26, 18; 1, 104. 3; 4, 30, 18; 5, 53 9; 7, 18, 8; 10, 64, 9.
74. *Rigvedic India*, vol. I, p. 72.
75. *ṚV*, VI, 27, 8.
76. *ṚV*, X, 33, 2.
77. 6, 27, 5-6.
78. See *Vedic Index*, pp. 29f.
79. See A. Cunningham's *The Ancient Goegraphy of India*, Notes, XXV; *The Sacred Books of the Āryans — The Matsya Purāṇa*, vol. I, pp. V-XII.
80. *Early India and Pakistan*, p. 113; *The Indus Civilization*, p. 27.
81. K.M. Srivastava, "The Myth of Aryan invasion of Harppan Towns" in B.B. Lal and S.P. Gupta (eds.), *Frontiers of the Indus civilization*, pp. 437-42.
82. See his *A History of Ancient Sanskrit literature*, pp. 11-14; *The Vedas*, pp. 1-3; *Lectures on the science of language*, vol. I, p. 275; vol. 2, pp. 445-46; *Biographies of Words and the Home of the Arya's*, pp. 80-154.

repeating the same theory which he expounded on the basis of the comparative study of so-called Indo-Āryan group of language.[83] But his theory gradually started losing its importance.

Romila Thapar has correctly stated that by identifying language with race some try to show "all speakers of Sanskrit as members of that nineteenth-century myth, the Āryan race".[84] She has questioned the validity of the theory of Āryan race as propounded by the Indologists and Philologists of the nineteenth century, for it is not supported by any historical evidence. She has rightly pointed out that the term Ārya stands for honoured person, and it does not have racial connotation.[85]

The Sapta-Sindhu region (Hapta-Hindu in the *Avesta*) encompassing seven rivers:— Sindhu, Śutudri (Sutlej), Vipāśā (Vyāsa), Paruṣṇī (Irāvatī-Rāvi), Asiknī (Cenāb) and Vitastā (Jhelum) — the five rivers of Punjab — and Sarasvatī, as described in the *R̥gveda*, was one of the flourishing centres of Āryan culture and civilization. A.C. Das[86] was one of the chief exponents of the theory of Sapta-Sindhu region as the original home of the Āryans. This has been accepted by many other India scholars.[87] But, actually, this was one of the prominent centres of their original settlement in the R̥gvedic period. It is significant to note that there is no evidence in the *R̥gveda* or elsewhere to prove the immigration of Āryans into this region from outside India. That is why, Muir[88] and many others[89] considered this region as the original home of the Āryans.

The Āryan territories in the north watered by the western tributaries of the Indus, the Cakṣu (Vaṁkṣu) and the said seven rivers also find mention in the Purāṇas.[90] Gordon Childe observes: "the hymns of the *R̥gveda*, the oldest Hindu sacred Book, describe the

---

83. *Biographies of Words and the Home of the Aryas*, pp. 89-90, 120, 127.

84. *Ancient Indian Social History*, p. 152.

85. "Which of us are Aryans?", *Seminar*, Monthly, No. 364 (Delhi, Dec. 1989), pp. 14-18.

86. *R̥gvedic India: Cultural History of India as depicted in the R̥gveda*, vol. I, pp. 8ff, 19-67, 122f.

87. See M.L. Bhargava, *The Geog. of R̥gvedic India*, pp. 129-30, 243f; V.N. Reu, *R̥gveda Par Ek Aitihāsika Dr̥ṣti*, p. 119f.

88. *Original Sanskrit Text*, vol. II, pp. 322, 523.

89. Rahul Sāṅkr̥tyāyana, *R̥gvedic Āryas*, pp. 58f; P.L. Bhargava, *India in the Vedic Age*, pp. 22f, 47-50, Curzon, *JRAS*, vol. XVI, pt. II (1854), pp. 187-200; See alo *The Vedic Age*, pp. 220-21 (App. — "India the Original Home land of the Aryan"); Z.A. Ragozin, *History of Vedic India*, pp. 49-56, 63ff.

90. *Vāyu*, 45, 93-96; *Matsya*, 114, 20-22; *Mārkaṇḍeya*, 54, 15-19.

Aryan tribes scattered about the north-west from the Kabul and the Kurram to the head waters of the Ganges and the Jumna."[91]

The comparative study of the Vedic, Epic and Purāṇic literature leaves behind an impression that there were several centres of Āryan culture within India which simultaneously flourished, and some of them like the Sārasvata region with Kurukṣetra as its nucleus were the original seats of the Āryans. This particular region was thickly populated during the R̥gvedic period. During this period, the Āryans had spread over different parts of Afghanistan, Punjab, Kashmir and the region lying between the Sarasvatī and Dr̥ṣadvatī. The original settlements of the Āryans in the region extending from the western bank of the Yamunā to Kurukṣetra (or Brahmāvartta) on the bank of Sarasvatī can be proved by the statement of V.S. Agrawala.[92] The *R̥gveda*[93] and the *Mahābhārata*[94] provide the details of the Sapta-Sārasvata region which also give some clues to their indigenous origin in contradistinction to their foreign origin.

F.E. Pargiter has strongly advocated in favour of the Indian origin of the Āryans. He has put aside all the conventional views relating to the Āryan invasion of India from Afghanistan in the north-west or their gradual advance from there eastward through the Punjab only as far as the Sarasvatī or Yamunā. On the basis of the Purāṇic evidence, he has attempted to prove Pratiṣṭhāna on the north bank of the Yamunā near Prayāg as their original home from where they are said to have spread over north-west and other parts of India. He also refers to the entry of Ailas or Āryans into India from the mid-Himālayan region on the basis of the ancient Indian historical tradition.[95] But he has not fully substantiated his arguments. However, H.D. Sankalia corroborates his views in his three different works[96] so far as Pratiṣṭhāna as the original home of the Āryans is concerned. No doubt, it flourished as one of the centres of the Āryan culture in the Gangetic Doāb or Madhya-deśa.

---

91. *What happened in History*, p. 175.
92. *Bhārata Sāvitrī*, I, pp. 255-56.
93. 6, 5, 61, 1-14.
94. *Āraṇyaka Parva*, 81, 1-7, 20, 97, 125, 175-78.
95. *Ancient Indian Historical Tradition*, pp. 296, 298-302.
96. *Prehistory and Protohistory of India and Pakistan*, pp. 557-58; "Prehistoric colonization in India: Archaeological and Literary evidences", in *Aspects of Indian History and Archaeology*, eds. S.P. Gupta & K.S. Ramchandran, pp. 308 & 310; *Prehistory of India*, p. 179.

The *Ariana* region to the west of the Indus in ancient Persian tradition was called *Eriene-Veejo* or *Airyana Vaejo* (the seat of pure or original Āryans). It was one of the 16 "good lands" as referred to in the Vendidad, Fargard I, of the *Avesta*.[97] J.D. Nadir Shah (an Iranian scholar) has described it as "the birth-place of the primitive Āryans". According to him, it was situated to the south-eastern foot of the Caucasus (now called the Central Hindukush).[98] Actually, it had a wider geographical extent than that of described by him. Curzon is of the opinion that ancient Iranian and Zend language have originated from the Vedic Sanskrit, and hence Iranians, one of the branches of the Āryans, expanded from the Sapta-Sindhu over the western region (Iran), and Āryans as such did not come from the west to the Sapta-Sindhu.[99]

The R̥gvedic Āryans and the Persians of the *Avesta* lived together in Ariana and Sapta-Sindhu and spoke one language for a considerable period of time which is attested by the similarity of the Vedic Sanskrit and Avestic language, the common names of the gods and goddesses and identical religious practices. The four important inscriptions — *Behistun inscription*, *Persepolis inscription*, *Naqsh-i-Rustam inscription* and *Hamadan Gold and Silver Tablet inscription* of Darius (*c*. 522-486 BC) bearing the names Ariya or Airya (Sanskrit = Āryavaṁśayaḥ), Sugudah or Sughdha, Sugdam, Gāndhārā, Bakhtri or Bakhdhi (Bāhlika), Hindu (Sindhu), Harahvaiti (river Harirudā of Herāt and not Sarasvatī), etc.,[100] show the intimate connection of both in the Ariana and Sapta-Sindhu region of high antiquity. After the separation of these two kindred peoples in Sapta-Sindhu, the Persian Āryans probably occupied Bactria or the region of Balkh, north of the Hindukush in Afghanistan, and Persia,[101] while the Vedic Āryans continued to exist in the Kabul valley, southern Afghanistan, Indus region and other parts of north-western India. The date of their separation cannot be determined with any reasonable degree of certainty. The dates varying from the third millennium BC to 1500 BC[102] are given in the sense of their separation from the so-called common home outside India. But we have every ground to admit the probability of their separation from each other in the Sapta-Sindhu

97. Eng. trans. by J. Darmesteter, SBE, vol. IV (Oxford, 1887, rept. Delhi, 1974), pp. 2-5.
98. "Aryana Vaejo, The Cradle of the Aryans", *Proc. & Transactions of First Oriental Congress*, 1920, pp. 84-94.
99. *JRAS*, vol. XVI, (1854), Pt. II, pp. 187-200; See also P.L. Bhargava, *op. cit*., pp. 47-50.
100. D.C. Sircar, *SI*, vol. I, pp. 4-11.
101. See *Camb. Hist. of Inida*. I, pp. 285ff; E.J. Rapson, *Ancient India*, p. 16. Also N.M. Chapekar, *Ancient India and Iran*, pp. 5-24.
102. *Vedic Age*, p. 210; Motichandra, *Sārthavāha*, pp. 39-40.

in the early Vedic Age. As a matter of fact, it was the Persian occupation of Gāndhāra, Kabul and Sindh during the time of Darius and their incorportaion into the Achaemenian empire which resulted in the division of Ariana as the country between India and Persia. It was this historic event which marked the demarcation of Indian and Persian boundary. The Indus became the western boundary of India and eastern boundary of Persia which remained unchanged till the time of Candragupta Maurya. This epoch-making event changed the entire geography and history of north-western India and made the confusion worse confounded about the geographical extent of Ariana as well as the origin and identity of the Vedic and Persian Āryans who lived together not only in Sapta-Sindhu but also in *Ariana* within India of the contemporary period. Hence, they in no way can be called an undivided branch of Indo-European stock.

It was the later Vedic Age which witnessed the expansion of Āryans (the Kurus representing the combination of two major sections, Bhāratas and Purus) in the valleys of the Gaṅgā and Yamunā. They passed from the stage of so-called pastoral economy to a settled life with kingdoms and urban centres, which have archaeologically been also proved. They were associated with Painted Grey Ware (PGW) and Northern Black Polished Ware (NBPW) cultures whose Carbon-14 dates vary from *c.* 1200 BC to 600 BC. Their further expansion in the upper and middle parts of the doāb, Pañcāla (Ahicchatra and Kāmpilya, northern and southern capital respectively), Matsya (Brahmarṣi-deśa), Madhya-deśa (in the east of Vinaśana, where Sarasvatī loses itself in the sand, and to the west of Prayāg), and that of other Āryan groups in Kāśī, Kośala, Aṅga, Magadha, Videha, etc., can be attested to by the combined study of the Veda,[103] Brāhmaṇas,[104] Purāṇas[105] and *Manu-Smṛti*.[106] Max Müller remarks that the five Vedic peoples (Purus, Aṇus, Yadus, Turvasas and Druhyus) were the builders of the civilization that flourished in the vast region extending from the Himālaya in the north to Kanyā-Kumarī in the south. He considers it as an event of historic importance in the annals of human civilization.[107]

The analyses of all the available data concerned help us arrive at a positive conclusion

103. *Atharvaveda*, 5, 22, 14.

104. *Ait. Br.*, 8, 3, 14; *Śat. Br.*, 1, 7, 2, 8; 1, 7, 3, 8; 5, 5, 2, 3; 13, 5, 4, 2; 13, 5, 4, 9; *Taitt. Br.*, 1, 8, 4, 1-2; 25,13, 1; *Tāṇḍya, Brāhmaṇa*, 25, 10, 16; *Taitt. Saṁ.*,7, 4, 19, 1; *Taitt. Āryan.*, 5, 1, 1.

105. *Matsya*, 114, 34-36; 121, 49-51; *Vāyu*, 47, 48-49.

106. II, 19-22; see also H.C. Chakladar, *The Aryan Occupation of Eastern India*, pp. 15ff.

107. *India — What can it teach us?*, pp. 5-10, 95-96.

that Ariana in the widest application of the term extending from the Vaṁkṣu (Oxus of the classical writers) basin south-east of the Hindu-Kush to the Kabul valley and lying within the geographical limits of ancient Bhāratavarṣa intact till the dawn of the sixth century BC was one of the earliest centres of the Āryans in north-western region to the west of the Indus in both pre-Ṛgvedic and Ṛgvedic period. It was a common home of the early Vedic and Persian Āryans as attested by the literary, epigraphic and linguistic evidences. Geographically, historically and culturally too Ariana, a part of India, was the cradle for both where they remained as the natives of one country till their separation from each other sometime in the Vedic Age and not between *c.* 2500 BC and 1500 BC as mistakenly supposed by some scholars. They were originally not an undivided branch of Indo-European family as established by some Indian and Western indologists on the basis of the study of comparative philology. Nor were they invaders or immigrants from outside. Rather, they were autochthones or indigenous inhabitants of India. The Vedic, Purāṇic, Persian and classical traditions confirm our belief.

Ariana was the *Ārjika* (not Ārjikiya — a river or lake) of the Ṛgvedic India and *Airyana-Vaejo* (*Āryāṇāṁ Vijaṁ* = the seat of pure or original Āryans) of the Persian *"Zend Avesta"* of Zarathushtra period (*c.* 660-585 BC). The classical geographers and historians of Alexander's time (*c.* 327-325 BC) applied the territorial designation *Ariane* to the land of the Āryans in north-west India. It was that part of the Āryāvarta, which stretched from the Himālaya to the Vindhyas and extended from eastern to western sea, as described by Manu. It corresponds to the *Ariake* of Ptolemy in the real sense of the term.

It was the Persian occupation of north-western India under Darius (*c.* 522-486 BC) and incorporation of Gāndhāra, Kabul and Sindh into Achaemenian Empire which in all likelihood resulted in the division of Ariana as the country between India and Persia, and in consequence the Indus became the western boundary of the former and eastern boundary of the latter which again underwent changes after the transfer of four important parts of Ariana — Kabul, Kandahār, Baluchistan and Herāt — to Candragupta Maurya by Seleucus in *c.* 305 BC. The post-Mauryan period's developments and particularly the Arabian occupation of Iran in AD 642 and Sindh in the first quarter of the eighth century AD resulting in the geographical transformation of the whole north-western region misled many scholars about the extent of the boundaries of India to the west of the Indus in the pre-sixth century BC and origin and identity of the Āryans of Ariana.

The fact remains that the Āryans were in possession of a vast territory extedning from the Vaṁkṣu valley to the Gaṅgā-Yamunā Doāb during the Vedic period. They were widely scattered over different parts of India. Hence, it will not be fair to show one particular region as their original home. Rather, it will be more accurate to say that there were many centres of their original settlements and expansion within India itself. Ariana within India like Sapta-Sindhu region, Gangetic Doāb and Sārasvata region was one of the noted early centres of Āryan civilization. Thus, India was undoubtedly the original homeland of the Āryans. Their settlements and expansion were all within the geographical limits of ancient Bhāratavarṣa. It will be in the fitness of things to mention that they do not represent any race of foreign origin, but a social group of Indian origin with a higher grade of culture.

The theory of Central Asiatic Origin of the Āryans was invented in 1820 by J.G. Rhode. According to him, the region watered by Oxus and Jaxartes north of the Himālayas and east of the Caspian Sea was the original home of the Āryans. He included Bactria (Bāhlika region) also in it. His view was endorsed by Schlegel and Pott. In 1848, Jacob Grim and in 1859 F. Max Müller also propounded more or less the same theroy which was later blindly supported by many.

As a matter of fact, Bāhlika on the river Vaṁkṣu or Oxus in northern Afghanistan was a part of Greater north-western India and not Central Asia. It was in the words of Strabo "the pride of Ariana". Without taking into account the geographical limits of India in the Vedic age, some European scholars included it in Central Asia which is not only a colossal blunder but also misleading.

It is worthwhile to mention that in a closed-door meeting held at the office of Royal Asiatic Society, London, on 9 April 1866 under the presidentship of Viscount Stronghold, Mr. Thomas invented a new theory about the origin and migration of the Āryans. According to his theory, Central Asia was their home where they lived together for considerable period of time. After leaving their original home they were divided into three branches. One migrated towards Europe and conquered the primitive inhabitants of the land. And other branch migrated towards Iran and Iraq and there also they repeated the same work which the Āryans did in Europe. The third branch entered India through the western passes of the Hindukush and settled in Afghanistan and Punjab and conquered the aboriginal Draviḍians, made some of them their slaves and the rest fled towards the south to save their lives. While advancing from the Punjab towards the east, the Āryans settled on the banks of the river Sarasvatī. The Āryans, according to him, belonged to a pastoral race, This was all concocted story and not a real history. An extract of the minutes of the meeting recorded in *JRAS* (new series, V, 1866, p. 420, fn) was passed over by Tilak to later scholars.

The Āryans or Vedic peoples were not nomads. They as indigenous peoples had rather settled life in Afghanistan, Punjab, Sindh, Madhya-deśa or Gaṅgā-Yamunā Doāb and Sarasvatī basin. They were civilized group. They had their own history and culture.

It can further be added that the comparative linguistic evidence adduced by some European philologists and ethnologists of the nineteenth century in support of the foreign origin of the Āryans became the root cause of the whole Āryan problem. By establishing the similarities between the seven principal languages (Greek, Latin, German, Celtic, Slavonic, Sanskrit and Zend) of so-called Āryan or Indo-European family and by placing their speakers in a common home in Asia or Europe and by showing their diffusion therefrom after their division and separation towards their respective countries sometime between *c.* 3000 or 2500 BC and 1500 BC, they propounded the Āryan race and migration theory.

Max Müller (1823-1900), a well-known Vedic and Sanskrit scholar, philologist and indologist of Germany, was one of the chief exponents of the theory of Central Asiatic home of the Āryans. In 1848, he settled at Oxford, where he continued to live till his death. In 1851, he wrote his first article in English wherein he used the word Āryan in the sense of a language and a race, which is on the record.[108] The Āryan problem was taken up for study in Germany and England along the same line. It may be noted here that Lassen (1800-76), the famous orientalist, was the first to use the word "Arian" (Āryan) in the racial sense in his *magnum opus*, a German work, *Indische Alterthumskunde* (*The History of Ancient India*) whose first volume came out in 1847. There may have been some impact of it on the writings of the former. Likewise, the theory of Central Asiatic origin of the Āryans propounded earlier might have influenced his thinking in the direction of finding their original home.

Max Müller joined the Oxford University as a professor of Sanskrit and Head of Vedic Research Department in 1855. On the basis of his study of science of comparative philology he tried to establish that the ancestors of the Greeks, the Romans, the Germans, the Celts (inhabitants of Wales and western France), the Russians, the Vedic Indians (or "Hindus") and the Persians belonged to the Āryan family. They were the speakers of the Āryan language. They were living together within the same fences in the common (or original) home in Central Asia and not Arctic region or Europe. The whole Āryan family as a result of their first separation about *c.* 3000 BC were divided into two distinct branches,

---

108. J. Huxley, *Race in Europe* in the series Oxford Pamphlets on World Affairs, No. 5, (OUP, London, 1939), p. 9.

the north-western and the south-eastern, which he himself calls it "only possible hypothesis". The north-western group comprising the first five migrated towards Europe. The south-eastern group comprising the Indians and Persians crossed over the narrow passes of the Hindukush, conquered or drove away before them the aboriginal inhabitants and settled in the north-western part of India in the new homes in the beautiful and fertile valleys. It is further said that within the sight of the Indus and its tributaries, the undivided south-eastern Āryans spoke the language common to Sanskrit and Zend but more primitive than both. The people spoke an Āryan language near the northern course of the Indus about *c*. 2000 BC. The Vedic Āryans and the ancestors of Persians remained united for sometime before their second separation between them. The primitive Āryans thrived in Persia. He has confessed that beyond this everything is uncertain and mere guesswork. He says that the Āryan conquerors of India came clearly from the north along the rivers of the Punjab. Ever since their settlements in the land of the seven rivers India has been called their home. Both the north-western and south-eastern Āryan groups are said to have been the prominent actors in the great drama of history.[109] His theory is not tenable at all. His description of the Āryans as nomads, a race, tribes, conquerors, etc., is not based on reality. It is equally not correct to say that they were speaking an Āryan language from which Sanskrit and Zend have been derived.

After 1871, Max Müller, of course, changed his views but only to a limited extent and not fully. In a lecture delivered at Strassburg in 1872, he pointed out that only the Vedic Sanskrit and Zend have some identical words. The other five languages of so-called Indo-European family are not very similar. He warned the scholars against wasting their time on an impossible task of discovering similarities between those five languages. He, however created the confusion by stating that "all the Aryan languages are cognate dialects".[110] He does not deny that the ancestors of the north-western branch of the Āryans may have remained together for sometime before they became finally separated, but maintains that "the linguistic evidence is too weak to support such conclusions".[111] He himself questions "Is it possible to fix the original home of Aryan speech, and to

109. For details see his *HASL*, pp. 11-14; 'The Veda and Zend-Avesta' — a lecture delivered at the Philosophical Institution, Leeds, in March 1865, pub. originally in *Chips from a German Workshop*, vol. I, rept. in *The Vedas* (a collection of his five lectures and one article published in different books), pp. 1-3; *Lecturers on the Science of Language*, vol. I, pp. 240 ff, 249; vol. II, pp. 445-46; *Biographies of Words and the home of the Aryas, op. cit*, pp. 80-103, 134, 153-54.

110. *Selected Essays*, vol. I, pp. 174, 225.

111. *Biographies of Words and the Home of the Aryas*, p. 87.

dertermine the migrations of the races who spoke Sanskrit, Persian, Greek, Latin, Celtic, Slavonic and Teutonic, in their progress from their original histoircal head-quarters"? And he himself answers that ". . . a commom language is by no means a certain proof of a common bee-hive".[112] He has admitted that "There is no Aryan race in blood. . . . Aryan, in scientific language, is utterly inapplicable to race. It means language and nothing but language; and if we speak of Aryan race at all, we should know that it means no more than a Aryan speech."[113] He says that ". . . . the first rough hypothesis was that the cradle of the Aryans may have been somewhere in Asia. There may have been a time when scholars were so much impressed with the primitiveness of Sanskrit that they would have preferred India as the cradle of the Aryas, and Sanskrit as the mother of Greek, Latin and the other Aryan dialects . . . we know that the Aryas were originally strangers in India."[114] He again says that Sanskrit is the most primitive language of the Āryan family. But the languages of Indo-European or Āryan family except Zend were not derived from it. He asserts that ". . . . the primitiveness of language is no proof whatever of the primitiveness of the geographical habitat of its speakers. It would be a mere revival of the exploded argument that all the Aryas must have come from the Sarasvati."[115] He clearly states that "I have declared again and again that if I say Aryas, I mean neither blood nor bones, nor hair nor skull; I mean simply those who speak an Aryan language. The same applies to Hindus, Greeks, Romans, Germans, Celts and Slaves. . . . To me an ethnologist who speaks of Aryan race, Aryan blood, Aryan eyes and hair, is as great a sinner as a linguist who speaks of a dolichocephalic dictionary or a brachycephalic grammar."[116]

It is significant to add that Max Müller further observed: "The actual site of the Aryan paradise, however, will probably never be discovered, partly because it left no traces in the memory of the children of the Aryan emigrants, partly because imagination

---

112. *Biographics of Words and the Home of the Aryas*, p. 88.
113. *Ibid.*, pp. 89-90.
114. *Ibid.*, p. 93.
115. *Ibid.*, p. 95.
116. *Biographies of Words and the Home of the Aryas*, p. 120.

would readily supply whatever the memory had lost. Nor is actual site a matter of great importane. Most of the Aryan nations in later times were proud to call themselves childern of the soil, children of their mother earth, autochthones. Some thought of the East, others of the North, as the home of their fathers; none of them . . . of the South or the West. New theories, however, have their attractions, . . . some patriotic scholars should have been smitten with the idea of a German, Scandinavian, or Siberian cradle of Aryan life. . . . But if an answer must be given as to the place were our Aryan ancestors dwelt before their separation. . . . I should still say, as I said forty years ago, 'Somewhere in Asia', and no more."[117]

From Max Müller's presentation of the subject it appears that he denied the existence of Āryan race and pleaded for its separation from language. He also did not favour the idea of determining the original home of the Āryans on the basis of linguistic similarities. He, however, retained his old view that the common Āryan home must have been "somwhere in Asia" — a vague expression — which gives scope to scholars to speculate on their original home any where in Asia.

The employement of the terminology of Comparative Philology in an ethnological sense has not produced anything substantial rather it has given birth to wrong theories about the origin of the Āryans. The "unholy alliance of these two sciences — Comparative Philology and Ethnology" had been protested not only by Max Müller himself,[118] but also by A.H. Sayce,[119] a distinguished philologist. E.B. Tylor aptly remarked that "A man's language is no full and certain proof of his parentange".[120]

V.G. Childe has correctly stated that the extension of the term Āryan to embrace all speakers of languages of Indo-European family is "illegitimate".[121] Collin Renfrew

117. *Biographies of Words and the Home of the Aryas*, p. 127.

118. *Ibid.*, pp. 244-45; *Lectures on the Science of Language*, vol. I, pp. 458-59.

119. *Introduction to the Science of Language*, vol. II, pp. 317-18; *Principles of Comparative Philology*, p. 175f; see also his "The Aryan Problem — Fifty years later", *Antiquity*, I, 1927, pp. 204-15.

120. *An Introduction to the study of Man . . . .*, pp. 112, 152.

121. *The Aryans, a study of Indo-European Origins*, p. 95; see also his "Retrospect", *Antiquity*, vol. XXXII, 1958, p. 73.

(Professor of Archaeology, University of Cambridge) has also rejected Max Müller's theory that the speakers of languages of that family had same original homeland where they lived together and following separation wandereds around Europe and western Asia.[122] S. Piggott's view that those Āryan-speaking people who established themselves in the Indus Valley in the second millennium BC after leaving the common home were predominantly conquerors[123] is also not acceptable.

The "highland of Central Asia, the region of the sources of Oxus and Jaxartes" was generally held to be original home of the primaeval Āryan community in the nineteenth century. Adolf Kaegi, a German Vedic scholar, also upheld the same view. According to him, the eastern branch of Āryans or Indians after their separation from the Iranians entered India by crossing over the western passes of the Hindukush. Their place of abode had been synchronised by him with "the time of composition of most of the hymns of the *Ṛig* — about 2000-1500 BC". It is further said that the chief settlement of the Vedic people was then in the territory of the Sindhu which was most thickly populated. They also settled in some parts of Afghanistan and along the five rivers of the Punjab.[124] Some other scholars have also harped on the same tune without examining the credibility of an evidence of linguistic palaeontology.

The proponents of the Central Asiatic origin theory have neither spelt out the reasons why the Āryans deserted this region and migrated towards Europe and Asia nor answered the questions if the Āryan original home was there why it became devoid of Āryans?, and why their descendants are not found there? This theory can now be completely discarded without any hitch and hesitation. The dates suggested by various scholars are also imaginary. They are not worthy of our acceptance.

The theory of Asiatic origin of the Āryans was rejected by some British scholars in the latter half of the nineteenth century. And they started looking for Āryan home in Europe. Isaac Taylor was one of them.[125] It was Giles who propagated the view that the

---

122. "Homelands in Question", from his *Archaeology and Language: The puzzle of Indo-European Origins*, In *Manthan*, JDRI, XV, 2-3, 1994, p. 79.

123. *Prehistoric India*, pp. 220, 239f; 246, 251.

124. *Studies in Ṛgvedic India*, trans. from the German, by R. Arrowsmith, pp. 21-22, 110, note 13.

125. *The Origin of the Aryans : An Account of Prehistoric Ethnology and Civilization of Europe* pp. 18-53.

Āryans migrated from Austria, Hungary and Bohemia to Persia, Bactria, Afghanistan and Punjab. O. Schrader, a German scholar, objecting to such view correctly stated that neither myth nor history nor language warrants any conclusion in support of their European origin. He strongly supported the Asiatic origin of the Āryans. But he suddenly shifted to European home theory. He himself could not find any positive answer as to whether Āryan home was in Europe or in Asia. He shifted from one hypothesis to the other.[126] L. Poliakov, a Russian author, questions the origin of so-called 'Āryan race' in Europe.[127]

The Āryan race theory, which is an invention of nineteenth-century Europe, has already been rejected by J. Huxley of England,[128] L.B. Synder of America,[129] Koenraad Elst of Belgium,[130] P. Choudhury,[131] Devendra Swarup[132] and many other Indian scholars. Romila Thapar also rejected this theory, as noted before, but she is still opposing the indigenous origin of the Āryans which is quite evident from her own statements as followes: "The linguistic evidence of the Vedic Sanskrit supports the coming into India of an Indo-European language from Iran, but does not support the notion that India was the homeland of the Āryan speaking people."[133] "Although the earlier notion of a systematic destruction of Harappan sites by Āryan invaders has been questioned from the evidence of archaeology, this does not allow us to maintain that the speakers of

---

126. "Sudden Shift to European home", an extract taken from his *Prehistoric Antiquiteis of the Aryan Peoples: A Manual of Comparative Philology and the Earliest Culture* (Eng. trans. of the 2nd edn. of original German book), in *Manthan, op. cit.*, pp. 57-62; also Isaac Taylor, *op. cit.*, pp. 48-52; K. Penka also advocated the European home theory in his famous work, *Origines Ariacae* (Wien, 1883).

127. "European Origins or Racism", in *Manthan, op. cit.*, pp. 22-35; also his *The Aryan Myth : A History of Racist and Nationalist Ideas in Europe* (Eng. trans. by Chattto-Heinemann), pp. 230 ff.

128. "The Myth of an Aryan race", in *Manthan, op. cit.*, pp. 63-65.

129. "The Origin and Development of the Aryan Myth", from his *The idea of Nationalism : Its Meaning and History*), in *Manthan, op. cit.*, pp. 70-78.

130. *Indigenous Indians : Agastya to Ambedkar* (Delhi, 1993).

131. *The Aryan Hoax that Dupes the Indians*, pp. 7, 15-16, 22, 31-34, 55, 93ff; also his *The Aryans : A Modern Myth* (Delhi, 1993).

132. "Genesis of the Aryan Race: theory and Its Application to Indian History", in *Manthan, op. cit.*, pp. 101-18.

133. "The perennial Aryans", *Seminar*, 400, 12, 1992, p. 22.

Indo-Āryan were therefore indigenous to India."[134] On the basis of affinities of the language of the *Ṛgveda* to old Avestan, she seems to be bit inclined to hold that there was a movement of Āryan speakers from West Asia to India.[135] But the truth is something different which I have highlighted here later.

It is worthy of note that on the basis of the evidence available in the *Ṛgveda* and the Purāṇic records, the facts brought to light by some Indian and foreign scholars through their researches during the last two decades and the recent archaeological discoveries, now it can conclusively be proved that the Vedic Āryans were of indigenous origin.

There were serious attempts by some Indian and foreign scholars in 1919 and late 1920s to project the image of Āryans as invaders.[136] But the views expressed by them in this connection have now become outdated, and hence they are no longer tenable. In fact, the whole concept of the Āryans as a race, immigrants, conquerors or invaders is totally wrong.[137]

Mortimer Wheeler's theory that the Āryans entered north-west India from outside, invaded and destroyed the Indus Valley cities (paritcularly Mohenjo-Dāro) in or about *c.* 1700 BC or about the middle of second millennium BC, massacred the people including women and childeren, defeated the aboriginal Draviḍians and pushed them towards the south, and thereafter they established themselves[138] was based on misinterpretation of the Ṛgvedic evidence of the destruction of some forts of the Dasyus by King Indra (1, 130, 7 and 10; 2, 14, 6; 2, 19, 6; 2, 20, 7 and 8; 4, 16, 13; 4, 26, 3; 4, 30, 20; 6, 20, 10; 7, 18, 13; 7, 99, 5; 8, 98, 6). This theory was a figment of his imagination and nothing else but only imagination. By no stretch of imagination the decline and fall of the Indus Valley

---

134. "The Theory of Aryan Race and India : History and Politics", *Social Scientist*, 24, 1-3, 1996, p. 13.

135. *Seminar*, *op. cit.*, p. 21.

136. For details see J. Kennedy, "The Aryan invasion Northern India", *JRAS*, 1919, pp. 493-529; J. Pathi, "Is Indo-Aryan Invasion a Myth?", *IHQ*, 1928, pp. 678-94, E.J. Thomas, "The so-called Indo-Aryan Invasion", *IHQ*, 1929, pp. 248-53; C.V. Vaidya, "Indo-Aryan invasion of India — not a myth", *ibid.*, pp. 253-60.

137. See also B.B. Chakravorty, *Itihāsa of Bhāratavarṣa From the Bhāratīya viewpoint*, p. 2.

138. "Archaeology and the Transmission of ideas", *Antiquity*, vol. XXVI, 1952, pp. 180-92; *EIP*, pp. 113, 131-32; "Ancient India: The Civilization of a subcontinent", In S. Piggott (ed.), *The Dawn of Civilization*, p. 249; *Civilization of the Indus Valley and Beyond*, pp. 79-83.

cities can be attributed to the Āryans. It is mainly on the basis of his theory that generally historians of ancient India believe that it is *c.* 1500 BC which marked the beginning of the Veidc age, and the Vedic civilization followed the Harappan civilization. But the fact remains that the former was much older than the latter. The antiquity of these two civilizations cannot be determined with any accuracy and precision; nor can their chronological order be decided with any degree of certainty because of the continuity of the former from the pre-Harappan to the Harappan period and beyond.

G.F. Dales was the first archaeologist to reject Wheeler's theory on the basis of his findings in the course of the excavation at Mohenjo-Dāro conducted in 1964. The skeletal remains spread all over the places at the site, according to him, were of "the people caught in a sudden and surprise flood". "None of them shows any cut-mark".[139] Following him many Indian and foreign savants demolished the said theory.

Asko Parpola has also disposed of Wheeler's view on the ground that the Dāsas or Dasyus' forts destroyed by the Āryans were not the Harappan strongholds. But his own view that the Āryans immigrated into India in successive waves and invaded it sometime before 1000 BC is not correct either. His statement that the R̥gvedic hymns do contain unmistakable reminiscences of the Āryan conquest and take over of the land from its earlier inhabitants (Dāsas)[140] is distortion of the history of R̥gvedic India. He has surmised that the earlier fight was more likely "in ancient Bactria or northern Afghanistan".

It will not be out of place to mention what Swami Vivekanada had said long ago: "And what your European pundits say about the Aryans swooping down from some foreign land, snatching away the lands of the aborigines and settling in India by exterminating them, is all pure nonsense, foolish talk. Strange that our Indian scholars, too, say amen to them; and all these monstrous lies are being taught to our boys. This is very bad indeed."[141]

The observation of an American archaeologist, J.G. Shaffer, is also worth-quoting here:

139. "The Mythical Massacre at Mohenjodaro", in *Expedition*, vol. VI, no. 3 (Phlladelphia, 1964), pp. 36-43; JOR, vol. XXXI, pp. 32-39; see also Wheeler's Review of "The Mythical Massacre at Mohenjodaro by G.F. Dales" in *Antiquity*, vol. XXXVIII, 1964, pp. 307-9.

140. "The Coming of the Aryans to Iran and India and the Cultural and ethnic identity of the Dasas", *Studia Orientalia*, vol. 64 (Helsinki, 1988), pp. 208-15; see also R. Heine Geldern, "The Coming of the Āryans and the end of the Harappa Civilization", *Man*, JRAI, vol. LVl, 1956, p. 151.

141. Quoted in *The East and the West* (Calcutta, Jan, 1990), p. 104.

"Current archaeological data do not support the existence of an Indo-Aryan or European invasion in the South Asia at any time in the pre or protohistoric period. Instead, it is possible to document archaeologically series of cultural changes reflecting indigenous cultural development from prehistoric to historic periods."[142]

The Āryan invasion of northern India is a mere myth which has already been exploded by a number of Indian and foreign scholars, notably, N.R. Waradpande,[143] S.G. Talageri,[144] N.S. Rajaram,[145] David Frawley (the American Vedic scholar popularly known as Vāmadeva Śāstrī)[146] and S.C. Kak.[147] They have all strongly advocated the indigenous origin of the Vedic Āryans with special emphasis on the Sārasvata region as their heartland.

B.G. Tilak's theory of the Arctic (North Polar region) home of the Āryans[148] was based on his supposition. He takes on astronomical ground the period from *c.* 6500 BC to 4500 BC as an important epoch in the history of Āryan civilization.[149] This theory was first critically examined by A.C. Das.[150] G.B. Levin, a Russian indologist, has also summarily rejected this theory.[151] Many other scholars taking Tilak's view as far-fetched imagination have disapporved it.

The Āryan migration or invasion theory propounded by some Indian and Western scholars so far in support of the foreign origin of the Āryans are purely hypothetical. We

---

142. "Indo-Aryan Invasions : Cultural Myth and Archaeological Reality", in J.R. Lukacs (ed.), *The People of South Asia: The Biological Anthropology of India, Pakistan and Nepal*, p. 88.
143. *The Aryan Invasion : A Myth*, pp. 2ff, 30ff, 90ff.
144. *The Aryan Invasion Theory : A Reappraisal*, pp. 290ff; also *Aryan Invasion Theory and Indian Nationalism* (Delhi, 1993).
145. *Aryan Invasion of India: The Myth and the Truth* (Delhi, 1993); *The politics of History Aryan Invasion Theory and the subversion of Scholarship* (Delhi, 1995).
146. *The Myth of the Aryan Invasion of India,* pp. 2ff, 59-63; Rajaram and Frawley, *Vedic Aryans and the origins of civilization: A Literary and Scientific perspective*, pp. 8-24, 45-60, 205.
147. "Vedic studies provide valuable Clues", *Manthan*, XV-4-XVI, 1 (1994-95), pp. 5-36.
148. *The Arctic Home in the Vedas*, pp. 145-48, 420.
149. *Ibid.*; *The Orion: Researches into the Antiquity of the Vedas*, pp. 200, 206ff.
150. *Op. cit.*, vol. II, pp. 372ff.
151. "Is Arctic the Original Home of Indians", *Soviet Land*, nos. 12-13, June-July 1968.

do not have any authentic evidence either historical or archaeological to accept such theory. But, on the other hand, we have a number of positive evidence including literary and archaeological to prove their Indian origin.

All the thirty-six times the word *Ārya* has been used in the *Ṛgveda* (the oldest Vedic text) in an adjective sense like noble, honourable, righteous, etc. Amarasiṁha in his *Amarakoṣa* (a lexicon) has given six characteristics of an *Ārya*. A true Ārya, according to him, is one who is a noble, civilized, gentle, of saintly disposition, born in a high family, etc.[152] Neither the evidence of the Vedic Sanskrit nor that of classical Sanskrit shows the Āryans as a racial group, linguistic group or ethnic group.

On the testimony of the *Ṛgveda*, the original settlements of the Vedic Āryans along the different rivers in Afghanistan (mentioned before) can be proved without any doubt. The valleys of Kabul and Swāt, Kandahār, Herāt and adjoining regions were the main centres of thier natural habitation. This was the *Ariana* region (the land of the Āryans) of classical writers the eastern boundary of which was the Indus and northern boundary the Paropamisos (Hindukush) mountains, or the same mountains of which the continuation formed the northern limit of India, as stated by Eratosthenes.[153] It is upon the authority of Apollodorus of Artemita (a town in Babylonia), an author of the *History of Parthia*, quoted several times by Strabo, that the name of *Ariana* was again so extended as to include some portions of Persian and Median territory, and even some of the northern parts of Bactria (the land on the other side of the Oxus extending northward to the Jaxartes) and Sogdiana (Samarkand) on the pretext that the people there spoke nearly the same language.[154] Apollodorus because of his vague knowledge of the northern limits of *Ariana* extended it to so-called Central Asiatic region.

There is not even the slightest indication in the *Ṛgveda* of the Āryan immigration into northern India from outside. Nor do we find any evidence in classical literature of their coming to India from Central Asia or from any part of Europe.

> "Hindus have lived in Afghanistan since ancient times, and it is believed to be the motherland of the Āryans — the cradle of the Āryan culture; it is from here that the Āryans are stated to have migrated to other lands."[155] But Afghanistan

152. *Amarakoṣa* with the "*Maṇiprabhā*" Hindi commentary of Haragovinda Sastri, 2, 7, 3.

153. Cf. Strabo, *Geog.*, XV, 2, 8, J.W. McCrindle, AICL, p. 86.

154. *Ibid.*, McCrindle, *op. cit.*, p. 88.

155. S.R. Lund and O.P. Pyasa, "Hindus in Afghanistan", in *Vivekanada Kendra Patrika*, II, 1 (Madras, 1973) p. 256.

> has been wrongly mentioned as a "mountain-locked country in central Asia".[156] While writing about the origin of the Āryans, many scholars have lost sight of the fact that Afghanistan remained an integral part of north-western India from the Vedic age down to the end of the seventh century AD.

Sapta-Sindhu or Sapta-Sindhavaḥ (the land of the seven rivers) mentioned in the *R̥gveda* (2, 12, 12; 8, 24, 27; 10, 43, 3; 10, 49, 9) included the Sindhu or Indus with its five principal tributaries on the West and the Sarasvatī on the east. The R̥gvedic references to the Sindhu (10, 75, 1-4, 6-8), the five rivers of the Punjab — the Paruṣṇī or Rāvī (5, 52, 9; 7, 18, 5, 8-9; 10, 75, 5), the Asiknī or Cenāb (5, 53, 9; 8, 28, 25; 10, 75, 5), the Śutudrī or Sutlej (3, 33, 1; 10, 75, 5), the Vipāśā or Vyāsa (3, 33, 1-3; 4, 30, 11) and the Vitastā or Jhelum (10, 75, 5)[157] — and the Sarasvatī (2, 41, 16-17; 7, 95, 1-6; 7, 96, 1-5; 10, 75, 5) bear witness to the fact that the Vedic Āryans were originally settled in the territories lying along these seven rivers.

The Sapta-Sindhu region was, no doubt, the cradle of the Āryans. Muir has unequivocally stated that there is no reference in any Sanskrit text to the Āryan settlements in Sapta-Sindhu after coming to India from outside which proves that they were the original inhabitants of this region which extended from the Sindhu to the Sarasvatī and included also the territory watered by the Kabul (where there was its confluence with the Indus), Kashmir and the Punjab.[158] B.C. Law's statement that "It is the Punjab where the early Āryans first settled themselves after their migration to India"[159] is wholly unworthy of our credence. Some scholars like K.M. Munshi,[160] S. Śrīkānta Śāstri[161] and Buddha Prakash[162] have strongly pleaded in favour of Sapat-Sindhu as their original home. Sampurnananda on the basis of his in-depth study of the subject has also convincingly argued in favour of this view.[163] He has categorically stated that

156. S.R. Lund and O.P. Pyasa, "Hindus in Afghanistan", in *Vivekanada Kendra Patrika*, II, 1 (Madras, 1973) p. 256.

157. See also A.C. Woolner, "The *Rigveda* and the Punjab", *BSOAS*, vol. VI, pp. 549-54.

158. *Op. cit.*, pp. 322, 523.

159. *Op. cit.*, p. 120.

160. *The Glory that was Gurjaradeśa*, p. 46.

161. "India, the Original Home of the Aryans", in *The Vedic Age*, *op. cit.*, Appendix, p. 220.

162. *Rigveda and the Indus Civilization*, p. XLV.

163. *Āryoṅ Kā Ādi Deśa* (in Hindi), 4th edn., pp. 27-37; A.K. Raman in his *Āryataraṅgini* (pp. 13, 22) has categorically stated that the Āryans moved from their original habitat, Afghanistan, the Indus Valley, and the Sapta-Sindhu region, into the Indo-Gangetic plain; L.N. Renu (*Indian Ancestors of Vedic Aryans*, pp. 35-37) has correctly stated that originally the Vedic Āryans were Indians.

the Āryans did not live either in the Arctic region or in Central Asia or in Western Europe but in their own original home — Saptasindhava — from where there was expansion of their culture in far distant land.[164] The information supplied by Z.A. Ragozin that the Āryans had been living in the valley of Kashmir (a part of Sapta-Sindhu) before the compilation of the *R̥gveda Saṁhitā*.[165] is of great worth.

The Sarasvatī was the greatest of the seven rivers. It was entirely an independent river and altogether different from the Indus. It was a mighty historical river. It was mightier than even the Indus. From the *R̥gveda* we learn that "it had flowed from the mountain (Himalayas) to the sea" (7, 95, 2). Now it is proven fact that Sirmora (the Plakṣa cataract) beyond Nāhana hills of the Śivālik range (near Shimla) was its source wherefrom it descended to the plains at a place called Ādi Badri in the Ambālā district. It had flowed from there in almost northwesterly direction through present-day Punjab, Haryana, Rajasthan and Gujarat down to the Arabian Sea. It was very very important river for the Vedic Āryans from various points of view. There are valuable references to it in the *R̥gveda* (2, 41, 16-21; 6, 61, 1-14; 7, 95, 1-6; 7, 96, 1-6) which highlight its importance as their sacred heartland. More than thirty-five hymns have been dedicated to this river. The composers of the hymns on this river have shown that their ancestors also used to laud it (6, 61, 10) which confirms the truth that the Āryans had been living on its banks since time immemorial. It has been diescribed as the "best of rivers" (2, 41, 16; 6, 61, 13; 7, 95, 2), the "best of mothers" (2, 41, 16) and the "best of goddesses" (2, 41, 18). The Vedic peoples pray to this river for their settlements on its banks in preference to other places (6, 61, 14). The places of original settlements of the Vedic Āryans along this river and its tributaries formed parts of Sārasvata region which they held as their motherland because of their special attachment to it. And the culture which flourished there was a Sarasvatī culture. From the description of this river in the said text it distinctly appears that the Āryans living there were advanced agriculturist enjoying all the facilities for leading a happy and prosperous life. Most of the *yajña*s were performed on the banks of this river by Vedic sages.

The allusion to Saptasvasā in the *R̥gveda* (6, 61, 10) or Sapta-Sarasvatī in the same text (7, 36, 6; 6, 61, 12)[166] as well as in the *Mahābhārata* (*Āraṇyaka Parva*, 81, 97; *Śalya* Parva, 36, 63; 37, 11; 39, 21) is indicative of its seven streams or tributaries. One of its major tributaries was Dr̥ṣadvatī (modern Citāṅga or Ghagghara) flowing west of the

164. *Āryoṅ Kā Ādi Deśa*, p. 178.

165. *Op. cit.*, pp. 170-71.

166. See also N.N. Godbole, "Rigvedic Sarasvati", *ABORI*, vol. LXII, 1963, pp. 1-40.

Yamunā. It had its origin from the Sirmora hills (south of the source of the Sarasvatī) and flowing through Ambālā, Sind, Bhādarā, Nohara, Rāvatasara and Hanumāngarh met the Sarasvatī about three mile north of Sūratgarh. And further it disappered in the sands of the Rājapūtānā. The another important tributary of the Sarasvatī was Āpayā (modern Āpagā) which flowed three mile away from Thāṇeśvara.

One of the Ṛgvedic hymns clearly illustrates the truth that the Vedic peoples so-called Āryans were settled along all the three rivers — Dṛṣadvatī, Āpayā and Sarasvatī (3, 23, 4). These three were also the places of *yajñas* for the Bharatas.

The land between the two rivers, Sarasvatī and the Dṛṣadvatī, has been called Brahmāvartta in both Purāṇa (*Vmn.*, 23, 12, 9) and the *Manu-Smṛti* (2, 17) which, according to the *Mahābhārata*, is identical with Kurukṣetra situated on the bank of the Sarasvatī and called Brahmakṣetra (*Āraṇyaka Parva*, 81, 1-7). Kurukṣetra situated south of the Sarasvatī and north of the Dṛṣadvatī has been called the sacred land (*ibid.*, 81, 175). It was also called Brahmavedī (*ibid.*, 81, 177; *Vmn.*, 23, 12, 15). Kurukṣetra, one of the important parts of Sārasvata region, was one of the earliest seats of the Vedic Āryans. They first started the plough cultivation here. The ancient Brahmāvartta corresponded with modern Thāṇeśvara, Ambālā and Karnāl districts, Sonepat, Pānīpat, Kurukṣetra and adjoining regions in Haryana.

The importance of Kurukṣetra on the Sarasvatī has been highlighted especially in the *Mahābhārata*.[167] According to the *Śalya Parva* (50, 19), the source of the Sarasvatī was Sarasūtī which originates from Brahmasara. The modern Sarasūtī has been located between the Sutlej and the Yamunā. We are told in the *Vāmna Purāṇa* that the Āryan settlement in the basin of the river Sarasvatī had its own importance (23, 21, 17-25). In the same Purāṇa it is clearly mentioned that the river Sarasvatī flowing from Kurukṣetra moved towards the west (23, 11, 1-2; 23, 12, 1-2). After reaching northern Rajasthan it disppeared in the sand. Manu has described that place as Vinaśana where it dried up.

The land between the Sarasvatī and Dṛṣadvatī called Brahmāvartta has been considered by Rāmadatta Sāṁkṛtya as the birth place of the Āryans.[168] He unequivocally states that the "Āryas were original inhabitants of Sapta-Sarasvatī region".[169]

Brahmāvartta region was, no doubt, the epi-centre of the Āryans. It is from here that they expanded over "Brahmarṣideśa" (between Brahmāvartta and the Yamunā)

167. *Āraṇyaka Parva*, 81, 1-178; *Śalya Parva*, 34, 12-36; 36, 1-63; 37, 1-4, 19-24.

168. *Ādi Mānava kā Ādi Deśa* (in Hindi), p. 96.

169. *Ibid.*, p. 142.

which, according to Manu, comprised Kurukṣetra, Matsya, Pañcāla, and Śūrasena regions and was less than Brahmāvartta in extent and beyond it (2, 19). Ganganath Jha took Brahmarṣideśa as the original home of the Āryans.[170] But it was not their original homeland rather a region of their gradual expansion form their main seat Brahmāvartta.

Aurel Stein (1862-1943) of Hungary was the first archaeologist to discover some lost Sarasvatī sites. He explored in 1940-41 a part of the dried up course of the river Sarasvatī in Bahāwalpur region (in erstwhile Punjab, now in Pakistan) and also in Bikāner and Gaṅgānagar districts of Rajasthan.[171] He further undertook an archaeological tour along the river Dṛṣadvatī (Ghagghara) in 1941-42 and discovered its old bed having a width of about 6 to 8 km form Shatrana in Punjab to Marcot in Pakistan.[172] The lost track of the river Sarasvatī have been found in Punjab, Haryana, Rajasthan and Gujarat through the researches of mainly archaeologists, geologists and other scientists. Of about 1200 sites of the Indus-Sarasvatī civilization explored so far nearly 500 have been located in Rajasthan and the Haryana on the Sarasvatī and its tributaries like Dṛṣadvatī (the rivers *par-excellence* of the Vedic Āryas). Sūratgarh, Hanumāngarh, Anūpgarh and Pīlībaṅgan in Rajasthan, Kurukṣetra in Haryana, Shatrana in Punjab and Prabhās Paṭan in Gujarat were some of the notable centres of purely Sarasvatī civilization that belonged to the Āryas.[173] The dry bed of the Sarasvatī in Punjab, Haryana and northern Rajasthan have also been brought to light by the scientists attached to Space Application Centre and Physical Research Laboratory, Ahmedabad, through their study and analysis of "Land Satellite Imagery, Aerial Phototgraphs" concerned in 1980.[174] They have, no doubt, done a great service to history and archaeology. A Research Team of eighteen scholars

---

170. "Aryan Invasion of India — Is it a myth"?, in *Ācārya Puṣpāñjalī* (D.R. Bhandarkar Commemoration Volume, Calcutta, 1940), pp. 1-2.

171. "A Survey of Ancient sites along the lost Sarasvatī River", *Geog. Jour.*, XCIX, 4, 1942, pp. 173-82.

172. "An Archaeological Tour along the Ghaggar-Hakra river", American Documentation Institute, Microfilm No. ADI 4861 (Washington, 1943).

173. For details see S.P. Gupta, "Studies in the Indus-Saraswati Civilization : Some New Developments", *Manthan, op. cit.*, pp. 79-97; "The Indus-Saraswati Civilization : An Overview", *Itihasa Darpan* (Research Journal of History), Delhi, vol. I, 1994, pp. 46-52; S.R.N. Murthy, "Geological Foundations of Vedic Civilization", *Manthan, op. cit.*, pp. 132-34; V.M.K. Puri and B.C. Verma, "Glaciological and Geological source of Vedic Saraswati in the Himalayas", *Itihas Darpan*, IV, 2, 1998, pp. 7-21; S. Kalyanaraman, "Sarasvati River: Historic Legacy and Developmental Challenge", *ibid.*, pp. 37-50.

174. D.P. Agrawal, 'What happened to the River Saraswati', *Science Age*, Feb. 1984, pp. 18-24; Yashpal, Baldev Sahai, R.K, Sood and D.P. Agrawal, "Remote Sensing of the lost Sarasvatī River", *Proc. of Indian Acad. Science, Earth and Planetary Science*, vol. 89, No. 3, Nov. 1980, pp. 317-31; *Manthan, op. cit.*, pp. 139-49; see also K.N.P. Magadh, *Vagdevi Sarasvatī*, p. 4.

including Sanskritists, archaeologists, historians, geographers and geologists led by late V.S. Wakankar also discovered a number of lost Sarasvatī sites in Rajasthan and Haryana in 1985-86. They have produced sufficient evidence of the original settlements of the Vedic Āryans on the banks of this river in both pre-Harappan and Harappan period.[175] A civilization that flourished along both the Sindhu and the Sarasvatī was predominantly Vedic.[176] The ceremonial structures like *vedīs* (fire-altars) and *yūpas* discovered at Kalibaṅgan (both Sarasvatī and Harappan site) in Rajasthan were connected with the Vedic *yajñas*.[177] It is believed that the Harappans in the Sarasvatī river basin were by and large Vedic peoples. It has been observed by S.R. Rao that "Their religious motifs, deities and sacrificial altars bespeak of Aryan faith".[178]

The Sarasvatī civilization of the Vedic Āryans had its own continuity. It had reached a high pitch in the R̥gvedic age. It is now established fact that it flourished in both pre-Harappan and Harappan times whose radio-carbon dates respectively are *c*. 2500-2200 BC and *c*. 2200-1700 BC. There were six different stages of the decline of the Vedic Sarasvatī. The hydrological factor was mainly responsible for its desiccation. The rivers Yamunā and Sutlej were earlier flowing with the Sarasvatī, but later changed their courses and absorbed its waters. The Yamunā brought in the waters of the Sarasvatī to join the Gaṅgā. The Sutlej turned towards the west and joined the Vipāśā and then the Sindhu. The Dr̥ṣadvatī also turning towards south-east became separate from the Sarasvatī. All these resulted in the lack of water in the river Sarasvatī which ultimately led to its desiccation and decay of the civilization that had once flourished on its banks. There might have been some other geological factors and natural calamities responsible for the end of this civilization. After the desiccation of the Sarasvatī the Vedic peoples moved towards the Gaṅgā-Yamunā Doāb towards the end of the R̥gvedic period. These events, according to carbon-dating, are placed between *c*. 1800-1700 BC. The geological studies indicate that the Sarasvatī river dried up early in the second millennium BC or

175. *A Quest After the Lost Vedic Sarasvatī River — An Expedition Report*, trans into Eng. by V. Dhundiraj Bapat and K.R. Umapathy from original in Marathi by L.S. Wakankar and C.N. Parchure (Mysore, 1994), pp. 1-26, 68-82; *Sarasvati Sodha* (a collection of articles), Nagpur, 1988, pp. 9-47.

176. See also 'The Indus Valley in the Vedic period', *MASI*, No. 31.

177. B.B. Lal, 'Some Reflections on the Structural Remains at Kalibangan', in *Frontiers of the Indus civilization*, ed. by him and S.P. Gupta, pp. 55-62: See also V.N. Misra, 'Lost Saraswati: The cradle of Harappan Civilization', *Manthan*, *op. cit.*, pp. 98-116; R.H. Dyson, 'Harappan Vedic Civilization — A continuum', *ibid.*, pp. 117-18.

178. Cf. S.G. Talageri, *The Aryan Invasion Theory — A Reappraisal*, p. VII.

around 1900 BC. Scientific techniques like carbon-14 dating, tritium analysis of water samples from deep wells all along the paleo-channels shown on the satellite image have helped S. Kalyanaraman in establishing that the Sarasvatī was a mighty river prior to 3000 BC and got desiccated around 1500 BC.[179]

H.D. Sankalia says that the present evidence indicates that the Sarasvatī-Dṛṣadvatī valley was inhabited by at least 2500 BC. Traditionally the Āryans lived at much earlier period, i.e., about 3000 BC. And then he raises a question, if we accept the traditional dates what would be the significance of carbon-14 dates around 1500 BC ?[180] In fact, neither all traditional dates nor all carbon-14 dates are absolutely correct. The former are sometimes purely suppositional and the latter are sometimes contradictory. The carbon dating of same sample of the same sight of the same civilization of the same period vary from each other. Some carbon dates are not accurate and, therefore, their reliability is doubted. Sometimes they are readjusted by applying MASCA correction factor. Chronologically speaking, there is no unanimity among scholars all over the world about the beginning or end of any civilization prior to the sixth century BC which includes both Vedic and Harappan civilizations. That is why, I have been consistently pointing out that all the dates before the sixth or fourth century BC are tentative. The antiquity of the original settlements of the Āryans and their expansion within India cannot be studied by putting them within chronological framework whether traditional or scientific.

Michel Danino, while demolishing the Āryan invasion theory in his monumental work, *The Invasion that never was*, observed: "The re-discovery of the Saraswatī deals a death blow to the invasion theory. Who will believe that the Aryans crossed up to six great rivers — the Indus and the Sutlej with its tributaries — only to settle down on the banks of a river that had gone dry five hundered years earlier. . . ."[181] This observation is of unique importance. Danino has correctly stated that no findings, either pottery or utensils or tools or weapons or graves or any form of art, have been made in the Indus-

179. *Op. cit.*, pp. 38-39.

180. *PPIP*, pp. 356-57, 403; see also his "Radio Carbon Dates in India, their consistency and Cultural implications" in D.P. Agrawal and A. Ghosh (eds), *Radio Carbon and Indian Archaeology*, p. 219; "Traditional Chronology and C-14 dates of Excavated sites", *JIH*, vol. 42, 1964, pp. 635-50.

181. Cf. *Organiser*, Delhi, 8 February 1998, p. 15.

Sarasvatī region which could be associated with an Āryan people coming into India from outside. Had the Indus-Sarasvatī civilization been pre-Āryan, an invading Āryan horde would have definitely left some trace of their arrival. The old view that a race of people — hordes of semi-barbarian or semi-primitive, cattle-rearing and Sanskrit-speaking pastoral nomads called the Āryans — poured from Central Asia or thereabouts into north-west India some 1500 years before the Christian era, invaded and destroyed the highly developed Indus Valley or Harappan civilization that had been flourishing there for over a millennium, defeated the native Draviḍians and pushed them towards the south and thereafter settled in the Punjab wherefrom in the later Vedic age expanded over the Gaṅgā-Yamunā Doāb and built the mighty Gangetic civilization has been totally rejected by him. Such view has now become completely outdated. This view was propagated by the British scholars to legitimise the British rule in India on the pretext that the Hindus were former invaders of the same family as the Europeans. When the British established their rule in India John Wilson called it a re-union of two branches of the same family (so-called Āryan or Indo-European family). There was a deliberate attempt on the part of some British scholars to distort the ancient Indian history and impose a British model of history on the Indians so far as the present subject is concerned. Danino's statement that neither the Vedas nor the Purāṇas nor any other Sanskrit texts make any reference to an original homeland of the Āryans outside India is absolutely correct.

The five allied Āryan peoples, viz., Purus, Yadus, Turvasas, Aṇus and Druhyus mentioned in the *Ṛgveda* (1, 108, 8) were originally settled in different parts of Sapta-Sindhu region. The areas occupied by Purus in the early phase of the Ṛgvedic age extended from the Paruṣṇī (Rāvī) in the west to the Sarasvatī in the east. In the later phase of that age the Bharatas (later merged into the Kurus) were confined to only Sārasvata region. The Yadus and Turvasas were closely associated with each other. They were settled in and around the Vitastā (Jhelum) west of the Paruṣṇī and between the latter and the Asiknī (Cenāb). The Aṇus were settled on the banks of the Rāvī and the Druhyus (their closest allies) near the Rāvī or between it and the Cenāb.

The original settlements of the Āryans in the valleys of the Gaṅgā and Yamunā during the Ṛgvedic period can be attested by the evidence of the *Ṛgveda* and the *Brāhmaṇas*. It is generally held by the scholars that since the rivers Gaṅgā and Yamunā appear only once along with the Sarasvatī, the rivers of the Punjab and other rivers of the west in the former (10, 75, 5), there was no Āryan settlement on their banks during the period concerned. But we find some more references to those two rivers in the said text showing the settlements of the Āryans in their valleys. The high bank of the Gaṅgā has been explicitly mentioned in the text (6, 45, 31) which shows the Āryan familiarity with the Gangetic valley. One of the hymns of the text (5, 52, 17) is a clear reflection of the truth that some of them were settled on the bank of the Yamunā. The Ṛgvedic evidence gets strengthened by what we find in the *Brāhmaṇas*. It is described therein that Bharata, the son of Duṣyanta, performed no less than seventy-eight *Aśvamedha* sacrifices on the bank of the Yamunā and fifty-five on the bank of the Gaṅgā (*Ait. Br.*, VIII, 4, 23, 3; *Śat. Br.*, XIII, 5, 4, 11, 21). There are sufficient evidence to show that the Āryans were in possession of the Gaṅgā valley towards the end of the Ṛgvedic age or before the composition of the hymns of the *Atharvaveda*. S.N. Pradhan, while dealing with "Aryan Settlement of India during the Ṛgvedic period", also admitted that "the valleys of the Gaṅgā and the Yamunā were inhabited by the Aryans during the Ṛgvedic peirod".[182] Thus, the Sarasvatī was not the eastern boundary of the land of theṚgvedic Āryans as held by some scholars. Sāyaṇa (AD 1300-80) includes both Gaṅgā and the Yamunā in the Sapta-Sindhu region which is partly true. A. Weber has also pointed out the Āryas divided into number of groups were settled on the banks of the Indus and the rivers of the Punjab in north-west India and in Kurukṣetra on the Sarasvatī in the Ṛgvedic age. And they further "spread towards the east beyond Sarasvatī as far as the Ganges".[183] There was, of course, diffusion of the Āryans from the Sarasvat region towards the east, but there is no mention in any text of displacing or defeating the other native people by them along the way.

The mention of the Cedis and their king Kaśu in the *Ṛgveda* (8, 5, 37-39) and other available evidences led Pradhan to conclude that "the Aryans were settled at the foot of the Vindhyas during the medieval Ṛgvedic period".[184] He is of the opinion that the full-fledged Āryan civilization had spread almost all over the Āryāvartta during that period. Āryāvartta of Manu (2, 22) and *Amarakoṣa* (2, 1, 8) also corresponds with the land between the two mountains, the Himālayas and the Vindhyas. "The tract of land between the Himalayas and the Vindhyas and the regions to the east of Kurukṣetra (or Sarasvatī) and west of Prayāga" called Madhyadeśa by Manu (2, 21) were decidedly occupied by the Āryans.

---

182. *Chro. Anct. India*, p. 202.
183. *HIL*, pp. 3-5, 8f, 37f.
184. *Op. cit.*

The expansion of especially the Kuru people in Madhyadeśa or the Gaṅgā-Yamunā Doāb in the later Vedic age is well-proven fact. The *Śatapatha Brāhmaṇa* (1, 4, 1, 10-19) speaks of the movement of the Vedic people across the rivers Sadānirā (Gaṇḍak) further to the east where they spread the Āryan culture.

The ancestors of the so-called Persian or Iranian Āryans were also originally living in Sapta-Sindhu region. They being the followers of *asura* culture and opposed to the Vedic Āryans — the followers of *deva* culture — were defeated by Indra in a battle which resulted in the separation of the former from the latter and dispersion from the original home towards ancient Persia (called Pārasika in the Purāṇic records) in the far west in the early Vedic age or after the composition of the Ṛgvedic *hymns* and *sūktas*. After reaching Persia through Afghanistan they became the followers of Ahura Mazda (= Asura Mahāna), the supreme God of Zoroastrianism. The memories of the places of the earlier settlements or which they were acquainted with are preserved in their scripture or religious document — the *Avesta*.

The sixteen place-names or so-called countries recorded in Part I (the *Vendidad*), Fargard (chapter) I, of the *Avesta* in the Zend language include the following: 2, 3(5) — *Airyana Vaejo* (Sanskrit *Āryāṇāṁ Vijaṁ* or *Bijyaḥ*) on the river Daitya, 5(13) — Sughdha (old Persian Suguda = Greek Sogdiana = modern Samarkand), 7(21) — Bākhdhi (Sanskrit Bāhlika = old Persian Bākhtri = modern Balkh), 9(29) — Haroyu (old Persian Haraiva = Greek Areia = the basin of river Harirūdaor Ṛgvedic Hariyupiyā = modern Herāt), 10 —Vaekerata (Kabul), 13(45) — Harahvaiti (old Persian Harauvati = the region extending from Harut to Kandahār watered by seven rivers including the Ṛgvedic Sarayū or Harirūda), 19(72) — Hapta-Hindu (Ṛgvedic Sapta-Sindhu = here only the basin of the affluents of the Indus) and 20(76) — Rangha (the basin of one of the tributaries of the Indus near Kabul called Rasā in the *Ṛgveda*).[185] *Airyana Vaejo* (the birth-place or motherland of the ancestors of Persian Āryans), which included the countries lying along the Indus and its tributaries, Kabul, Kandahār and Herāt, is identical with *Ariana* of classical writers. Their inhabitants have been called by Strabo *Arianoi*. *Airyana Vaejo* is said to have been situated on the bank of the river "Daitya", which must have been a river in Sapta-Sindhu region on the bank of which the ancestors of the Pārasīs were defeated at the hands of Indra. The river called Daitya is a manifestation of their hatredness to the river (probably the Indus) on which the incident took place. It is sometimes identified without any basis with the river Araxes (or Aras) north of Azarbaizan (in

185. *"The Zend-Avesta"*, Pt. 1. the Vendidad, Eng. trans. by James Darmesteter, SBE, vol. IV, pp. 2-10.

former USSR) in an attempt to locate *Airyana Vaejo* there and thereby to prove their central Asiatic origin.[186] After leaving Sapta-Sindhu region they lived in *Ariana* region (the land of the Āryans) of India for a considerable period of time and finally dispersed in different groups on their way to Persia. Some of them might have settled for sometime in Bāhlīka region lying south of the Vaṁkṣu or Oxus river covered by north Afghanistan. The settlement of one section of them in Sughdha or trans-Oxus Sogdiana in Central Asia for sometime before reaching Persia cannot, however, be denied.

The *Ṛgveda* and the *Avesta* (the two oldest surviving records) contain sufficient evidence of the intimate connection that existed between the Vedic Āryans and the ancestors of the Persian Āryans. The Vedic Sanskrit is very much akin to Zend, the language of the *Avesta*. The Vedic Ārya, Aryamana, Asura and Indra are identical with the Avestan Airya, Airyimana, Ahura and Indra respectively. Likewise, the Vedic divinities like Mitra (sun), Varuṇa (the sky-god) are exactly similar to the Avestan Mithra and Varana. And further, the Vedic Soma, Yajña, Āhuti, Atharvana and Vṛtra are identical with the Avestan Haoma, Yasna, Ajuhati, Athravana and Verethraghan. The Pārthavas and the Pārśavas mentioned in the *Ṛgveda* (6, 27, 8; 10, 33, 2) were no other than the ancestors of the Parthians or Persians. The Vedic Sanskrit is also similar to the old Iranian language — Pahalavī — to some extent. The linguistic similarity and affinities in the matter of religious beliefs, ritualistic observances, manner and customs and thought and tradition constitute unmistakable proof of their close relationship in the Vedic age.

The evidences produced above proves conclusively that Sapta-Sindhu (called Hapta-Hindu in the Persian *Avesta* and the *Bhaviṣya Purāṇa*, Pratisarga Parva, ch. 5) was the original home of both the Indian and Iranian Āryans, the two kindred peoples, before their separation. This invalidates the theory that the ancestors of the Vedic Indians and Iranians — the eastern branch of the Āryan or Indo-European family — were living together in their common home in Central Asia before coming to Sapta-Sindhu through the north-western passes in pre-Vedic age.[187] It is said that there were various areas of cultural interaction between the two. The main interaction zone lay between the Oxus and the Indus.[188]

Of twenty-one parts of the *Avesta,* two were destroyed by Alexander the Great during his military campaign and some were taken away by his companions to Greece. The

186. See also SBE, vol. IV, pp. 2-3 and 5, note 2.

187. See also A.C. Das, *op. cit.*, vol. I, pp. 173ff; *JRAS*, XVI, II, 1854, pp. 187-200.

188. B. and F.R. Allchin, *The Rise of civilization in India and Pakistan*, pp. 301ff.

Avesta in its present form was discovered by some Western scholars in India itself sometime before 1885. However, this is the only Persian document which throws light on the subject under discussion. The informations supplied by the Greek and Roman geographers and historians about the subject also deserve our notice. J.W. McCrindle while giving an etymological explanation of the term *Ariane* used by Strabo in his *Geography* (XV, 2, 1) observed that this (derived from *arya*) "still survives in the form *Iran*, the modern name of Persia. . . . The term *Arya* designated in common the Iranians and the Indians of the North".[189] Herodotus says that the Persians at one time called themselves *Artaioi* and the Medes were originally called *Arioi*. The Medes were none other than the Maga Brāhmaṇa priests living in Media province, north-western part of Iran. Their parentage can be traced back to the Indian Āryans. They were the performers of the Vedic Atharvan or the Avestan Atharvana *yajñas*. It is because of the intimate relationship of the Indian and Persian Āryans that Strabo observed that the southern parts of the Paropamisos or Hindukush mountains (which correspond to the considerable portion of Afghanistan like territory of Arachosia or Kandahār) belonged to India and *Ariana* (Persia).[190] Persians because of having lived earlier in the *Ariana* region of India were called Airya and their country *Ariana*. Strabo on the authority of Apollodorus included some parts of Persia and Media, northern parts of Bactria, and Sogdiana within the geographical limits of Ariana only on the ground of the similarity of language spoken by thier inhabitants.[191] As a matter of fact, the ancestors of Persian Āryans while on their way to Persia after their separation from the Vedic Āryans left impact of the language they picked up from the latter on the inhabitants of all these places which they passed through.

The original abode of the Vedic Āryans and the ancestors of Persian Āryas can also be fixed at a place where a plant called Soma in the *Ṛgveda* and Haoma in the *Avesta* grew naturally. Max Müller was the first scholar to make attempt in this direction as appears from some of his letters of 1884, but he could not succeed.[192] This plant was used by them for various purposes. It had its own importance in their religious life. The *soma* juice in particular had an equal importance in Vedic and Avestic sacrifices. Charles James Lyall wrote in 1884 that "If we can find the Soma anywhere in the region of the

189. *AICL*, p. 80, note 2.
190. *Geog.*, XV, 2, 10, cf. *ibid.*, p. 90.
191. *Ibid.*, XV, 2, 8, cf. *ibid.*, p. 88.
192. See his *Biographies of Words and the Home of the Aryas*, pp. 222-24.

Hidhu-kush, it at once fixes the region as the mother-country of Indians and Iranians and locates them together in the Vedic age, or at least its beginning."[193]

The Ārjika region mentioned in the *Ṛgveda* (9, 65, 23; 9, 113, 2) was famous for its *soma* plant. We know that this plant grew in abundance on the Muzavant mountain on the southern bank of the river Kabul north of Hindukush in Afghanistan. There was an Āryan settlement there. Thus, in all probability this Ārjika region, which formed a part of *Ariana,* was also inhabited by them in the early Vedic age.

The evidence recorded in the Purāṇas about the origin and expansion of the Āryans in India is of exceptional value. On the basis of this evidence it can firmly be established that Pratiṣṭhāna on the confluence of the Gaṅgā-Yamunā in Prayāg (modern Jhūnsī near Allahabad) was one of the earliest seats of their original habitation. It was from here that the sons of Manu Vaivasvata spread out in different directions. Ikṣvāku, his eldest son and the founder of the Solar dynasty, obtained Madhyadeśa with its capital at Ayodhyā. His name figures also in the *Ṛgveda* (10, 60, 4). His descendants further continued to rule there. The names of many kings of the Ikṣvāku dynasty are found in the Vedic literature. Ikṣvāku's son Nimi also called Videha was the founder of the Videha dynasty. One of the descendants of Manu established rule at Vaiśālī.[194]

Purūravā or Purūravas Aila, the progenitor of the Lunar dynasty and the contemporary of Ikṣvāku, was the most famous Āryan king. He ruled at Pratiṣṭhāna, the capital city of Madhyadeśa,[195] for about sixty-four years.[196] He was succeeded by his son Āyu at Pratiṣṭhāna, while his another son Amāvasu founded a kingdom with its capital at Kānyakubja (Kanauj). Āyu's eldest son, Nahuṣa, continued the main line at Pratiṣṭhāna, and his another son, Kṣatravṛdha, founded the dynasty that ruled at Kāśī. According to the *Brahma Purāṇa* (chs. 10-12) and the *Linga Purāṇa* (1, 63), Nahuṣa, Yayāti and his successors, Puru, Duṣyanta and Bharata — all ruled at Pratiṣṭhānapura. Will any sensible person whether he or she be a historian, archaeologist or scholar or even a layman will ever believe that they came from outside India to rule over there? The descendants of Purūravā contributed a lot towards the propagation of the Vedic

---

193. *BIographics of Words and the Home of the Aryas.*, p. 223.

194. For details see G.P. Singh, *EIHTA*, pp. 29-49.

195. *Vy.*, 91, 1-2, 5-8, 18, 51; 92, 1-7; *Vṣṇ.*, 4, 1. 8-64; *Bhāg.*, 9, 1, 42; *Bmd.*, 3, 60, 21; 3, 65, 45-46; 3, 66, 19-22; *Mts.*, 12, 18; 104, 5; 106, 30; H.H. Wilson, *Vṣṇ.*, Eng. tr., pp. 318-19, 324-25; *Br.*, Chs. 9-11; *Bhv.*, vol. I, vv. 43-47, pp. 292-93.

196. *Vy.*, 91, 5.

religion and culture and bringing of the peoples within the fold of Āryanism.

Nahuṣa's son and successor named Yayāti was another famous Āryan king who extended his sway over whole of Madhyadeśa west of Ayodhyā and Kānyakubja kingdoms, the Sārasvata region, the north-west and the country west, south and south-east of his territory of Pratiṣṭhāna. He divided his territories among his five sons, Yadu, Turvasa, Druhyu, Aṇu and Puru, who are popularly known as five Āryan or Vedic peoples. His youngest son Puru ruled over Madhyadeśa — the southern half of the Gaṅgā-Yamunā Doāb — with its capital at Pratiṣṭhāna. Yadu got the south-west, Turvasu the south-east, Druhyu the north-west and Aṇu the north and the east.[197] It is only the Purāṇic records in which the entire details of the original settlements and expansion of their descendants are given. The pedigree and progeny of each Āryan king also occur therein. The Purāṇic genealogies of the kings of different Āryan dynasties are without any parallel in the history of the Āryans. The Ṛgvedic heartland — the Sarasvatī-Dṛṣadvatī Doāb — was ruled by kings in the line of Puru. The Pauravas' settlements in the first phase in the Sarasvatī and upper Doāb are archaeologically associated with Ochre-Coloured Pottery (OCP) of the late Harappan phase dated *c.* 2200-1700 BC. The Pauravas, who had their original seat at Pratiṣṭhāna, gradually expanded over the whole of the Gaṅgā and Yamunā plain from the Śivālik hills to Magadha and ruled over the kingdoms of Hastināpura, Pañcāla, Cedi, Vatsa, Karuṣa and Magadha (in all of which the ruling families were mainly the Bhāratas). The Yadus expanded over Rājpūtānā desert, south-east Berār and then north of Yamunā. Their realm lay in the areas watered by Carmaṇāvatī (Cambal), Vetrāvatī (Betwā) and Sūktimatī (Ken). The Āṇavas held the northern parts of the Gaṅgā-Yamunā Doāb. They also spread out all over Punjab or Vāhlika including Madra, Kaikeya and Sindhu-Sauvīra, and east Bihar, Bengal (exept the north and east) and Orissa. The Druhyus were originally settled in the territory west of the Yamunā and north of the Cambal. They further expanded over the Punjab and finally settled in Gāndhāra region (Afghanistan). The Turvasus established themselves in Karuṣa region which extended to Rewā and beyond.[198] It amy be added here that Śivi, an Āṇava emperor, drove the Druhyus out of Gāndhāra towards the Central Asia at much later stage. It is believed that the Āryans of Druhyu dynasty spread Āryan culture in Central and Western Asia. It is also assumed that some sections of the Āryans of Aṇu dynasty spread Vedic culture in Western Asia.

---

197. *Vy.*, 93, 87-92; *Agn.*, 274, 1-23; *Vṣṇ.*, 4, 10, 30-32; *Br.*, 12, 18-19; *Mts.*, 36, 5; *Bmd.*, 3, 68, 90-92; *Krm.*, 1, 21, 9-11; *Lg.*, 1, 67, 11-12; Wilson, *op. cit.*, IV, X, pp. 331-2; *Hv.*, 30, 1-2, 5, 17-18.

198. For details see G.P. Singh, *op. cit.*, pp. 53-97.

The Purāṇic evidence is an amplification of the Ṛgvedic evidence of "Vivasvāna's son Manu and his descendants" (10, 63, 1), "Purūrava and his sons" (10, 95, 11), Nahuṣa (1, 122, 8; 7, 95, 2; 9, 91, 2), his son Yayāti (10, 63, 1) and his five sons or five Āryan peoples mentioned above (1, 108, 8; also 7, 18, 6, 12-14; 10, 62, 10).[199] The Ṛgvedic references to the Āryan kings are all isolated whereas in the Purāṇas they are all consolidated. The Vedic and Purāṇic tradition concerning the Āryas are complementary to each other. By correlating these two traditions and synchronising the data concerned we can have an integrated picture about them. I am in perfect agreement with P.L. Bhargava,[200] A.D. Pusalker,[201] R.B. Pandey,[202] S.G. Talageri[203] and all those scholars who hold that on the combined testimony of the Vedas and Purāṇas it can incontrovertibly be proved that the Āryans were autochthones of the land. Neither in the *Ṛgveda* nor in the Purāṇas we find any evidence of coming of Āryans from outside India. F.E. Pargiter has also pointed out that Vedic literature knows nothing about the entrance of the Āryans from the north-west into India. He further adds: "If one puts aside all preconceived ideas and examines the Ṛgvedic hymns in the light of historical tradition, nothing will be found in them really incompatible with traditional history, and a great deal is elucidated thereby."[204]

Pargiter after collating all the eighteen main Purāṇas put forward the theory that the earliest home of the Ailas or Āryans was Pratiṣṭhāna in Madhyadeśa. They originally belonged to the mid-Himālayan region (Ilāvṛta) which has always been the sacred land of the Indians. Purūravas Aila who began his rule at Allahabad came from this region.[205] The Āryans "conquered and spread out north-west, west and south, and had by Yayāti's time occupied precisely the region famed as Madhyadeśa".[206] "They possessed that Mid-

199. For five Āryan peoples see Macdonell and Keith, *VI*, vol. I, pp. 466-67; vol. II, pp. 11-13; R.C. Jain, *EAB*, pp. 70-92; A.D. Pusalker, "Aryan Settlements in India", in *The Vedic Age*, pp. 249-66; "Traditional History from the Earliest Time to the Accession of Parikshit", in *ibid.*, p. 310.

200. *India in the Vedic Age : A History of Aryan Expansion in India* (Lucknow, 1971).

201. "Aryan Expansion in India", *Purāṇa*, vol. 6, No. 2, pp. 307-32.

202. "The Puranic data on the Original Home of the Indo-Aryans", *IHQ*, 1948, pp. 94-103; see also his view in *Nāgarī Pracāriṇi Patrikā*, Kāśī, vol. 54, No. 2006, pp. 63-73.

203. *Op. cit.*, pp. 293ff, 327-28.

204. *AIHT*, pp. 301-2.

205. *Ibid.*, pp. 296-99.

206. *Ibid.*, p. 296.

land definitely and made it their own thoroughly, so that "it was their true pure home",' as G. Grierson[207] describes it linguistically. "They expanded afterwards into the Punjab and East Afghanistan, into West India and the north-west Dekhan, into East and south Bihar and into Bengal"[208] which Grierson calls the "Outer Band".[209] Some scholars have postulated not only an invasion of Āryans from the north-west, but even a double invasion, and the theroy is that "the inhabitants of the Midland represent the latest stage of Indo-Aryan immigration", and that the latest invaders entered "into the heart of the country already occupied by the first immigrants, forcing the latter outwards in three directions, to the east, to the south and to the west".[210] Pargiter does not lend his support to such hypothesis.

Pargiter with full confidence says that ". . . ancient Indian tradition knows nothing of any Aila or Āryan invastion of India from Afghanistan, nor of any gradual advance from thence eastwards (as far as the Sarasvatī or Yamunā). On the other hand it distinctly asserts that there was an Aila outflaw of the Druhyus through the north-west into the countries beyond, where they founded various kingdoms and so introduced their own Indian religion among those nations."[211] He further says that the theory, that the Āryans invaded India through the north-west after separating from the Iranians, and entered in two streams, is hardly tenable. The connection of Persia with India does not prove that the Āryans entered India from that direction. The north-west and the Punjab were not regarded their ancient home. He has reasonably concluded that tradition has preserved copious and definite accounts giving an entirely different description of the earliest Āryans and their beginnings in India. They elucidate the Āryan domination and occupation of India geographically and linguistically. He remarks that it is wrong to say that all this copious tradition was falsely fabricated, and the truth has been absolutely lost.[212] Lastly, he raises a pertinent question for the advocates of the foreign origin of

207. *Imp. Gaz. Ind.*, I (1907), p. 357 cited in *ibid.*
208. *AIHT.*, p. 296.
209. *Imp. Gaz. Ind.*, p. 358, cf. *ibid.*
210. *Imp. Gaz. Ind.*, p. 358.
211. *AIHT*, p. 298; see also *JRAS*, 1919, pp. 358-61.
212. *Ibid.*, p. 302.

the Āryans to ponder over: "If all this tradition is false, why, how, and in whose interests was it all fabricated?"[213]

Pargiter's theory has been fully supported by A.D. Pusalker.[214] H.D. Sankalia corroborating Pargiter's views observes: "Accepting the Puranic view that the Aryans originated somewhere in mid-western UP around Pratisthana or Allahabad and spread in all directions, we find that this view fits in surprisingly well with the present known origin and distribution and nature of the PGW and the associated Early Iron age culture."[215] "Pargiter's further argument that his theory of Madhyadesa around Allahabad as the original home of the Aryans (the Ailas) no way goes against Grierson's theory of the "Outer and the Inner Band" of Aryans might also be corroborated by this interpretation of the archaeological evidence."[216] But his view, that the Purāṇic tradition cannot go beyond a few centuries before the Christian era, and all the early accounts purporting to go back to 3000 BC are imaginary,[217] is partly debatable. In fact, the Purāṇic accounts of the Āryan origin in India do not and cannot coincide with PGW phase of culture whose Carbon dating varies from archaeologist to archaeologist. The Purāṇic evidence in this regard is much older than the archaeological one. The Āryan settlements in Madhyadeśa goes back to Ṛgvedic age. Sankalia further casts this doubt on the validity of Pargiter's theory only in terms of the antiquity and expansion of culture in mid-eastern India. He opines that mid-eastern India civilization is not earlier than north-western India civilization. The earlier cultures are found to have flourished in Baluchistan and Afghanistan showing distinct affinities with those of Iran and western Asia, and then in Sindh, the Punjab and northern Rajasthan. To that extent Pargiter's theroy, according to him, remains "unsubstantiated and contradicted".[218] Actually, there were various centres of Āryan culture in India. This culture flourished contemporaneously in the north and the east in the early Vedic age. Thus, it is very difficult to say which one is

---

213. *AIHT*, p. 302.
214. *Op. cit.*
215. *AIHA*, p. 308.
216. *Ibid.*, p. 310; also *PPIP*, p. 557; *Prehistory of India*, p. 179.
217. *Ibid.*, pp. 308-9.
218. *PPIP*, p. 558; *Prehistory of India*, p. 179; also *AIHA*, p. 310; see also his "New Light on the Aryan Invasion of India: Links with the Iran of 1000 BC discovered in Central India", in *The Illustrated London News*, London, 24 September, 1958, pp. 478-79.

earlier and which one is later. There is no reason to doubt the veracity of Pargiter's statements. His theory is not based on postulation but on the evidence recorded in some of the historical Purāṇas.

According to L.D. Kalla, Kashmir and the Himālayan region were two important centres of Āryan's original settlements.[219] Umapada Sen propounded the view that R̥gvedic Āryans had lived in Kashmir between 3500 BC and 3000 BC. During the *Brāhmaṇa* period they had descended into the eastern Punjab and gradually spread eastward.[220]

There was an outflow of the Āryans form India into Iran, West Asia and Europe before the sixteenth or fifteenth century BC and they spread Āryan religion and culture there.[221] These facts are hardly reconcilable with the theory propounded earlier about the entrance of the Āryans into north-west India from those countries. The north-west was a route for the Āryan expansion outside India. The movements of the Āryans were from the East to the West and not vice-versa. The want of space and time does not render it possible to dilate upon this aspect of the subject.

In the recent past, many Indian and foreign scholars by throwing away the old theories of foreign origin of the Āryans into the dustbin of history have indisputably proved that India was their original homeland. The most prominent among them are N.S. Rajaram and David Frawley whose views and works have already been mentioned here before. As already stated, the Āryans being the original inhabitants of India were settled in its different parts. I beg to differ from those scholars who have shown a particular place or region as their original home. In the R̥gvedic age, the Āryan land extended from the Vaṁkṣu basin in the north to the Gangetic basin in the east. They were originally settled in Bāhlika region, south of the river Vaṁkṣu, in north Afghanistan, in the territories lying along almost all the rivers of Afghanistan mentioned in the *R̥gveda*, the Indus and the five rivers of the Punjab, and in the valleys of the Sarasvatī, Yamunā and Gaṅgā. Both the early and later Vedic age witnessed the expansion of the Āryans, as discussed before.

We close the discussion here with an observation that any attempt on the part of Indian or foreign scholars to prove the foreign origin of the Āryans whether Central

---

219. *Poc.* VI, pp. 723-74.

220. *The Rigvedic Era (3500-2000 BC)*, p. 176.

221. See G.P. Singh, "The Colonial and Cultural Expansion of the Āryans Outside India as Gleaned from the Vedic Literature", *Journal of the Deptt. of History*, Manipur University, Imphal, vol. II, 1987, pp. 17-30.

Asiatic or European will amount to falsification of their history recorded in the *Ṛgveda* and depreciation of the evidence furnished in that text and the Purāṇas in support of their Indian origin, and devaluation of classical sources which abound with valuable references to *Ariana* as a land of their original settlements which lay within the geographical limits of India if viewed from the perspective of contemporary geography.

2

The Origin, Antiquity and Identification of the Cīnas

As Depicted in Ancient Indian Literature and Inscriptions*

THE primary purpose of undertaking this research work is to identify the Cīnas in the light of the evidence recorded in ancient Indian literature and inscriptions and some other corroborative sources and thereby to prove that they were not the Chinese people of Mongolian origin as erroneously supposed by some historians, anthropologists and philologists but a non-Āryan race of Indian origin who had settled in north-western and north-eastern India in anceint times. Some of those who had occupied the territories in Tibet and Burma had no connection with the Chinese proper. As a matter of fact, the appellation signifies both a geographical designation and a ethnic group. Attempt has also been made to throw some light on their origin and antiquity. The subject under review constitutes an important part of ethnology of ancient India.

In the *Vālmīki-Rāmāyaṇa*, Cīna appears to be a place in the Himālayan region of northern India.[1] But, on the other hand, in the *Mahābhārata* they have been depicted as the people living within the frontiers of the kingdom of Prāgjyotiṣa during the time of its king Bhagadatta. They along with the Kirātas (the hill tribes of ancient Assam), the dwellers of marshy regions near the sea (i.e., the alluvial tracts and islands near the mouths of the Ganges and the Brahmaputra or Lohita Sea also known as the Eastern Sea) called Sāgarānūpavāsins, *mlecchas* and other formidable warriors formed the retinue

* From *Adhyayan*, JBIAS, vol. V, nos. 1 & 2, 1995, pp. 1-17.

1. Kiṣkindhā Kāṇḍa, 43, 13; See also R.K. Rai, *Vālmīki-Rāmāyaṇa Koṣa* — Descriptive Index to the Names and Subjects of *Rāmāyaṇa*, pp. 58 ff for identification of places in north-western India with which the Cīnas are associated.

of the said king and took part in the battle of Kurukṣetra under his leadership as an ally of Duryodhana after being defeated by Arjuna in their own kingdom.[2]

It will not be correct to say that Bhagadatta's kingdom extended up to the confines of China and Himālayan regions of Nepal and his army consisting of the Cīnas and Kirātas belonged to these two countries respectively.[3] Since no evidence has been furnished as yet in any authentic source showing the participation of the Chinese soldiers in the *Mahābhārata* war or tracing the lineage of the Cīnas from the Chinese, we do not find any basis to support their identification with the Chinese. As a matter of fact, Prāgjyotiṣa kingdom of Bhagadatta during the period concerned comprised the hilly areas of Assam, north and south-east Bengal, the areas on both sides of the Lauhitya stretching as far as Gangetic Delta or the sea, the sub-Himālayan ranges of Bhutan and some parts of Tibet and Burma.[4] Therefore, we have every reason to believe that the Cīnas of the epic age during this particular period possibly might have formed the part of non-Āryan tribal population inhabiting the areas concerned. This can be further corroborated by other statements.

Motichandra in his analysis of the data contained in the *Mahābhārata* has rightly pointed out that the Cīnas of the epic age were the "Chinas of upper Burma".[5] Even Alberuni has expressed more or less the same view. While describing the countries of eastern India including Prāgjyotiṣa, he refers to the Cīna, Kirāta and Suvarṇabhūmi and further makes it clear that Cīna is Chin Hills (Burma) bordering Maṇipur.[6] Actually, they were known as Cīnas because of their settlements in the mountainous region (=Ching). The people of this race are still found in Burma and Maṇipur and believed to

---

2. Sabhā Parva, 23, 19-20; Udyoga Parva, 19, 14-15; also R.K. Rai, *Mhābhārata Koṣa* : A Descriptive Index to the names and subjects in the *Mahābhārata*, pp. 28, 190-91 and 460; V.S. Agrawala, *Bhārata Sāvitrī*, 2, p. 40; Pargiter, "The Nations of India at the Battle between the Pāṇḍavas and Kauravas", *JRAS* (1908), p. 334; D.C. Sircar, *SGAMI*, pp. 104, 160, 163-64.

3. P.N. Bhattacharya, *Kāmarūpa Śāsanāvalī*, Int., p. 2, fn. For details about the Kirātas see G.P. Singh, *The Kirātas in Ancient India*, pp. 59-164.

4. See Pargiter, "Ancient Countries in Eastern India", *JASB*, LXVI, pt. 1, (1897), pp. 104-61.

5. *Geographical and Economic Studies in the Mahābhārata*, Upāyana Parva, pp. 60-61.

6. E.C. Sachau (tr.), *Alberuni's India*, 1, pp. 201-299-303.

be of different racial stocks. One of the medieval sources[7] also confirms the inclusion of Burma in the Cīna (=Cheen) country.

Pargiter has alo observed that the Kirātas were the mountain tribes of N.E. India and the Cīna comprised the country of Tibet along the whole range of the Himālayas. The Cīnas of the epic age were linked with the Kāmbojas in the north-west, the kingdom of Bhagadatta of Assam in the north-east and with the people living near the source of the Ganges in the country lying midway between the two regions. He refers to the Cīna king Dhautamūlaka (as mentioned in the *Udyoga Parva*), who is said to have extirpated their kinsmen, and hence they were marked as kṣatriyas and became degraded because of the extinction of sacred rites.[8] Here he indirectly supports the view of Manu which will be discussed here little later. But in the other source[9] he has identified the Cīnas with the Chinese and considers them as well as the Kirātas as Mongoloids which contradicts his earlier statement, as quoted above.

James Taylor is of the firm opinion that "the country of Cīna described as adjacent to Kāmarūpa on the east can be no other than the eastern part of the valley of Assam".[10] The word Sina, Senae, Thina or Thinae, as mentioned by the classical (Greek and Roman) writers, notably, an anonymous author of the *Periplus* (first century AD),[11] Ptolemy (middle of the second century AD)[12] and Arrian (second century AD), is supposed to be corruption of Cīna or Cheena and connotes wider meanings. After having made a thorough investigation into the classical sources, I have come to the conclusion that Sina or Sinae corresponds to Assam and Thinae or "This" to China proper. An unknown writer who follows Eratosthenes (*c.* 240 BC) and Ptolemy has categorically stated that "the Indians whose dominions are bounded by the Sinae on the east. . ."[13]. In this connection, he also

---

7. Abul Fazl's *Ain-i-Akbari*, tr. by H.S. Jarrett and Sir J.N. Sarkar (Dellhi, 1988), II, pp. 118-19, 131-32.
8. Eng. tr. of *Mārkaṇḍeya Purāṇa*, II, Pt. II, pp. 284, 319 note, and pp. 322-23; also *Indian Culture*, p. 319.
9. *JASB*, LXVI, Pt. 1 (1897), pp. 85, 109f.
10. *JASB*, XVI, Pt. 1 (1847), pp. 29-30.
11. W.H. Schoff, *The Periplus of the Erythraean Sea*, pp. 48, 260-61, 266, 269, 273-74.
12. McCrindle, *Ancient India as Described by Ptolemy*, pp. 220, 244-46, 263.
13. McCrindle, *Ancient India as Described in Classical Literature*, p. 212. McCrindle's Identification of Sinae with Southern China (*ibid*, note 1) is not absolutely correct.

refers to China but quite separately as Thinae. Taylor has also remarked that "Ptolemy places it in 38 N.L. but it is probably 28 N.L. in the vicinity of Sadiya in upper Assam".[14]

A.K. Majumdar's statement, that the "Cīnas of the *Mahābhārata* were the Tsan or Tsin people or Tibeto-Burman from a part of central Asia who settled and the people of low lands bordering Bengal",[15] does not convey clear meaning. However, the relevance of the latter part of the statement cannot be doubted.

D.C. Sircar identifies them with the Tibeto-Chinese people.[16] But here it must be made clear that the validity of the use of the term "Tibeto-Chinese" conjointly in context of the period preceding the seventh century AD is very doubtful from the historical as well as linguistic points of view because there was no contact of the both before this period. A local authority on the history of ancient Assam has judiciously applied the term Cīnas, as referred to in the said epic, only to the Tibetans and the Bhutanese.[17] M.R. Singh also identifies them with the people of Tibet and maintains that they, according to Manu, were originally kṣatriyas and later became degraded race.[18]

H.C. Ray[19] and Suniti Kumar Chatterji[20] have identified the Cīnas of the epic of the time of Bhagadatta with the non-Āryan Tibeto-Chinese race of Mongolian family without adducing any solid proof in support of their contentions. They have not taken other data contained in the epic about them into consideration. Sudhakar Chattopadhyaya, on the one hand, calls them "a Tibeto-Mongoloid people" and, on the other, supporting the views of Pargiter and depending on other epic accounts of the subject has stated that "The Cinas denoted the Tibeto-Mongoloid people of the Himālayan region, who extended from the territory of the Kambojas in the West to the kingdom of Bhagadatta in the east with their main habitation centring round the source of the Ganges. . . . they are the Shin tribe of the Gilgit region. The Cinas should be distinguished from the Apara Cinas, further Cinas, possibly China proper, mentioned in the lesser Epic".[21] Their identification

---

14. *Op. cit.*
15. *Early Hindu India : A Dynastic Study*, II, p. 423.
16. *SGAMI*, p. 34 note 6.
17. K.L. Barua, *Early History of Kāmarūpa* (Gauhati, 1966), p. 2.
18. *GDEP*, p. 173.
19. *The Dynastic History of Northern India*, I, pp. 240, 248 f.
20. *Kirāta-Jana Kṛti*, pp. 26 ff.
21. *RENIT*, pp. 73 and 100.

with the Tibeto-Chinese Mongoloids seems to be a common blunder on the part of scholars concerned. The space does not permit me either to go into the details concerned or to examine the credibility of statements made by various other scholars in this regard.

The other references to the subject concerned in the *Mahābhārata* also cannot be passed over in silence. They along with the Yavaṇas, Kāmbojas and other *mleccha* races have been placed in the north-western India.[22] They have been further listed among eighteen different races called Dasyus like the Kirātas, Gāndhāras, Kāmbojas, Śabaras, Pahalavas, etc., and described, on the one hand, as descendants of the brāhmaṇas and kṣatriyas, and as the vaiśyas and śūdras, on the other. They also appear to have been brought within the pale of Āryandom[23] probably in the post-epic age. We do not have anything at our disposal to examine the correctness of the statement with regard to their origin. However, certain observations have been made by other scholars in this regard. Romila Thapar, while referring to this particular evidence, has called them *mlecchas* who did not follow the law of *varṇa* and later they were to be admitted within the fold of Āryan religion and culture.[24] Vasudeva Sharan Agrawala on the basis of an in-depth study of the *Mahābhārata* has also admitted that they were one of those non-Āryan races or Dasyus who had settled in India before the Gupta period and later accepted the social system of the Āryans.[25]

In the Purāṇas, the Cīnas mentioned along with the Gāndhāras, Sindhu-Sauvīras, Śakas, Yavaṇas, Kāmbojas, Daradas, Tuṣāras, etc., were the people of the north-west.[26] S.M. Ali refers to their settlements on the bank of the river Indus and also locates them in Ladakh.[27] The Purāṇic dictionary refers to it as northern state where the *śrāddha* ceremony was forbidden.[28]

---

22. Bhīṣma Parva, 10, 64-65.
23. Śānti Parva, 65, 13-14, 15-23.
24. *AISH*, p. 176.
25. *Bhārata Sāvitrī*, 3, pp. 60-63.
26. *Vy.*, 1, 45, 118; 1, 58, 78-83; *Mts.*, 114, 51-58; *Mkd.*, 54, 35-41; 57, 39; *Vām.*, 13, 41; *Bmd.* (Bareli ed., 1988), Pt. I, 10, 46-48, p. 103; (Vankatesvara Press, Bombay, 1913), 2, 16, 7; 18, 46.
27. *The Geography of the Purāṇas*, p. 171.
28. R.P. Sharma, *Paurāṇic Kośa*, p. 175.

B.C. Law on the basis of the epic and Purāṇic sources has resonably drawn the conclusion that the Cīnas as such were certainly not the people of China rather they had settled down along the Indian side of the Himālayas from the north-west to the extreme east. They are very much associated with the country (Kāmboja) in the north-west, which was famous for a particular breed of horse. They were also settled not very far from the sources of the Ganges. They being of *mlecchas* were outside the pale of Āryan culture and lived on the border of Prāgjyotiṣa in the epic age along with the Kirātas.[29]

They along with the Kirātas, Khasas, Daradas, Draviḍas, Kāmbojas, Oḍras, Yavaṇas, Śakas, Paradas, etc., are said to have been degenerated to the rank of śūdras from their original position of kṣatriyas because of the neglect of the prescribed Vedic religious system, the established Brāhmaṇical Code of Conduct, omission of the sacred rites, etc.[30] This view of Manu with particular reference to their indigenous origin and their status as Vrātya or degenerate kṣatriyas has been acknowledged by a number of Indian and foreign scholars, notably, Romila Thapar,[31] V.S. Agrawala,[32] D.C. Sircar,[33] P.V. Kane,[34] M. Krishna Machariar,[35] R.P. Chanda,[36] S. Chattopadhyaya,[37] Sylvain Levi[38] and Lassen.[39] The statement of Manu has been interpreted by different scholars in different ways in this particular context. However, we cannot deny the interpolation in his statement because some of those tribes who are obviously of foreign descent have also been

29. "Countries and Peoples of India", *ABORI*, XVII, Pt. III (April 1936), pp. 236-37 and 241.

30. *Manu-Smṛti*, X, 43-44; See also G. Bühler's tr. "The Laws of Manu with Extracts from Seven Commentaries", SBE (ed. F. Max Muller, OUP, 1886, Delhi 1964), XXV, p. 412., A.C. Burnell, *The Ordinances of Manu*, pp. 310-11; N.V. Banerjee, *Studies in the Dharma-Śāstra of Manu*, p. 67.

31. *AISH*, pp. 164-65; *The Past and Prejudice*, p. 37.

32. *India as Described by Manu*, pp. 5f.

33. *Studies in the Society and Administration of Ancient and Medival India*, I, pp. 48-49, 101-3 and 132 fn.; *Studies in the Religious Life of Ancient and Medival India*, p. 91, *JARS*, XIV (Sept., 1978), pp. 4-5.

34. *Dharmaśāstra Kā Itihāsa*, I, 129-30 and 131.

35. *History of Classical Sanskrit Literature*, Int; ix-ixi.

36. *The Indo-Aryan Races*, pp. 43-44.

37. *RENIT*, pp. 32 & 73.

38. *Pre-Aryan and Pre-Dravidian in India* (tr. from French by P.C. Bagchi), Pt. III, p. 89.

39. *Indische Alterthumskunde*, I, pp. 441 ff.

incorporated in the list of kṣatriya tribes. There is no denying the fact that some Āryan and non-Āryan tribes were reduced to the position of śūdras and they also perhaps cannot be an exception to this. R.S. Sharma[40] has thrown a good deal of light on this aspect of the subject.

Varāhamihira has referred to the Cīnas altogether nine times out of which seven times he has placed them in the north-west (Vāyava) associating them with the Kāmbojas, Gāndhāras, dwellers of the Indus region, Kāśmīras, Pulindas, Yavaṇas, Vāhlikas, Afghans, etc,[41] one time in the north-east division (Īśāna)[42] and one time towards the east of Narmadā mentioning them together with Prāgjyotiṣa.[43] But Ajaya Mitra Shastri in his thesis has mentioned them as a people of only north-east division,[44] and H. Kern has, mistakenly, equated those of north-western disvision with the "Chinese".[45]

They also find mention the Buddhist texts. The *Apadāna* describes the Cīnas as a people "who came to Haṁsavatī on the Ganges from a distant land (ārā va cīnaraṭṭhā ca āga-cchanti)".[46] In the Pāli *Śāsanavaṁsa Himavantapadesa* (p. 13), they are mentioned as the people of Cīnamaru watered by the river Oxus, i.e., Vaṁkṣu or Cakṣu. It shows that during the Buddhist period they had spread as far as Central Asia beyond north-western extremity of India. They are further placed by B.C. Law[47] in the Himālayas beyond Cilāta or Kirāta. In the Pāli *Milindapañha* (compiled by a Buddhist scholar, Nāgasena), there occurs an expression "Cīna-Vilāta" = Cilāta = Kirāta. In this particular text, Cīnas figure in three different lists. Collectively speaking, they have been mentioned

---

40. For details see *Śūdras in Ancient India*, pp. 33-41, 44f, 262f, 280f.
41. *Br. Sam.*, V, 77, 78, 80; X, 7, 11; XI, 61; XVI, 38.
42. *Ibid.*, XIV, 30.
43. XVI, 1.
44. *India as seen in the Bṛhat Saṁhitā of Varāhamihira*, p. 73.
45. Ed. *Br. Sam.*, 5, 77, 78, 80; tr. cf. *JRAS*, 1970, pp. 430ff; 18871, pp. 45ff; 1873, pp. 36ff; 1875, pp. 81ff.
46. II, pp. 358-59, cf. B.C. Law, *India as Described in Early Texts of Buddhism and Jainism*, p. 86; See also *Apadāna*, I, ii. (Pali text Society, London, not yet ed.).
47. *Historical Geography of Ancient India*, pp. 73, 98-99.

along with Kāśī, Kośala, Vaṅga, Takkola, Śaka, Yavaṇa, Kāśmīra, Gāndhāras, etc.[48] But details are unfortunately missing.

The Cīna-deśa as referred to in the Tantra literature — the *Sammoha Tantra* (List 1, v. 6) and *Śaktisaṅgama Tantra* (Bk. III, Ch. VII, v. 34) — can be placed to the south-east of Mān-Sarovar that is Tibet called "Bhoṭa-deśa" in the verse.[49] This exactly tallies with the statement of Pargiter, as already mentioned. Here it must be made clear that Cīna and Mahā-Cīna, as mentioned in the *Vālmīki-Rāmāyaṇa*,[50] Tāntric texts, *Sammoha Tantra*,[51] *Śaktisaṅgama Tantra*[52] and *Laghu-Kālatantra-jatika*, the Buddhist text, *Sādhanamālā*, and *Mānasollāsa* (2, 6, 17-20)[53] of Someśvaradeva (AD 1127-38), are two different countries. Both can be distinguished from each other.

The Mahā-Cīna country, as mentioned particularly in the *Śakatisaṅgama Tantra*, is said to have extended from the Kailāsagiri (that part of the Himālayan range, which lies to the north of Mān-Sarovar) and from the place of the origin of the Sarayū as far as Monga (Mongolia to the north of China). Mahā-Cīna, therefore, refers to China proper.[54] This is further supported by the evidence recorded by the Chinese traveller, Hiuen-Tsang, himself who visited India in the seventh century AD. He said that "his native country was the Mahācīna or Mahāchina of the Indians and that it was situated some myriade of *li* to the north-east of India".[55] One of the priests of India is said to have informed him that Cīna is a country of the *mlecchas*[56] which constitutes a testimony to the fact the Cīnas were not the people of China but the *mleccha*s of India. B.C. Law[57] has rightly called the people — "Apara-Cīnas" — as Western Cīnas.

There are some other views which are worthy of our attention. Robert Shafer supports

48. IV, 8, 94cf Trenckner's edn., pp. 327, 331 & 359; R.D. Vadekar's edn., p. 321; M. Pelliot, *Journal Asiatique* (Paris, 1914), II, pp. 379f.
49. D.C. Sircar, SGAMI, pp. 78, 84 and 103.
50. Kiṣkindhā Kāṇḍa, 43, 13.
51. List I, V, 6.
52. Bk. III, Ch. VII, V, 35.
53. *GDEP*, pp. 171-73.
54. D.C. Sircar, *SGAMI*, p. 104.
55. Thomas Watter's *On Yuan Chwang's Travels in India* (AD 629-45), I, p. 349.
56. Samuel Beal, *The Life of Hiuen-Tsiang*, p. 167.
57. *ABORI*, XVII, III, (1936), pp. 236-37.

the view of Śrī Raṅgācārya who suggested that the Cīnas were the modern Sina who spoke a Dardic language of the same name (which was also spoken by the Durds of Hindukush).[58] K.P. Jayaswal also supports this view. While dealing with the races as described by Manu, he observes that the "Chinas are the Sina race or tribe of Gilgit Region".[59] Mr. Shafer does not consider them either as the foreign race as thought of in the Buddhist and Jaina literature or as Mongoloid or Chinese as considered by S.K. Chatterji. He further makes it clear that the epic Āryans knew nothing about the east or north-east and the Cīnas always remained associated with the people of north and north-west. The appearance of the Chinese on the eastern frontier of early India has been doubted. He places the Cīnas of the Purāṇic age beyond the Himālayas on the upper Indus and in Kashmir. The Chinese, according to him, do not seem to have been able to penetrate Tibet proper before the seventh century AD and Baltistan before the eighth century AD. The Cīnas were not those powerful Chinese who invaded India but a people who were forced to pay tribute during the epic age. He also refers to the view of Sir Aurel Stein who also admits that the Cīnas were in the upper Indus Valley at a very early period. The Chinese before the establishment of the dynasty of Tsin (*c*. 249-210 BC) were outside the border whom the "Indo-Āryan" did not recognise.[60]

H.H. Wilson's identification of the Cīnas, as mentioned in the epics, the Purāṇas and *Manu-Smṛti*, with the Chinese (the so-called people of Chinese Tartary) is not correct.[61] Klaproth in an attempt to prove them Chinese suggested merely on the basis of an inferential evidence that the ancient Indian texts referring to the Cīnas are not older than the third century BC when the reigning dynasty of Thsin first gave that name to "Chinae".[62] It is true that the designation "China" was first derived during Tsin dynasty which commenced in *c*. 260 BC. But it is not acceptable that the texts mentioning the Cīnas are not older than the third century BC. It has been made very clear that the "Hindus became acquainted with the Chinese only about 200 BC when their arms extended to the Oxus".[63] This evidence also suggests that before the third century BC the word

58. *Ethnography of Ancient India*, pp. 130-32.
59. *Hindu Polity*, Pt. I, p. 124, note 33.
60. *Op. cit.*
61. See his Eng. tr. of *Viṣnu Purāṇa*, Bk. II, Ch. III, No. 145, p. 160; Bk. IV, Ch. III, p. 300.
62. *Ibid.*
63. *Ibid.*

"Chinese" was not in use. Thus, the Cīnas, as mentioned in early literature, are evidently not the Chinese people.

The epigraphic records also supply some information about them. The Cīnas mentioned along with the Cilāta = Kirāta, Kāśmīr, Gāndhāra, etc., in one of the Nāgarjunakoṇḍa Inscriptions (in the Prākṛt language with southern Brāhmī script and dated second half of the third century AD) of the Ikṣvāku king Vīrapuruṣadatta (successor of Sātavāhanas) of Kṛṣṇa-Gunṭūr region[64] have been placed in Tibet and beyond the Kirāta region.[65] This inscription records that they were profoundly influenced by the doctrine of Buddhism, as propagated by Buddhist monks of the period concerned. Their regular visits to Nāgārjunakoṇḍa, the important seat of Buddhist culture, to attend the religious discourses of the *arhats* with the monks afford testimony to their inclination towards Buddhism. It appears that during 14th regnal year of the said king the Cīnas along with the Kirātas, Gāndhāras, Kāśmīras, Vanavāsīs, Damilas, Yavaṇas, etc., were converted to Buddhism by Ceylonese Buddhist monks.[66]

In Hāthīgumphā Cave Inscription (Udayagiri Hills near Bhubaneśvar bearing Prākṛt language resembling Pāli and Brāhmī script) of king Khāravela (second-first century BC) of Kaliṅga the word figures as Sino (Vasikaroti), which has variant readings.[67] From whatever clue is available it can be safely presumed that they might have been one of the hill-tribes who were brought under control. The influence of Jainism on them is not known.

Bālaghāṭa plate of Pṛthvīsena II (*c.* AD 470-90),[68] a ruler of the Vākāṭaka dynasty of the Deccan, and Bhatūrya Inscription of Rājyapāla (*c.* AD 991-1018),[69] a Pratihāra ruler of northern India, bear witness to the victories of the rulers concerned over the Cīna,

---

64. J. Ph. Vogel, *Ep. Ind.*, XX, I, p. 22, line I; D.C. Sircar, *SI*, I, p. 234; See also *Ep. Ind.*, XX, 1, pp. 6f, 16f, 19f.
65. *SI*, p. 235, Note. 1.
66. *Ep. Ind.*, XXXV, 1, p.1; See also *Ep. Ind.*, XXXIII, pp. 248-49.
67. K.P. Jayaswal and R.D. Banerji, *Ep. Ind.*, XX, pp. 72f, Line 14, fn. 11; K.P. Jayaswal, *JBORS*, III, (1917-18), pp. 425ff; IV, pp. 364f; XIII, pp. 221f; XIV, pp. 150f; R.D. Banerjee, *JBORS*, III, (1917-18), pp. 486f; D.C. Sircar, *SI*, 1, pp. 213-17; Prinsep, *JASB*, VI, pp. 1075-91; *Corp. Ins. Ind.*, 1, pp. 27f, 98, 101, 132ff; Fleet, *JRAS* (1910), pp. 242ff, 824f. For the revised text of the Inscription see B.M. Barua, *IHQ* (1938), pp. 461 ff. Different Scholars have interpreted the text in different manners.
68. *Ep. Ind.*, IX, p. 270.
69. *Ep. Ind.*, XXXIII, p. 150.

mleccha, Aṅga, Kaliṅga, Vaṅga, Oḍra, Pāṇḍya, Karnāṭa, Lāṭa, Sumha, Gurjara, etc., and their subjugation by them. Whatever may be the truth it is almost certain that the Cīna, as referred to in this particular context, was not China but in all probability the neighbouring areas consisting of tribal population.

The analysis of all the available data concerned gives us the result that the Cīnas were a widely diffused non-Āryan race in ancient India. They were neither the Chinese nor the people of Mongolian family but the tribal people of indigenous origin having their settlements in eastern and western extremities of northern India, in other parts of India, particularly the hilly regions, and in Tibet and Burma. Relying on the testimonies of *Mahābhārata* and *Manu-Smṛti* and on other supporting evidence, they can be considered as the descendants of the brāhmaṇas and kṣatriyas, later degenerated to the rank of the śūdras. It was Mahā-Cīna which roughly corresponds to modern China. The antiquity of China as a country cannot be pushed back earlier than the third century BC. Therefore, we do not find any valid reason to trace the ancestry of the so-called Cīnas to the Chinese or to connect them with only the Chinese people. Their racial ethnology, as highlighted in ancient Indian literature and inscriptions, does not permit us to do so. As a matter of fact, they represent both the countries and peoples of ancient India.

PART II
Society, Economy and Religion

3

Ancient Indian Society and Economy in the Jain and Buddhist Traditions

THIS essay aims at portraying a vivid picture of ancient Indian society and economy, as recorded in the Jain and Buddhist traditions. The social structure, *varṇa* system, the caste hierarchy, the position held by various Āryan and non-Āryan social groups in the contemporary society, the family and the marriage system, position of women in the society, the prevalent social customs, slavery, agriculture, animal husbandry, land ownership, production and distribution system, the condition of peasantry, land tenure system, arts and crafts, indigenous industries, trade and commerce, market economy, taxation system, professional and occupational groups, guild system, various other socio-economic institutions, feudalism, land-grant system, currency system, weights and measures, etc., are some of those relevant aspects, which fall within the purview of the treatment of the subject. An attempt has been made to draw a comparative picture of the subject based on the data available in the Jain canon comprising the *sūtras*, *niryuktis*, *cūrṇis*, *bhāṣyas*, etc., (fifth century BC to the sixth century AD), commentaries or *ṭīkās* (eighth to seventeenth century AD), non-canonical texts and the Purāṇic records of the early period (seventh to tenth century AD), the canonical Pāli literature, mainly the *Nikāyas* and the *Jātakas* (fifth to first century BC), the post-canonical Pāli texts (first to fourth century AD) and commentaries (by Buddhaghoṣa and Dhammapāla, the two celebrated Buddhist commentators, who flourished in the fifth century AD) and the Sanskrit texts (of the early centuries of the Christian era) of the Buddhists, and some other useful collateral sources.

The four-fold divisions of early Indian society of the Jains and Buddhists represented by the brāhmaṇas, kṣatriyas, vaiśyas and śūdras constitute the common feature of their social life during the period concerned. The social order of the later Vedic age in respect of *varṇa* organisation appears to have been little reversed by the Jain and Buddhist scholars. In the early Buddhist texts and the Jain canonical and Purāṇic literature, the order of the first two *varṇa*s was reversed with the result that the kṣatriyas came to be placed first and the brāhmaṇas just next to them from the point of view of social grades. As regards the remaining two *varṇa*s the order was left undisturbed. The Jains and Buddhists always stood for the social superiority of the kṣatriyas over the brāhmaṇas. According to both Jain and Buddhist traditions, the kṣatriyas enjoyed the highest status than the brāhmaṇas in the contemporary society. However, the reversal of the order of the first two *varṇa*s did not alter the basic structure of their society. Like the later Vedic society the *varṇa* distinction was maintained to a considerable extent in their society too. The divisions of Jain and Buddhist society into four *vaṇṇa*s were more or less based on the brāhmaṇical concept of *varṇa* organisation. In the Jain and Budhist society we find the reflection of the conception of society as an organism in the sense of the origin of the brāhmaṇas, kṣatriyas, vaiśyas and śūdras from the mouth, the arms, the thighs and the feet of Brahmā respectively, which the Brāhmaṇist stood for in the pre-Buddhistic phase of ancient Indian history. The organic conception of society and its allegorical expressions eventually resulted in the formulation of a theory, which was later put into practice. The allegorical fancy led the Brāhmaṇist to name the four divisions in terms of *varṇa* and *jāti*. The term *varṇa* was interpreted literally in the sense of distinctive colour or complexion and *jāti* in that of distinctive mode of birth. The *varṇa* and *jāti* forming the basis of social distinctions received two-fold interpretation : biological and psycho-ethical, biological and socio-cultural. The *varṇa* as a biological term meant colour or complexion and as a psycho-ethical term, man's internal nature. The *jāti* as a biological term meant birth, pedigree or relationship, and as an ethical term, a particular mental or moral trait. The persistent brāhmaṇical tendency to give a hereditary character to occupational distinctions by birth-right ultimately led to the formation of castes and castes within castes. The impact of brāhmaṇic tradition on the social organisation of the Jains and Buddhists is clearly discernible. The early records of Jains and Buddhists bear an eloquent testimony to the fact that there was a powerful movement of thought for counteracting the rapidly increasing brāhmaṇical tendency.

It is significant to note that the Jains did not accept the social system based on the four *varṇa*s till the dawn of the seventh century AD, which marks the beginning of their Purāṇic period. The Vedic concept of four *varṇa*s was conspicuous by its absence in Jain society in its early phase, but subsequently (during the period : seventh to tenth century AD) it received wide social recognition. The fact stated above can be confirmed by the evidence adduced in the *Ādi Purāṇa* (which constitutes the first part of the *Mahāpurāṇa*),[1]

1. II, 38, 45.

composed by Jinasena III in *c.* AD 840. The four classes : *bambhaṇa* (brāhmaṇa), *khattiya* (kṣatriya), *vaissa* (vaiśya) and *sudda* (śūdra) have, of course, been mentioned in the Jain canon,[2] but this division was fundamentally based on occupations and not birth. The study of the Jain Purāṇas also reveals the fact that Jain society was originally based on the law of *karma* and not rules of *varṇa*. The people were free to choose their profession voluntarily. No specific duty was assigned to any *varṇa*. Guṇabhadra, disciple of Jinasena III, in his *Uttarapurāṇa* (which constitutes the second part of the *Mahapurāṇa*),[3] composed towards the close of the ninth century AD (*c.* AD 898), has denounced the social distinctions on the basis of *varṇa* or caste. Raviṣena (who belonged to the seventh century AD) in his *Padma Purāṇa*[4] also laid emphasis on judging the status of an individual in the society on the basis of virtuous deeds and not caste. It is further stated therein that the *cāṇḍālas* representing lower caste performing the duties generally assigned to the brāhmaṇas could be entitled to be called as brāhmaṇas. But after sometime their social system underwent some changes.

After having thoroughly investigated the data available in the Jain Purāṇas, we find that the contemporary political situation emerging out of the foreign invasions of northern India after the decline of the Guptas or during the compositional period of the Jain Purāṇas, which resulted in the anarchy and upset the social balance, had actually compelled the Jain *ācāryas* to bring the society within the bounds of the four *varṇas* for maintaining the social order. Raviṣena in his *Padma Purāṇa* (*c.* AD 676 or 677), Jinasena II in his *Harivaṁśa Purāṇa* (*c.* AD 783) and Jinasena III in his *Ādi Purāṇa* (ninth century AD) upheld the validity of the four-fold divisions of society of the Vedic times, further codified the rules of *varṇa* (*vaṇṇa*) and thereby paved the way for the perpetuation of the *varṇa* system in Jain society. Thus, the Jain *purāṇakāras* became instrumental in persuading the people to strictly follow the *varṇa* rules, which had taken a distinct shape in the pre-Purāṇic period, as evidenced by the facts stated in Jain canonical texts and commentaries.

The four classes called brāhmaṇa, kṣatriya, vaiśya and śūdra distinctly figure in the Jain Purāṇas.[5] The theory of their origins as propounded therein bears the stamp of the

---

2. *Uttarādhyayana* (*Sūtra*), 25, 31-33; *Ācārāṅga*, *Niryukti*, 19, 27.
3. 74, 492.
4. 11, 203.
5. *Ādi Purāṇa*, 1, 16, 243-46; *Padma Purāṇa*, 5, 194; see also "Account of the Jains" in *As. Res.*, IX (Delhi, 1979), pp. 247 ff.

Brāhmaṇic tradition. It is said that the kṣatriyas, vaiśyas and śūdras originated respectively from the arms, thighs and feet of the first Jain *tīrthaṅkara*, Ṛṣabhadeva, and the brāhmaṇas originated from the mouth of his son, Bharat. Each of the four *varṇas* was assigned the similar duties which characterised the Brāhmaṇical social order. The brāhmaṇas were entrusted with the duties of studying and teaching *śāstras* and performing worships, rituals, etc., the kṣatriyas were the warriors; the vaiśyas were engaged in agriculture, trade and commerce, etc., and the śūdras, who were recognised as the fourth social order like that of Vedic system, had to render their services to the other three upper classes. The śūdras were further sub-divided into touchables and untouchables.[6] Jinasena clearly states that each of the four *varṇas* had to remain within the limits of their respective duties.[7] According to him, the laws were framed by the state to punish those who violated the established rules of *varṇa* organisation.[8] He is said to have laid emphasis on the *daṇḍa* (or coercion), whose application was taken as an essential factor for the maintenance of the existing social order.[9] Restrictions were also imposed on the people in regard to the performance of marriage within the limits of *varṇa* so as to perpetuate the *varṇa* system and to maintain the social balance.[10]

The above description gives us an impression that there was definitely some impact of the Hindu culture or the influence of the Brāhmaṇical traditions on Jain society of early medieval period. The Jain Purāṇas bear witness to the assimilation of Brāhmaṇical ideas and institutions in the Jain society. The social changes concerned marked the fundamental departure from the original teachings of Jainism. As a result of the changes which the Jain society underwent during the period concerned and also later, the Jains of south, particularly Karnataka, lost their social identity. On the basis of the study of *Yaśastilaka* of Somadeva (*c.* AD 959), G.C. Jain has pointed out that even the followers of Jainism, who originally raised the voice of protest against the *varṇa* system of Vedic times could not keep themselves away from the undercurrents of the time. By the ninth

6. For details see *Ādi*, 1, 16, 183-86, 243-46; II, 38, 46; *Padma*, 3, 256-58; 5, 194; 11, 201-2; *Harivaṁśa Purāṇa*, 9, 39, (for different versions on the origin of the brāhmaṇas see *Ādi*, II, 38, 7-20; *Padma*, 5, 195; *Harivaṁśa*, 11, 105-7).
7. *Ādi*, 1, 16, 187.
8. *Ibid.*, 1, 16, 248.
9. *Ibid.*, 1, 16, 251-53.
10. *Ibid.*, 1, 16, 247.

century AD the *varṇa* rules of the Vedic times received the stamp of Jainism from Jinasena.[11]

With regard to the social status and duties of each of the four *varṇas*, we shall here first recount that of the brāhmaṇas. At the outset, it will be quite befitting to the context to state that throughout early Jain and Buddhist texts a sharp distinction was sought to be drawn between the brāhmaṇas as they ought to have been and the brāhmaṇas as they actually were, that is to say between the ideal and the factual. In drawing a correct picture of the social life in India as revealed in the ancient Jain and Buddhist texts, we are concerned with the brāhmaṇas as they actually were. For the Jains and Buddhists ideally perfect brāhmaṇas of the time were those who became degenerated on account of their gradual deviations from the ancient path of purity or morals.

The brāhmaṇas, who occupied the highest position in Hindu society before the advent of Jainism and Buddhism in the sixth century BC, were sunsequently put into the lower grade than the kṣatriyas in Jain and Buddhist society. From Jain canon, particularly the *sūtras*, it appears that the brāhmaṇas (called *bambhaṇs*) were contemptuously looked down upon. The term *dhijjāi* (*dhik-jāti*) or "condemned caste" has been frequently used for them.[12] Their former position, which they held in the Āryan society, was actually restored in the early medieval period, as it appears from the Jain Purāṇas. The Purāṇic evidence fairly attests to their supremacy during the period concerned.[13] They were generally held in high esteem. They enjoyed certain privileges like immunity from taxes and capital punishment.

The primary duties of the brāhmaṇas were to study the Vedas, acquire the knowledge of the *śāstras*, teach them to others, offer sacrifices, accept the gifts, etc.[14] They were alo expected to have perfect command over the fourteen branches of knowledge (*Cauddasa-Vijjaṭṭhāna*), i.e., six *aṅgas* : *śikṣā*, *vyākaraṇa*, *nirukata*, *chanda*, *jyotiṣa* and *kalpa*; four Vedas : *Ṛgveda*, *Yajurveda*, *Sāmaveda* and *Atharvaveda*; Mimāṁsā, Nyāya, Purāṇa and Dharmaśāstra.

It is curious to note that Jain writers like those of the Buddhists laid stress on

11. *Yaśastilaka kā Sāṁskṛtika Adhyayana*, pp. 59, 68-70.
12. J.C. Jain, *LAIJC*, p. 187; see also his, *Jain Āgama Sāhitya Mein Bhāratīya Samāj*, pp. 224-25.
13. *Ādi*, II, 39, 130-32; II, 40, 182-84.
14. *Niśītha-Bhāṣya*, Jinadāsagaṇi Mahattara, ed. Upādhyāya Kavi Amar Muni and Muni Kanhaiyalal, 13, 4423; *Adi*, 1, 16, 246.

judging the brāhmaṇahood of the people on the basis of their deeds and not birth.[15] It is clearly stated in the Jain Purāṇas that those brāhmaṇas (followers of Jainism), who did not perform the duties as prescribed in the Jain texts or strictly followed the Vedic tradition or did not eschew the path of violence, were deprived of their brāhmaṇahood and considered only an ideal brāhmaṇa.[16]

In one of the Purāṇas, a brāhmaṇa named Pravarak has been referred to as an agriculturist, who used to earn his livelihood through plough cultivation.[17] But this may be an exception. Because the brāhmaṇas usually employed the śūdras for agricultural works.

The order of the four *vaṇṇa*s or *varṇa*s : *khattiya* (kṣatriya), brāhmaṇa, *vessa* (vaiśya) and *sudda* (śūdra), as arranged in the Buddhist tradition[18] from the point of view of social grades, also shows that the position of the brāhmaṇas was inferior to that of the *khattiya*s.

In the *Dasa-brāhmaṇa Jātaka*, the brāhmaṇas have been divided into ten categories, classes or types, viz., the brāhmaṇas who moved around like physicians (*tikicchakasama*); those who acted like servants (*paricārakasama*); those who in the garb of ascetics behaved like tax-collectors (*niggāhakasama*); those who begged alms; those who like tradesmen (*vāṇijakasama*) used to sell various things; those who like the *ambaṭṭha*s and the *vessa*s carried on agricultural trade, etc., the *purohita*s who interpreted omens, castrated and branded animals and acted as butchers (*go-ghātaka*); those who armed with the sword and the shield guarded the business-quarter; those who in the garb of hermits behaved like hunters (*luddakasama*) and the *yājñika*s who performed the *soma-yajña*, etc.[19]

The criticism of the brāhmaṇa position offered in the Pāli *vāseṭṭha Sutta* clearly implies that the brāhmaṇas of the time followed the pursuits of agriculturists (*kassak*) craftsmen (*sippika*), order-carriers (*pessika*), tradesmen (*vāṇija*), soldiers (*yodhājiva*),

15. *Uttarādhyayana*, 25, 29 ff.
16. For details see *Ādi*, II, 38, 43, 47; II, 39, 133; II, 41, 46-58; II, 42, 179-92; *Padma*, 4, 115-20; 11, 201; 109, 80-82.
17. *Harivaṁśa*, 43, 116.
18. *Aṅguttara Nikāya*, ed. Richard Morris and Edmund Hardy, III, p. 214; *Sutta-Nipāta* (one of the 15 books of *Khuddaka Nikāya*), 1, 7; III, 9; *Vinaya-Piṭaka*, ed. H. Oldenberg, IV (for three upper social grades); T.W. Rhys Davids, *BI*, pp. 53-54; B.C. Law, *HPL*, 1, pp. 87-88; see also his *IETBJ*, pp. 139-40.
19. B.C. Law, *IETBJ*, pp. 150-51.

sacrificers (*yājaka*) and landlords (*rājañña*) as various means of their livelihood.[20]

From the Fragment on *sīla*s it distinctly appears that the brāhmaṇas earned their livelihood by such low pursuits as those of apothecaries, druggists, physicians, priests, occultists and sorcerers, landholders, traders, cattle-breeders, farmers, etc. They were actually expected to live up to their highest religious ideal, but in practice they appeared as hoarders of wealth and as persons who cared to lead luxurious and voluptuous life in an aristocractic style.[21]

A more correct picture of the brāhmaṇa position in the society of the Age may be drawn on the basis of the Buddha's classification of the brāhmaṇas into five types: *brahmasama* or resembling the Brahmā, represented by those who were of high and pure birth and renounced the world to live the life of lonely meditation; *devasama* or resembling the gods, represented by those who took up the position of married householders; *mariyādā* or those who strictly adhered to their ancient tradition; *sambhinna-mariyādā* or those who disregarded their ancient tradition and married girls from all social grades including the *sudda*s and untouchables; and brāhmaṇa-*cāṇḍāla* or those who lived a vulgar life.[22]

The classification of the brāhmaṇas in Jain and Buddhist traditions presents two sides of the picture in contrast. On the one hand, they commanded respect in the society because of their supreme worth, moral virtues, intellectual perfection and spiritual fervour, and on the other, their position degenerated on account of their worthlessness, moral degradation, deviation from the established social norms, etc.

In both the Jain and Buddhist traditions, valuable description of the brāhmaṇas, who followed different professions of their own, have been provided. Of those who were in the service of the king (*rājakammika*), the most important was the *purohita*. From the *Jātaka*s it appears that he acted as the *ācariya* or preceptor, the sacrificial priest and the house-priest of the king.[23] One of his principal duties was to guard the king's treasures.[24] He was not only king's officer,[25] but also *senāpati* in the matter of judicial

---

20. *Sutta-Nipāta*, p. 122; R. Fick, *The Social Organisation in North-East India in Buddha's Time*, p. 221f.
21. *Dīgha Nikāya*, ed. T.W. Rhys Davids & J.E. Carpenter, I, p. 4f; T.W. and C.A.F. Rhys Davids (tr.), *Dialogues of the Buddha*, X, p, 6f.
22. *Aṅguttara*, III, p. 223f.
23. *Jāt.*, II, p. 376; IV, p. 270; V, p. 127.
24. *Ibid.*, III, p. 513 f.

duties.[26] The role played by the *purohita* as king's officer has also been highlighted by Mr. Fick.[27] The *Sarabhaṅga-Jātaka* speaks of Jotipāla, son of the *purohita* of the king of Benāres, who was appointed commander-in-chief (*senāpati*).[28] The *purohita*s received fees and gifts from the kings, which constituted their main source of income. The gifts included land-endownments, women, maidens, slaves, male and female, and livestocks. Here lay the origin of the landed property and wordly prosperity of the *purohita*s. The brāhmaṇas belonging to this very class became rich and powerful only because of certain permanent land-grants and endowments and other royal grants (*rājadeyyam-brahmadeyyam*).[29] Next to the *purohita* in importance were the *amāccas* or *mahāmatta*s (councillors and ministers) who offered their sevices to the king. The *yācaka*s were the sacrificers. The brāhmaṇas were occasionally employed by the king as *dūta*s (ambassadors). They also filled the office of *senāpati*s (generals) and *yodhājivas* (soldiers).

The brāhmaṇas pursued various other vocations of life as well in their own independent capacities as private citizens. In the Buddha's time (sixth to fifth centuries BC), a brāhmaṇa of the Bhāradvāja clan living in Dakkhiṇagiri was a rich agriculturist. It is said that five hundred ploughs were needed to cultivate the fields owned by him.[30] The *Somadatta-Jātaka* relates the story of a poor brāhmaṇa farmer who himself ploughed his field.[31] The *Jātaka*s record many instances of the brāhmaṇa farmers driving the plough with their own hands.[32]

The *Mahāsutasoma-Jātaka* refers to a wealthy brāhmaṇa who was engaged in trade. He carried on trade between the east-end and the west-end of India transporting his goods in 500 wagons.[33] There is also an allusion to ordinary brāhmaṇa tradesmen and hawkers who roamed about in the country to sell their wares.[34]

---

25. *Jāt.*, I, p. 439.
26. *Ibid.*, II, p. 187 f.
27. *Op. cit.*, p. 164.
28. *Jāt.*, V, p. 127 f.
29. Fick, *op. cit.*, p. 244f.
30. *Sutta-Nipāta* (Kāśī-Bhāradvāja Sutta), pp. 12-16 cf. *HPL*. I, p. 242; *Saṁyutta-Nikāya*, ed. M.L. Feer and Mrs. Rhys Davids, I, p. 171f.
31. *Jāt.*, II, p. 165.
32. *Ibid.*, III, p. 162; IV, p. 276.
33. *Ibid.*, V, p. 471.
34. *Ibid.*, II, p. 15.

The *Phandana-Jātaka* narrates the story of a brāhmaṇa who adopted the profession of a carpenter (*vaḍḍhaki*).[35] We also find an instance of a brāhmaṇa youth who lived in a frontier village earning his livelihood by selling the hunted beasts[36] obviously because of economic reason.[37]

Some of the *Jātakas* speak of brāhmaṇas who possessed enormous wealth. There were some brāhmaṇas whose wealth amounted to eighty crore (*asitikoṭi-dhanavibhava*).[38] According to the celebrated Pāli scholiasts, it were the *mahāsāla*-brāhmaṇas, whose hoarded wealth amounted to eighty crore.[39] But the *Mahāgovinda Suttanta* describes them as heads of the Vedic institutions.[40]

The privileges enjoyed by the brāhmaṇas like immunity from taxes and rents in so far as the land-endowments were concerned are, of course, elucidated in the brāhmaṇa and Jain texts. But the Pāli texts do not bear testimony to any privileged position enjoyed by them in the eye of the law. It is clearly stated in the *Madhura Sutta* that a criminal, whether a brāhmaṇa or not, was liable to execution.[41] The *Jātakas* also provide unmistakable evidence of the execution of brāhmaṇas.[42]

In the Buddha's time, brāhmaṇas claiming descent from Kurupañcāla occupied a pre-eminent position among the brāhmaṇas as a class.[43] So far as occupation of the brāhmaṇas as a basis of social distinction was concerned, we find in both Jain and Buddhist traditions that the study and teaching of the Vedas with all the auxiliary sciences and arts useful to the state and to the people at large, and the priestly duties in connection with all socio-religious ceremonies constituted their monopoly.

The economic conditions of the brāhmaṇas as a class, other than those in high royal service, the *mahāsālas*, and the few farmers and traders was pitiable. Most of them belonged to the poor class as they were wholly dependent on an uncertain income from fees, gifts and alms.

35. *Jāt.*, IV, p. 207.
36. *Ibid.*, II, p. 200.
37. Fick, *op. cit.*, p. 247.
38. *Jāt.*, II, p. 272; IV, pp. 15, 22.
39. *Paramatthajotikā* (a commentary on *Sutta-Nipāta* by Buddhaghoṣa), ed. Helmer Smith, II, p. 313.
40. *Dīgha*, XI, p. 236.
41. *Majjhima-Nikāya*, ed. V. Trenckner & R. Chalmers, II, p. 83f.
42. *Jāt.*, I, p. 439; Fick, *op. cit.*, p. 212.
43. *Ibid.*, I, pp. 324, 356.

In contrast to the Brāhmaṇical works emphasising the social superiority of the brāhmaṇas, Jain writers like those of the Buddhists repeatedly point to the higher social rank of the *khattiyas* or kṣatriyas than the brāhmaṇas. The *khattiyas* of the time included princes, warriors or nobles, who acquired the right to rule the country by the strength of their arms. A number of *khattiya* kings and princes, who renounced the world, achieved the ideal of *jina*-hood an embraced Jainism, are mentioned in the Jain texts. They are said to have learnt seventy-two arts and achieved proficiency in the art of fighting. According to the Jain Purāṇas,[44] they were primarily concerned with the maintenance of internal order and peace and protection of their territories against their enemy. Their main duty was to protect the weaker section of the society from being exploited by other powerful class.

In the Buddhist tradition too, the *khattiyas* represented the ruling class, family, tribe or clan, who claimed descent from the leaders of the Āryan tribes. Wherever they founded a territory or colony, they lived either under a monarchical or tribal, oligarchical or republican form of government. In monarchies, the kings were their best representatives. In oligarchies, such as those of the Licchavis, Mallas and Śākyas, all the members bore the family title of *rājā*, which means a leading members of the ruling clan.

It should also be noted that the reigning king was not necessarily a man of the *khattiya* family. From the *Jātakas* we gather the information that where the reigning kings were considered unworthy of the throne, the people in a body replaced them each by a brāhmaṇa.[45] When a king died without an hier, the duty fell upon the *purohita* to find out a worthy successor.[46] The king was freely recognised as the foremost of men.[47]

Though the *khattiyas* were the warriors *par excellence*, the soldiers of a kingdom or a territory were not necessarily all *khattiyas*. Even those born of brāhmaṇa families adopted the profession of *yodhājivas*. However, in the *Jātakas* the Uggaputtas occupying superior military ranks are all described as *khattiyas*. There is a notable instance of how a *khattiya* prince renounced his right to kingship and took to trade as his profession on

---

44. *Ādi*, I, 16, 184; II, 42, 4, 13; II, 44, 30; *Padma* 3, 56, 246, 11, 202; 78, 12; *Harivaṁśa*, 9, 38.
45. *Jāt.*, I, p. 326.
46. *Ibid.*, III, p. 238; IV, p. 39.
47. *Mahāvagga* (part of the *Vinaya Piṭaka*), VI, 35, 8.

the condition that his brothers, the reigning kings would exempt him from the payment of duties and taxes.[48]

The society was composed of two other social grades, namely, those represented by the vaiśyas (*vaissas* of the Jains and *vessas* of the Buddhists) and śūdras (known as *suddas* in both Jain and Buddhist traditions).

The vaiśyas formed the third grade of the society with trade and commerce, agriculture and farming as their distinctive occupation. They basically belonged to the mercantile class.[49] In the Jain Purāṇas they have been mentioned as *seṭha*, *vaṇika*, *śreṣṭhi*, *sārthavāha*, etc.[50] Besides trade, they kept themselves enaged in agricultural work and cattle rearing,[51] which they later abandoned because of fear of violence in such activities.[52]

The term *gāhāvai*s used in the Jain sources[53] or *gahapati* or the canonical Pāli texts[54] in its general sense was applicable to all who lived the life of a householder, irrespective of classes or social grades. The term corresponds to the traditional vaiśya order of the Hindus of ancient India. By general usage the term was restricted to the *seṭṭhi*s or bankers who were the best representatives of the *vessa*s. They were the *gahapati*s *par excellence* just as the *khattiya*s were the warriors *par excellence*. In fact, it was from the families of the *gahapati*s that there emerged the *seṭṭhi*s. The interchangeability of the *gahapati* and the *seṭṭhi* as members of the same family is supported from references to them in the Buddhist sources.[55] As *seṭṭhis* they controlled the whole of trade and commerce, agriculture and industry. They were, no doubt, the business magnates in a city or town.

It is noteworthy that there was hardly any social grade which did not participate in production, distribution, export and import, sale and purchase of trade commodities. So on the basis of occupation alone it is difficult to ascertain as to how far the social distinction accorded to the *vessa*s as a class was maintained. Trade and farming as the occupation of

---

48. *Jāt.*, IV, p. 84.
49. *Padma*, 55, 61, 83, 80; *Harivaṁśa*, 21, 78-80; *Uttara Purāṇa*, 70, 150.
50. *Ādi,* II, 47, 215.
51. *Padma*, 3, 256-7; 4, 202; *Harivaṁśa*, 9, 39; *Ādi,* I, 16, 184.
52. K.C. Jain, *Prācīna Bhāratīya Sāmājika evaṁ Ārthika Saṁsthāyen*, p. 41.
53. *LAIJC*, pp. 190-91.
54. *Saṁyutta*, I, p. 71; *Niddesa* (part of the *Khuddaka Nikāya*), II — *Cullaniddesa*, Sec. 135.
55. *Cullavagga* — the part of the *Vinaya*, VI, 4, 1, *Aṅguttara*, IV, 282.

the vaiśyas could be taken to mean that the economic aspect of social life was dominated by the *vessas* especially the *gahapatis*.

The *suddas* or śūdras, who belonged to the servile class and low caste, constitute the lowest strata of both the Jain and Buddhist society like that of Hindu society. According to the Jain Purāṇas, they had a degraded posititionin the society and were not allowed to have access to the *śāstras*.[56] Those, who were in the service of the kṣatriyas and vaiśyas, were treated as śūdras.[57] They have also been referred to as *dāsasudda* in both the Jain[58] and Buddhist sources,[59] who were no other than the slaves devoid of any legal status or right. According to the Jain *Mahāpurāṇa*, they were divided into two different sections. One section called *kāru* śūdra had two-fold divisions : (1) touchables, e.g., barbers, potters, washermen, etc., and (2) untouchables, e.g., *cāṇḍālas*. The others were called *akāru* śūdra.[60] There is also an evidence to show that they were not allowed to wear the sacred thread on account of their low birth.[61] In the commentatorial tradition of the Jains (*Uttarādhyayana* commentary) as well as *Jātaka*[62] we find an illustration of their exploration by the high caste people. The śūdras are said to have included the bulk of the people of non-Āryan descent who were engaged in the service of upper class and were darker in colour.[63] It is worthy of note that in spite of the preachings of the doctrines of Jainism and Buddhism, their social position was not much improved. As a matter of fact, nothing substantial was done to ameliorate their condition However, one noticeable change was that they were not treated in Jian and Buddhist society as much scornfully as in the Brāhmaṇical society. It is said that some of the *tāntrik ācāryas* belonged to the śūdra class.[64]

Those who accepted the social system based upon the four broad divisions of people were distinguished as Āryans from the rest of the populace looked down upon as *milakkhas* or *milakkhus* (= *mlecchas*). They were known as *anāriyas* (non-Āryans) because their

56. *Padma*, 3, 28; *Harivaṁśa*, 9, 39.
57. *Ādi*, I, 16, 185.
58. *Padma*, 8, 258.
59. *Dīgha*, I, 104.
60. *Ādi*, X, 16, 185-88.
61. *Ibid.*, II, 40, 170-71.
62. *Uttarādhyāyana Ṭīkā*, 13, p. 185a; *Citta-Sambhūta Jāt.*, no. 498.
63. *BI*, p. 54.
64. K.C. Jain, *op. cit.*, p. 4.

language, dress, food, habits and style of living completely differed from that of the Āryans. They are also characterised as *dasus*. This can fairly be substantiated by the evidences adduced in the Jain canonical literature[65] and early Buddhist literature (Pāli texts and commentaries).[66]

In the Jian Purāṇas, the *mlecchas*[67] have been mentioned along with other non-Āryan tribes like *āvarttas*,[68] *carata*,[69] *cilātas* (Pāli and Skt. *kirātas*][70]— all three cognates of the *mlecchas*, *pulindas*,[71] *śabaras*,[72] *niṣādas*[73] and *bhīlas*.[74]

Besides non-Āryan social group, there were many other despised classes, untouchables, low-born races and low-caste professional groups, who have been mentioned in both Jain and Buddhist traditions below the four recognised social grades of *khattiya*, brāhmaṇa, *vessa* and *sudda*.

In Jain canon and commentaries we come across a long list of despised castes. The *pāṇas*, the *ḍombas* and *morattiyas* have been referred to as condemned castes (*jāti-duguñchiya*).[75] The *mātaṅgas* more or less belonged to the same category.[76] The *pāṇas* correspond to the *cāṇḍālas*, who were living outside a village. They were employed to carry corpses.[77] The *ḍombas* sold the basket and other articles.[78] The *Mahāpurāṇa* specifically refers to the *cāṇḍālas*.[79]

---

65. *Niśītha, Sūtra*, 19, 26; *Bhāṣya*, 16. 5727ff.
66. *Dīgha*, III, p. 264; *Saṁyutta*, V, p. 466; *Jāt.*, VI, p. 207; *Sumaṅgalavilāsinī* (commentary on the *Dīgha* by Buddhaghoṣa), ed. Rhys Davids, I, p. 176; *Paramatthajotikā* (commentary on *Sutta-Nipāta*), II, p. 236.
67. *Padma*, 27, 5; 41, 69.
68. *Ādi*, II, 32, 76.
69. *Ibid.*, I, 16, 161.
70. *Ibid.*, II, 32, 76.
71. *Padma*, 41, 3; *Ādi*, I, 16, 161.
72. *Ibid.*, 7, 296-98; 32, 29; *Ādi*, I, 16, 161.
73. *Padma*, 85, 80.
74. *Uttara Purāṇa*, 62, 87.
75. *Niśītha Cūrṇi*, 4, 1618.
76. *Uttarādhyayana Ṭīkā*, 13, 186.
77. *Vyavahāra Bhāṣya*, 2, 37; *Antagaḍadasāo*, 4, 22.
78. *Niśītha Cūrṇi*, 4, 1816.
79. *Ādi*, II, 41, 342.

The professional group of low castes included peacock-tamers (*mayūra-posaga*), hunters (*vāha*), butchers (*sogariga*; *khaṭṭiga*), cobblers (*padakāra*), barbers (*ṇhāvita*), etc.[80]

In contradistinction to the upper grades, the canonical Pāli text enumerates the five *hīnajātis* (despised castes or low tribes) as the *cāṇḍāla*, *veṇa*, *niṣāda*, *rathakāra* (= *cammakāra*) and *pukkusa*. The *cāṇḍālas* are distinguished from the *pukkusas* as corpse-throwers (*chavachaddhaka*) and from the *methars* and sweepers (*pupphachaddhaka*). The *venas* are the workers in bamboo, the *rathakāras* the workers in leather and the *niṣādas* the hunters.[81] Both Jain and Buddhist sources make mention of *cāṇḍālas* and *pukkusas*, who were more despised than others.[82] In the opinion of Rhys Davids[83] they were aboriginal tribes. In the *Jātakas* the *cāṇḍālas* have been described as *bahinagare*,[84] i.e., living outside the town in separate village as excluded groups. The *kirātas* find mention in the Pāli commentaries as a forest tribe who linguistically belonged to the *mleccha* group.[85]

The heterogeneous structure of the society and the multiplications and proliferation of castes stood as barriers in the removal of social distinctions. Before we deal with the question of caste, it will be worthwhile to point out that no hard and fast line was drawn on the basis of birth, so far as the selection of an occupation was concerned. There was greater possibility of change of the social ranks. The advent of Buddhism brought about a great change in the Indian social system prevalent in the pre-Buddhist period. We find that great amount of laxity was granted to three upper social grades in the society of the Buddhist period, in respect of change of their vocations. These changes set in motion the process of social transformation. There are some instances from the *Jātakas* to show that a kṣatriya prince adopted the occupations of a potter, a basket-maker,[86] trader,[87]

---

80. *Niśītha Bhāṣya*, II, 3708; 4, 1618; *Vyavahāra Bhāṣya*, 3, 94.
81. *Aṅguttara*, I, p. 107; II, p. 85.
82. *Ibid.*, I, p. 162; III, p. 214; H. Jacobi (tr.), *Jaina Sūtras*, *Sūtrakṛtāṅga*, I, 3, 9, in SBE, XLV, II (Oxford, 1895, rept. Delhi, 1973), p. 301; see also BI, p. 55.
83. *BI*, p. 55.
84. *Mātaṅga Jāt.*, no 497; *Amba Jāt.*, no 474.
85. *Sumaṅgalavilāsinī*, I, p. 176. for details see G.P. Singh, *The Kirātas in Ancient India* (Delhi 1990), pp. 59-121.
86. *Jāt.*, II, 5, 290.
87. *Ibid.*, IV, 84; IV, 169; see also *Peta-Vatthu* (part of the *Khuddaka Nikāya*), (Commentary by Dhammapāla), ed. E. Hardy, p. 111f.

etc., without any dishonour or penalty of loosing his caste. The brāhmaṇas engaged themselves in trading activities.[88] A brāhmaṇa is said to have taken the post of an assistant to an archer, who had himself been previously a weaver.[89] The brāhmaṇas also lived as low-caste hunters and trappers.[90] Brāhmaṇas are also frequently mentioned in the *Jātakas* as engaged in agriculture. A *seṭṭhi* is said to have worked as a tailor and as a potter retaining the respect of his community.[91] It appears that the Āryan social group did not strictly adhere to their respective occupations to which they were attached in the pre-Buddhist period. The four-fold divisions of the society was reasonably based on the theoretical concept. The *varṇa* distinction was not strictly followed in the Buddhsit tradition. This can also be corroborated by the statement of Mrs. C.A.F. Rhys Davids.[92]

Scholars are divided in their opinion about the prevalence of caste-system in India during the period concerned. The views expressed by them in this regard are irreconcilable. Even in the original Jain and Buddhist sources the evidences appear to be so much so contradictory that it is difficult to arrive at any positive conclusion. However, it cannot be denied that in spite of slight modification in the *varṇa* system, reversal of the Brāhmaṇical social order in respect of the first two *varṇas* and the socio-religious reformation movement of the sixth century BC, the social distinctions were maintained in some form or the other whether it be on the basis of occupations, birth or lineage or social position. Both Mahāvīra and Buddha as true champions of social equality denounced the caste-system, but they also could not do away with age-old restrictions of caste. At the time of the rise of Jainism and Buddhism the social scenario was somewhat different and there was nothing like rigorous caste system in India. The caste as such had not become an established social institution. The caste structure was no doubt intially flexible, but it gradually became rigid. On the basis of the comparative analysis of the data available in the Jain and Buddhist texts we find that a clear-cut line of distinction was drawn by the Jains between high castes (*jāti-ārya*) and low castes (*jāti-juṅgiya*) and by the Buddhists between the upper and lower classes (*ukkaṭṭhajāti* and *hīnajāti* respectively).

From the Jain canonical texts[93] it appears that the Jains initially opposed the caste

88. *Jāt.*, IV, 15f; V, 22, 471.
89. *Ibid.*, III, 219; V, 127f; 1, 356f.
90. *Ibid.*, II, 200; VI, 170ff.
91. *Ibid.*, VI, 372.
92. "Economic Conditions According to Early Buddhist Literature", in E.J. Rapson (ed.), *CHI*, vol. 1, Ancient India, p. 186.
93. *Uttarādhyayana*, 12, 37; also 25, 29 ff; 29 ff'; *Ācārāṅga*, 2(3), 49.

system. There was no place for caste in thier society. The *Padma Purāṇa*[94] confirms it that till the seventh century AD the caste-system was not strictly followed by them. But by the ninth century AD the caste distinction received a wide social recognition, which can irrefutably be prove by the *Mahāpurāṇa*.[95] Thus it is quite evident that the Jains became strong supporters of caste-stystem during the early medieval age. The system further received support from the Jain writers of the later period.[96] This was one of the factors responsible for the decline of Jainism.

The *Ambaṭṭha Sutta* of *Dīgha Nikāya*[97] deals mainly with the subject of caste, but this *Sutta* cannot be safely utilised as a source for the study of castes in ancient India. In the *Vāseṭṭha Sutta* of the *Sutta Nipāta*[98] the Buddha opposes the caste system. The Buddhist tradition theoretically upheld the concept of equality of *khattiya*, brāhmaṇa, *vessa*, *sudda*, *cāṇḍāla* and *pukkasa*, as evidenced by the data contained in the *Sutta Nipāta*[99] and supported by Fick.[100] But in practice the social equality was not fully maintained. There are some evidences to show that brāhmaṇas were deprived, by their fellow-brāhmaṇas, of their status as brāhmaṇas, for drinking water mixed with the rice water which a *cāṇḍāla* had used.[101] We are further told how this was done: "three brahmins for some offence or other, outlaw a brahmin, shaving him and cutting him dead by pouring ashes over him, thus banishing him from land and from the township."[102] We have also a clear instance of a brāhmaṇa "eating the food of a *cāṇḍāla* and repenting of doing so".[103] Certain restrictions, rigid more or less, were imposed as to commensality or the right of eating together. T.W. Rhys Davids had differentiated between *vaṇṇa* or *varṇa* and *jāti*. The former, according to him, stands for colours and not castes and the latter for birth, which had nothing to do with the building up of caste prejudices.[104] But

94. 11, 195-202.

95. *Ādi*, II, 38, 47; *Uttara Purāṇa*, 74, 491-93.

96. Phulchandra, *Varṇa, Jāti aur Dharma*, pp. 159-64; see also G.P. Singh, "The Concepts of Varṇa and Jāti in the Jain and Buddhist Traditions", *Adhyayan*, JBIAS, vol. VII, nos. 1 & 2 (1997), pp. 49-50.

97. *Digha*, I, pp. 87-110 cf. *HPL*, I, pp. 86-88.

98. *HPL*, I, p. 88.

99. 1, 7; III, 9.

100. *Op. cit.*, p. 29.

101. *Jāt.*, IV, 388.

102. *Dialogues of the Buddha*, 1, 120.

103. *Jāt.*, II, 82.

104. *BI*, p. 62.

in Pāli and other contemporary Indian texts these two terms occur as synonyms.[105] The *vaṇṇa* and *jāti* (caste), no doubt, formed the basis of social distinctions, *jāti* was one of the factors for determining the social status of the people.[106] Rhys Davids' statement that at the Buddha's time in India the caste system was not in existence[107] seems to be absolutely correct. But his view that "The caste system, in any proper or exact use of the term, did not exist till long afterwards",[108] is not tenable. Whatever may be the facts, it is undeniable that the early Indian society of the time was free from the rigidity of caste distinction and restrictions as prevalent in the pre-Buddhist India. The evidences furnished in the Jain and Buddhist sources, however, testify to the prevalence of caste system in early Jain and Buddhist society.

The family was most important unit of the society. The age-old joint family system was in vogue. It was more or less a partriarchal society. The law of succession was mostly based on hereditary principles.

The customs of endogamy and exogamy (marriage within and outside one's own clan, *jāti* or tribe respectively) were prevalent among both the Jains and Buddhists. In theory the members of both upper and lower classes were to follow the rules of endogamy. But in practice the members of two upper classes, in spite of restrictions as to connubium or the right of inter-marriage (which were imposed to prevent the loss of colour through intermixture and to preserve the racial, tribal or family type), resorted to the practice of exogamy. The brāhmaṇas and kṣatriyas enjoyed the privileges of marrying the girls from the vaiśya and śūdra families, whereas, on the other hand, the vaiśyas, śūdras and outcastes could not aspire to marry the girls from the kṣatriya and brāhmaṇa families. the members of two lower grades marries within their own class (*samāna jāti* and *samāna gotta*). Though, it was an established rules, but in practice it was not always possible to prevent the intermingling of various classes. The kṣatriyas in particular married girls and women from all social grades. Their royal harem was filled with maidens and women from all soical grades. It is only those kṣatriyas, among whom the tribal tradition formed

---

105. B.C. Law, *Concepts of Buddhism*, p. 11 cf. *IETBJ*, p. 143.

106. See *Dhammapada-aṭṭhakathā* (Commentary by Buddhaghoṣa), ed. H.C. Norman and L.S. Tailang, II, p. 218; *Dīgha*, I, p. 99.

107. *BI*, p. 62.

108. *Ibid.*, *Dialogues of the Buddha*, I, 95-107.

a strong social tie, who stirctly adhered to the rules of endogamy. The Jains[109] and Buddhists[110] had almost an identical tradition in regard to all that has been stated above.

The three froms of marriage, viz., marriage arranged by the parents of both parties, *svayaṁvara* (the choosing of a husband by girl from amongst the persons assembled on the occasion) and the *gāndharva* marriage (the bride and bridegroom made their own choice without the knowledge of their guardians and were married without any rites or ceremonies) were the most popular according to both Jain[111] and Buddhist sources.[112] Besides these three, there were various other forms of marriage and irregular unions, which are not worthy of explication. Both Jain and Buddhist traditions bear testimony to the prevalence of monogamy and polygamy in their society. Generally the people were monogamous. But for the ruling class and rich people of the society the polygamy was the rule and monogamy the exception.[113] Polyandry was also practised, but unlike polygamy it was rare, as it appears from the Jain[114] and Buddhist texts.[115]

The dowry system also existed in different forms, according to both Jain[116] and Buddhist sources.[117] Both Jain and Buddhst traditions refer to the prevalence of divorce system[118] and remarriage of men and women including widows.[119] The female members strictly observed the *purdah* system either by putting the veil on their faces or by using

---

109. J.C. Jain, *LAIJC*, pp. 206-7; *Ādi*, I, 16, 247-48.

110. *IETBJ*, pp. 166-67, 174-75, 180; *Dhammapada-aṭṭhakathā*, I, p. 390; II, p. 218; see also *Jāt.*, 1. 477f, 257f; *Therigāthā-Aṭṭhakathā* (Comm. by Dhammapāla) ed. E. Muller, p. 260.

111. J.C. Jain, *op. cit.*, pp. 206-12; *Jain Āgama Sāhitya mein Bhāratīya Samāj*, p. 253; *Uttarādhyayana Ṭīkā*, 9, p. 141; *Padma*, 6, 19f, 70f; 8, 78-80, 101-8; 10, 6-10, 15, 25-26; 24, 89-90, 121; 66, 91; 93, 18; *Harivaṁśa*, 29, 68; 31, 35, 43-55; 45, 37; 21, 26; *Ādi*, II, 43, 195-98; 45, 34, 54, 170-78; *Uttara Purāṇa*; 62, 82, 63, 8; also P. Thomas, *Indian Women Through the Ages*, p. 107.

112. *Dhammapada-Aṭṭhakathā*, I, pp. 278-79; *JBBRAS*, vols. 31-32, pp. 137-38.

113. *LAIJA*, p. 213; *Ādi*, I, 15, 69; II, 37, 34-36; *Utara Purāṇa*, 62, 41; 68, 169; *Harivaṁśa*, 44, 50; *Padma*, 58, 69; 94, 17-18; *Niśītha Cūrṇi*, 9, 1513; P. Thomas, *op. cit.*, p. 116; *Jāt.*, nos. 514, 538; *IETBJ*, p. 168.

114. *Āvaśyaka Cūrṇi*, Jinadāsagaṇi Mahattara (Ratlam, 1928), p. 549.

115. *Kunāla Jāt.*, no 536; *Jāt.*, V, 412ff; *IETBJ*, p. 168.

116. *Uttarādhyayana Ṭīkā*; 4, p. 88; *Uvāsagadasāo*, ed. P.L. Vaidya, 8, p. 61; *Padma*, 38, 9-11; *Ādi*, I, 8, 36; II, 45, 3-4.

117. Rockhill, *Life of the Buddha*, p. 62; G.P. Malalasekera, *DPPN*, II, p. 901.

118. *Ādi*, II, 47, 203-6; *Uttara Purāṇa*, 71, 226-28; 72, 93; *Padma*, 16, 9, *Therigāthā* Com., p. 260.

119. *LAIJC*, p. 214; *Uttarādhyayana Ṭīkā*, 4k p. 97; *Jāt.*, I, 306ff; I, 257ff; II, 115, 158; V, 412ff.

curtain to keep themselves concealed from public view.[120] The custom of *satī* or self-immolation was also practised. According to the custom, the widows got themselves burnt alive along with the funeral pyre of their dead husbands. In the Jain canon the evidences are very meagre, but the Jain Purāṇas[121] are replete with such instances.

Prostitution as a social institution was also in existence in ancient India. The Jain and Buddhist writers seem to be in perfect agreement with each other in this regard. According to both Jain and Buddhist sources, besides the kings, wealthy nobles and rich people, there were many others who could well afford to keep and maintain the courtesans (*gaṇikā*s, i.e., girls of perfect beauty) or prostitutes, the reasons for which are not far to seek. The Jain canon and commentaries[122] make general references to them, whereas, on the other hand, the Jain Purāṇas classify them into two groups. One group of them earned their livelihood through dancing and singing and others by indulging in flesh trade.[123] In the Pāli text mention has been made of *satta-vaṇijja* or trade in living beings[124] or traffic in human beings, which implies among other things traffic in women and slave trade. The Pāli literature clearly attests that some of the leading *gaṇikā*s or courtesans of the time made a profitable trade of prostitution by maintaining a regular brothel containing five hundred prostitutes.[125]

Some of the noted courtesans of the time who find mention in Jain texts, include Kosā and Upakosā of "Pādaliputta", Devadattā of Ujjain, a rich courtesan of Campā, etc.[126] The Jain Purāṇa mentions Buddhisenā as a prostitute of Sāketa.[127] The *Jātaka*s also refer to the characteristic style of living of courtesans.[128] The Pāli texts and

---

120. *Uttarādhyayana Ṭīkā*; 2, 28; *Kalpasūtra*, 4. 64; *Nāyadhammakahāo*, ed. N.V. Vaidya, I, p. 8; *Ādi*, II, 43, 43; *Padma*, 8, 70; *Dhammapada-Aṭṭhakathā*, III, p. 100f.

121. *Ādi*, II, 44, 296-302; *Uttara Purāna*, 75, 93.

122. *Ācārāṅga*, *Cūrṇi*, Jinadāsagaṇi Mahattara (Ratlam, 1941), 2, p. 97; *Sūtra-Kṛtāṅga Ṭīkā*, 4, 1, 24; *Uttarādhyayana Ṭīkā*, 3, p. 64.

123. *Ādi*, I, 4, 73; 1, 7, 243-44; II, 46, 300-8; *Uttara Purāṇa*, 50, 48; *Harivaṁśa*, 21, 42, 56-66; 27, 101; *Padma*, 17, 10; see also Nemichandra Śāstrī, *Ādi Purāṇa mein Pratipādita Bhārat*, p. 184.

124. *Aṅguttara*, III, p. 208.

125. *Jāt.*, III, pp. 60f and 435f.

126. *LAIJC*, pp. 217-19.

127. *Harivaṁśa*, 27, 101.

128. *Jāt.*, V, pp. 425, 448, 452.

commentaries mention the names of Ambapāli, Padumavatī, Salavatī, Sirimā, Samā, and Sulasā who were the famous courtesans of the Buddha's time. Ambapāli of Vaiśāli,[129] Sirimā, daughter of Salavatī[130] and Samā of Benares[131] have been mentioned as courtesans-cum-prostitutes. The Jain text[132] and a extracononical Pāli work[133] make incidental allusions to the courtesans along with dancing girls and slave girls who were living in all big towns or cities.

Both the Jain and Buddhist tradition confirm the existence of slavery as a social institution in early India. There is striking similarity between the two traditions with regard to the classifications of slaves and their social status. There were some male and female slaves (*dāsa*s and *dāsī*s respectively) who were employed by the master of the family as domestic servants for performing all sorts of household work. Besides the above, the other different kinds of slaves were those who were born of slave parents or born to slave women over whom the master had the legitimate right of ownership (born slaves called *gabbha* in the Jain texts and *antojātā* in the Buddhist texts); those who were purchased by kings and rich people kept in the palace and harem (*kiya* of the Jains and *dhanakkītā* of the Buddhists); those who were captured in predatory raids or taken as prisoners of war and reduced to slavery under coercion (*ruddha* of the Jains and *karamarānītā* of the Buddhists); those who took to slavery of their own accord under compelling circumstances; those who were deprived of their freedom as a judicial punishment for certian crime; those who were made slaves because of non-payment of debts, etc. The authenticity of the above description, as a whole, may be tested on the

---

129. *Dīgha*, II, pp. 95-98; *Vinaya Mahāvagga*, VI, 30, pp. 231-33; VIII, 1, 2; *Vinaya Piṭaka*, I, p. 268; *Suttanipāta* Com., 1, 244; *Vinayavastu* of the Mūlasarvāstivāda, Gilgit Manuscript, vol. III, pt. 2, p. 19. *Therigāthā*, ed. Rāhul Sānkṛtyāyana, p. 19.

130. *Vimāna-Vatthu*, ed. E.R. Goonaratne, p. 27; *Dhammapada* Com., III, 106-9.

131. *Jāt.*, III, 59ff.

132. *Ācārāṅga Cūrṇi*, p. 71.

133. *Milindapañha*, ed. V. Trenckner, p. 331.

basis of the data supplied in Jain[134] and Buddhist sources.[135] We also find some parallelism between the two regarding the nature of treatment meted out to the slaves. The household servants were generally treated well. The emancipation of slaves is often referred to. There were various ways and means for the slaves to free themselves from the bondage of slavery.

Judging by available data, the status of women in the contemporary society was very low. They were considered as an article of trade, which often used to go to the highest bidder. The *Anadabhuta Jātaka*[136] contains instances of the sale of daughter. The Jain Purāṇa also confirms it.[137] They were merely a source of enjoyment for ruling class and wealthy people. They were not allowed to take part in any important social and political activities. This is attested by both Pāli literature[138] and the Jain *Mahāpurāṇa.*[139] They were not allowed by their husbands to enjoy sufficient freedom.[140] It was in the early medieval period that some Jain *ācāryas* raised their voice against the exploitation of women in the society.[141]

The sixth and fifth centuries BC, which were the blooming period from the point of view of the rise of Jainism and Buddhism, witnessed the remarkable improvements in the general economic conditions of the people of particularly northern India. The evidences drawn from various sources suggest that there was a regional diversity in the prevalent economic system of the contemporary period. While making an attempt to reconstruct

---

134. *Uttarādhyayana Sūtra*, 3, 17; *Bṛhatkalpa Bhāṣya*, 1, 825; *Ovāiya* Com., Abhayadeva (Surat, VS. 1914), 5, p. 20; *Niśītha Bhāṣya*, II, 3676; *Harivaṁśa*, 8, 52; 33, 47-50; 43, 2, 23; *Padma*, 6, 381-422; 5, 122-23; 29, 35; 71, 64; *Ādi*, I, 14, 165; 1, 16, 114-25; 1, 20, 56; II, 42, 157; II, 44, 125, 234-35; II, 43, 33; *Uttara Purāṇa*, 75, 494-95; also K.C. Jain, *Bauddha aur Jain Āgamoṅ me Nārījīvan*, p. 136.

135. *Vinaya Piṭaka*, 1, 72; III, 15, 135, 161; IV, 224; *Mahāvagga*, 1, 39, 1; *Cullavagga*, IV, 4, 7; VI, 4, 1; *Vinaya Texts*, 1,191; *Dīgha*., 1, 72; *Sumaṅgalavilāsinī*, 1, 168; 1, 300; *Majjhima*., II, 149; *Dialogues of the Buddha*, 1, 101; *Dhammapada* Commentary, 1, 208ff: III, 321; *Thera-gāthā Aṭṭhakathā* (Commentary by Dhammapala), vol. I, p. 140; vol. II, p. 220; *Jāt*., 1, 200; III, 3433; IV, 220; VI, 135; VI, 486; VI, 521; VI, 577.

136. *Jāt*., I, p. 290.

137. *Padma*, 71, 64.

138. B.C. Law, *Women in Buddhist Literature*, p. 32f.

139. *Uttara Purāṇa*, 68, 71.

140. *Padma*, 16, 28.

141. *Harivaṁśa*, 19, 16; *Padma*, 15, 173.

a picture of the economic conditions of the people at large, we shall first begin with agriculture which constituted the backbone of ancient Indian economy.

The socio-economic structure of India was broadly based upon the village. According to both Jain and Buddhist tradition, the rural economy of India was based chiefly on a system of village communities of landowners or what is generally known as peasant proprietorship. The common occupation of the villagers was agriculture or farming. The peasants enjoyed the right of absolute ownership over the land they cultivated. The peasantry were not deprived of their inalienable rights. Their position was indeed much improved. The recognised terms for peasants in the Jain tradition were *kariṣaya*[142] and *karṣaka*[143] and in the Buddhist tradition *kassaka*, *karṣaka* or *kr̥ṣaka*[144]. The agricultural work or cultivation has been referred to in the Jain source[145] as *kisikamma* and in the Buddhist source[146] as *kasī*. The cultivable lands around the villages were known as *gāmakhetta*s, accoding to both the traditions. The organisation of different villages varied from one another in the matter of village economy, in the customs of land-tenure and in the rights of individual householders as against the community. The land tenure system was governed by the esatablished customs an rules. Both the Jain[147] and Buddhist[148] souces bear clear testimony to the fact that enough care was taken to irrigate the fields. Various methods of irrigation were applied by the farmers in various parts of the country for increasing the fertility of the soil. The irrigation channels were laid by the community and the supply of water was regulated by rule under the supervision of the headman.

As a general rule, the great field was divided into plots corresponding in number to that of the heads of houses in the villages and each family took the produce of its share. According to early Buddhist literature, the holdings were small which were managed by the members of one family or with the help of a hired man as well as big extending over one thousand *karisa*s (acres) or more.[149]

---

142. *Āvaśyaka Ṭīkā*, 947, p. 426a; *Ovāiya*, Com. Abhayadeva, I, p. 7.
143. *Uttar Purāṇa*, 54, 12; *Padma*, 6, 208.
144. *Dīgha*, I, 61.
145. *Uttarādhyayana Ṭīkā*, I. p. 10a.
146. *Majjhima* (*Mahādukkhakkhandha Sutta*) I, pp. 83-90.
147. *Br̥hatkalpa Bhāṣya*, I, 826; I, 1239; *Niśītha Cūrṇi*, *Piṭhikā*, 329; *Ādi*, I, 16, 157; I, 17, 24; I, 4, 72, 79; I, 5, 104, 259; II, 35, 40; *Padma*, 2, 6, 23; *Harivaṁśa*, 43, 127.
148. *Jāt*, IV, 167; V, 412.
149. *Ibid.*, I, 277; III, 293.

According to both the traditions, agriculture was carried on by ploughing. The *khettas* were cultivated by means of ploughs driven by oxen. The iron-tipped plough cultivation was practised. The pursuit of agriculture was greatly associated with social prestige.[150] In order to maintain a well organised agricultural system as well as for higher production, the state provided all sorts of financial assistance to the farmers. Agricultural implements, manures and good quality of seeds were made available to them by the king. Attempts were made through the initiative of the state to bring land under cultivation.[151] We find that the productive land yielded bumper crops.[152] The expansion of aggrarian economy led to the prosperity of the country.

As matters relating to ownership over the land were settled by the established customs and with the general consent of the community, the general rule did not recognise the right of primogeniture, particularly in the Buddhist tradition. No individual could acquire either by purchase or inheritance any exclusive rights in any portion of the common grassland or woodland. According to the early Pāli literature, kings owned private lands, and the ceremonial ploughing or sowing by them as also by other big farmers, was one of the seasonal festivals of the year.[153]

Various kinds of crops were grown on the soil. Rice, which was the chief article of food,[154] was grown abundantly. Of the other food crops, the chief were barley (*yava*), wheat, millet, grams, beans and sugar-cane.[155] Besides these, there were agicultural produces, which included spices like pepper, mustard, dry ginger, garlic, oilseeds like castor, fibre crops like cotton, etc.[156] Various kinds of fruits, vegetables and flowrs were also cultivated.

Among the domestic animals, cattle were held in high estern as a source of wealth. Cows, buffaloes, oxen and sheep constituted the main livestock of the people.[157] Each

---

150. *Bṛhatkalpa Bhāṣya*, 4, 4891; *Āvaśyaka Cūrṇi*, p. 81; *Padma*, 2, 3; 3, 67; 4, 63; 34, 60; *Harivaṁśa*, 7, 117; *Ādi*, II, 37, 68; *Jāt*., II, 165; Malalasekera, *DPPN*; II, p. 901.
151. *Ādi*, II, 42, 177; see also *Jayadissa Jāt*., no. 513.
152. *Padma*, 2, 7.
153. *Jāt*., IV, p. 167.
154. *Bṛhatkalpa Bhāṣya*, 2, 3301, 3397-98; *Jāt*., I, 340; II, 43, 135, 378; III, 383; IV, 276.
155. *LAIJC*, pp. 116-20; *Padma*, 2, 3-9; *Ādi*, I, 3, 186-88; *Harivaṁśa*, 14, 161-63; 19, 18; 58, 32, 235; *Jāt*., I, 339; II, 110; *Majjhima*, I, 57; *Vinaya Mahāvagga*, VI, 35-56.
156. *LAIJC*, p. 116 f; *IETBJ*, p. 182.
157. *Ibid*., pp. 121-22; *Padma*, 2, 10-24; 4, 8, 63-64; 83, 15-20; *Harivaṁśa*, 9, 36; 8, 134-36; 35, 50-53; 58, 211; *IETBJ*, p. 182.

village had grazing ground for the cattle. The cattle belonged to the householders of village, but no one had separate pasture.

According to both Jain[158] and Buddhist sources,[159] agriculture, cattle rearing and trade and commerce (*vanijja* or *vānijya*) were the chief sources of the livelihood of the people.

We know very little as to how the principles of distribution were governed and the taxation policy followed in early India, according to these two traditions. However, the Jain tradition shows that one-ninth of the share of the produce from land went to the king and the rest was distributed among the people.[160] The Buddhist tradition, on the other hand, clearly affirms that the land was enjoyed by the cultivators by the payment of a *tithe* to the kings in the monarchies. The *tithe* or tax was calculated as a share of the raw produce and levied in kind, which was measured out either by the village syndic or headman (*gāma-bhojaka*) or by an official (a *mahāmatta*) at the barn doors[161] or by survey of the crops.[162] The amount which was levied according to the wish of the ruling power, varied from 1/6 to 1/12 portion of the produce.[163] In the *bhojaka* or headmen, the peasant proprietors had a nominal head as their representatives at political headquarters.[164] In the monarchies, the king had a right to a *tithe* on raw produce, which was collected as a yearly tax as per customary rule, and only to this extent he could be considered as the ultimate owner of the soil. The king could dispose of all abandoned and forest lands[165] as he liked and all ownerless lands were acquired by the crown,[166] which bears a reflection of the growth of the feudal tendencies. The king could remit the *tithe* to any person.[167] In case of cultivated lands, owners could sell or dispose of them in any way they liked. There is no clear testimony to isolated large estates or to great feudatories. However, there is an evidence of a village grant to a priest.[168] The *raṭṭhika*s, *pettanika*s and *bhojaka*s

158. *Ādi*, I, 16, 179-81.
159. *Dīgha*, I, pp. 83-90.
160. *LAIJC*, p. 146.
161. *Jāt.*, II, p. 378; see also *Dīgha*, I, 61; *Aṅguttara*, I, 229, 239, 241.
162. *Ibid.*, IV, p. 169.
163. *Ibid.*, III, p. 9.
164. *Ibid.*, I, p. 119.
165. *Dīgha*, I, p. 87.
166. *Jāt.*, III, p. 302; IV, p. 485; VI, p. 348.
167. *Ibid.*, IV, p. 169.
168. *Dialogues of the Buddha*, I, 108; *Jāt.*, VI, 344.

have been reflected to as three classes of royal officers as well as hereditary feudal lords, landowners and landholders. They are said to have been represented mostly by the *khattiyas.*[169] It is stated in the early Buddhist literature that land might be given away in the kingdom of Magadha, whereas land might be sold in that of Kośala. In the former case, a brāhmaṇa landowner offers as a gift a thousand *karisas* of his estate,[170] and in the latter a merchant entangles an unwilling noble in the sale of a park.[171] The Jain sources also throw some light on the feudal life of the ruling class.[172]

Of all the republics or oligarchies mentioned in the Buddhist canon, it were only Śākyas, who levied *tithe* or other tax on the people, as a source of the state revenue, which goes attested by Aśoka's inscription on the Lumbinī or Rummindei pillar.[173] The *tithe* thus remitted on the occastion of Aśoka's visit to the birthplace of the Buddha must have been imposed by the Śākyas at a date anterior to the Mauryan hegemony. The taxation system was more or less flexible, but there are some Buddhist sources[174] which hint at the oppressive taxation operative in certain cases.

Both Jain and Buddhist tradition give us an impression that the occupational groups, who were associated with different arts and crafts included the weavers, the spinners, basket-makers, metal-workers, blacksmiths, goldsmiths, silversmiths, workers in lead, tin, brass, copper, zinc, lead and bronze, jewellers, potters, carpenters, leather-workers, ivory-workers, painters, dyers, washermen, tailors, workers in stone and wood, etc.[175] Spinning and weaving were the most important handicraft industries. Among the other important indigenous industries were washing and dyeing, ivory work, leather work, etc. These were the recognised and specialised branches of arts and crafts. The craftsmen achieved a considerable proficiency in their respective fields. The art of house-building (architecture) was in a very flourishing stage during the period concerned.

It is significant to note that in order to lessen the scope of class struggle and

---

169. *IETBJ*, P. 173.
170. *Jāt.*, IV, 281.
171. *Vinaya*, II, 1581f (*Cullavagga*, v, vi, 4, 9).
172. J.P. Jain, *The Jaina Sources of the History of Ancient India*, p. 251.
173. *JRAS*, 1898, p. 546 f.
174. *Saṁyutta Nik.*, I, 170-71; *Kāma Jāt.*, no 467; *Bilārikosiya Jāt.*, no. 450.
175. *LAIJC*, pp. 127-37; *Ādi*, I, 4, 26; I, 16, 176, 182, 185-86; II, 32, 29; *Padma*, 5, 287; 14, 17; *Harivaṁśa*, 27, 71; 38, 68; 56, 57; 55, 92; *Apadāna*, II, p. 357f; Law, *Concepts of Buddhism*, p. 24f; *Dīgha Nik.* (*Sāmaññaphala sutta*), I, pp. 47-86; *BI*, pp. 88-96; *Jāt.*, I, 356; I, 320; II, 18, 197, 405; III, 281, 376; IV, 81, 159, 207; VI, 7; *Therig.* (Comm.), 20.

professional competition, the Jain scholars in the ninth century AD propounded a new theory of division of labour which was based on the *varṇa* system. According to this theory; the people were advised to choose their occupations remaining within the limits of their respective *varṇa*s, so that they could be able to achieve competency and proficiency in their fields.[176] The other motto behind such proposition was to check the tendency of the people to abandon their own hereditary professions and adopt that of others.

The artisans, traders, merchants, craftsmen and other professional groups organised themselves into various guilds (*seṇis*, *pūgas*), agreeing to be governed by their own laws and customs. It seems that a guild was organised in the form of a union or association for the welfare of its members enjoying the right to approach the king for seeking redressal of their grievances and to demand justice. It is curious to note that both Jain[177] and Buddhist traditions[178] refer to eighteen guilds. In the Jain texts the guilds of the goldsmiths,[179] the painters[180] and washermen[181] are specifically mentioned. According to the Jain Purāṇas, like the hereditary craftsmen the merchants also formed their own guilds. The *seṭṭhi* happened to be the chief of the eighteen guilds or *seṇis*.[182] Being the caravan leader he was popularly known as a *satthavāha*.[183] Out of the eighteen guilds only four that of the "the wood workers, the smiths, the leather-dressers, the painters and the rest', expert in various crafts are mentioned in the *Jātaka* records.[184] But there are some other Buddhist sources, which contain a list of the whole eighteen guilds, including those of architects, mechanics, carpenters, smiths, masons, workers in stone, weavers, ivory-workers, conch-workers, leather-workers, dyers, potters, jewellers, the barbers, garland-makers, sailors, basket-makers, painters and the rest.[185] According to

176. *Ādi*, I, 16, 187; II, 29, 29.
177. *Jambuddīvapaṇṇati*, 3, 43, p. 193f; *Āvaśyaka Cūrṇi*, p. 260; *Ādi*, II, 46, 112-42; *Harivaṁśa*, 49, 27.
178. *BI*, p. 90; *CHI*, vol. I, 183.
179. *Nāyādhammakahāo*, ed. N.V. Vaidya, 8, p. 105.
180. *Ibid.*, p. 107.
181. *Āvaśyaka Cūrṇi*, II, p. 182.
182. *Ādi*, II, 46, 112-42; *Harivaṁśa*, 49, 27; also *Bṛhatkalpa Bhāṣya*, 3, 3757; *Jāt.*, I, 131, 231.
183. G.C. Jain, *op. cit.*, p. 193.
184. *Jāt.*, I, 267, 314; III, 281, IV, 411; VI, 22, 427.
185. *Mahāvastu*, ed. E. Senart, 3, p. 113; pp. 442-43; *BI*, pp. 90-96; Mrs. C.A.F. Rhys Davids "Notes on Early Economic Conditions in Northern India", *JRAS*, October 1901, pp. 863-72; B.C. Law, *IETBJ*, p. 179.

the *Mahāvastu*, the guilds of *śilpāyatana* played very important role in the development of the material culture of the country. At the head of each guild was a president (*pamukha*) or Alderman (*jeṭṭhaka*), who held distinguished position at the court.[186] The guilds were invested with the powers of arbitration between the members of the guild. The disputes between one guild and another fell within the jurisdiction of the *mahāseṭṭhi* or "the lord High Treasurer", who acted in the capacity of a chief Alderman over the Aldermen of the guilds.[187] As a matter of fact, the guilds exercised the executive, legislative and judicial functions.[188] During the time of the Buddha the guilds were well-organised and found an important place in the economic life of the country. With the growth of trade and commerce in the early centuries of the Christian era the rules were framed relating to the guilds.

By their habitual adherence to the rules of marriage and eating within their own class or group, the guilds were being hardened into caste. The general tendency to segregate one class of workers from another within the same profession socially and economically widened the gap between them and consequently the newly emerging commercial organisation suffered a great setback. However, this organisation as an economic institution continued to thrive.

The traders and merchants occupationally attached to their respective guilds played significant role in providing boost to trade and commerce during the period concerned. It is important to note that there was no co-ordination among the different traders who maintained the guilds. However, the trades were carried on both individually and corporately. The agricultural produces and industrial goods were sold in markets, inland and foreign. The inland and foreign trades flourished side by side. The export and import of goods were carried on along land (*thala*) routes and water (*jala*) routes. According to the Jain canon *Bṛhatkalpasūtra Bhāṣya* (fourth or fifth century AD),[189] *thalapaṭṭana* stands for those market towns where the goods were supplied by bullock-carts and *jalapaṭṭana*, on the other hand, was the sea-port from where the Indian goods were shipped outside and foreign goods were unloaded. "Ānandapura, Mahurā and Dasaṇṇapura are the examples of *thalapaṭṭana* where trade was carried by land. Diva, Kānanadiva and Purima

186. *CHI*, vol. I, p. 184; *BI*, pp. 96-97.
187. *BI*, p. 97.
188. *Vinaya*, IV, p. 226.
189. Ed. by Muni Puṇyavijaya, *Vr*; 1.1090.

were *jalalpaṭṭana* market towns where trade was carried by water".[190] There were some *doṇamuha* market towns or port-towns such as Bharuyakaccha or Bharukaccha (Broach in Gujarat) and Tāmalitti (Tāmralipti or modern Tāmaluk in Midnāpur Dist. of West Bengal) where trade was carried both by land and sea.[191] Nigama was a town, which was exclusively inhabited by traders.[192] Puṭabhedana was such a trade emporium where the seals of goods coming from different parts of the country were broken.[193]

The means of transport for inland trade was the cart or wagon.[194] The rivers were another means of communication. The boats were used for carrying on trade through the rivers.[195] The boats are denoted by the words : *nāva*, *agṭṭhiyā*, etc. The foreign trade was generally carried on by sea, and in some instances partly by sea and partly by lnad. The maritime trade seems to have been quite developed. The sea-going vessel was known as *poya* (*pota*), *poyavahana* (*potavahana*), *vahana*, *pavahana* or *jānapaṭṭa*, *yānapatra*.[196] The *Ācārāṇga Sūtra* refers to *alitta* (*oars*), *piḍhaya* (rudders), *rajju* (rope), etc.[197] The pilot (*niryāmaka*) piloted the ship. The sea-voyages were undertaken frequently, but the journey was perilous. The *Aṅgavijjā* provides an important list of boats and ships, which includes *nāva*, *pota*, *koṭṭimba*, *sālikā*, *saṁghāda*, *tappaka*, *plava*, *pindikā*, *kaṭṭhā*, *velu*, *tumba*, *kumbha* and *dati*. Out of these, *koṭṭimba*, *tappaka* and *saṁghāda* have been respectively identified with *cotymba*, *trappaga* and *sangar* of the Greeks, as it appears from the Greek text[199] of the first century AD.

The merchants and traders who used wagons or bullock-carts were known as *satthavāhā* (*sārthavāha*) or caravan merchants. They used to travel in a caravan from the point of view of their safety. The caravans carried their goods by carts and wagons,

---

190. *LAIJC*, p. 148.
191. *Bṛhatkalpa Bhāṣya*. *Vr*., 1, 1090.
192. *Ibid*., 1, 1091.
193. *Ibid*., 1, 1093.
194. *Niśītha Cūrṇi*, 20, 6533; *Pdma*, 33, 46.
195. *Harivaṁśa*, 8, 134.
196. *Ācārāṅga* (tr. H. Jacobi, SBE; XXII, Oxford, 1884), 2.3, I, 10-20; *Padma*, 55, 61; 83, 80.
197. *Ācārāṅga*, 2.3, I. 342.
198. *Aṅgavijjā*, ed. Muni Puṇyavijaya, p. 166.
199. *Periplus*, pp. 40, 46, 182, 243, 245.

camels, mules and bullocks.[200] Sometimes they had to face attacks on them by *dasyus* or robbers on the way.[201]

The merchants have been referred to in the Jain Canon[202] as *vaṇi* and *vivaṇis* and in the Purāṇas[203] as *vaṇika*, *vanija* or *vaiśya*. There were some merchants (*vaṇi*), who sold their commodities at their shops, and others (*vivaṇis*), who had no shops of their own, moved from place to place to sell thier wares.[204] We learn from the Jain *Mahāpurāṇa*[205] that there were some dishonest merchants who by putting their own seals on the commodities of others used to sell them.

Campā was one of the important trade centres in respect of both inland and foreign trade. It had trade connection with Mithilā. According to the Jain canonical text, *Nāyādhammakahāo*, the sea-faring merchants of Campā loaded their boats with various saleable goods such as betel-nuts, sugar, rice, flour, oil, ghee, molasses, vessels, medicines, drugs, clothes, jewels, etc., and proceeded to the port city of Gambhira. They set out on sail for Mithilā, where they ultimately reached for trade.[206] The merchants of Campā used to travel up to Ahicchattā (Ahicchatra, i.e., Rāmanagar, Bareilly) with their bullock-carts, laden with their goods for trade.[207] The ships laden with merchandise also set out on sail from Campā to Suvarṇadvīpa (Malay Peninsula and Indonesian islands) and Kāliyadvīpa (perhaps on the sea-coast of East-Africa) via Tāmralipti.[208] Ujjain was another great centre of trade. The traders from here journeyed to the town of Campā with a caravan.[209] The trade was carried on between Ujjain and Campā through Kauśāmbī and Vārāṇasī.[210]

Mathurā was also famous as an emporium of trade.[211] The merchants from Mathurā

---

200. *Bṛhatkalpa Bhāṣya*, 1, 3066ff.
201. *Harivaṁśa*, 49, 27-29.
202. *Niśītha Bhāṣya*, 16, 5750.
203. *Padma*, 3, 257; 6, 154; 55, 60; *Ādi*, I, 1, 68.
204. *Niśītha Bhāṣya*, 16, 5750.
205. *Ādi*, I, 1, 68.
206. *Nāyā*, 8, pp. 97-98; J.C. Jain, "Trade and Commerce in Ancient India" (from less known Jain sources), *QRHS*, vol. XVII, no. 1, 1977-78, pp. 48-49, *LAIJC*, pp. 149-51.
207. *Nāyā*., 15, p. 159; see also *Āvaśyaka Cūrṇi*, 9, 472.
208. Motichandra, *Sārthavāha*, pp. 166-68.
209. *Āvaśyaka Niryukti*, 1276 f.
210. *Āvaśyaka Cūrṇi*, 9, 448.
211. *Ibid*., p. 709 (a); *Bṛhatkalpa Bhāṣya*, vr. 1, 1239.

used to travel to Dakṣiṇa-Mathurā (Madhurā) for trade.[212] Soppāraya, Sūrpāraka or Suppāraka (modern Sopārā in the Ṭhāṇe district to the north of Bombay) was another emporium of trade where five hundred tradesmen used to carry their business.[213] The trade was also carried on between Suraṭṭha (Surāṣṭra or Saurāṣṭra) and Pāndumahurā (Dakṣiṇa Madurā) by sea.[214]

The merchants of Uttarāpatha used to carry gold and ivory to Dakṣiṇāpatha for sale. Cloth was an important article of trade. It was an exchangeable commodity. Mathurā and Vidiśā were manufacturing centres of cloth. Gauḍa was famous for silken garments. Various kinds of cloth were taken from east to the country of Lāṭa and sold at higher prices. Tāmalitti, Malaya, Kāka, Tośalī, Sindhu, Dakṣiṇāpatha and China were famous for various kinds of textiles. Nepal was famous for blankets. Woollen blankets were sold at high prices in different parts of Maharastra. According to *Bṛhatkalpasūtra Bhāṣya* (-3912), Nepal, Tāmralipti, Sindhu and Sauvīra were noted for the trade of fine clothes.

The non-canonical Jain text, *Kuvalayamālā*, ascribed to Udyotana Sūri (AD 778) provides an interesting account of the trading merchants who flocked to the city of Vijaya (one of the three cities of Annam along the eastern coast of Indo-China) from different countries, such as Golla (the region near Godāvarī), Madhyadeśa, Magadha, Antarvedī (the region between the Ganges and the Yamunā river), Kira (Kullu, Kāṅgrā), "Dhakka", Sindh, Maru (Rajasthan), Gurjaradeśa, Lāṭa, Mālava, Karnataka, Tājika (Tajikistan), Kośala, Maharashtra and Āndhra in connection with their trade.[215]

From the Jain canon it appears that the traders of Uttarāpatha or the frontier countries traded in horse. A trader of Uttarāpatha came to Dvārakā during Kṛṣṇa's time to sell his horse.[216] The Jain Purāṇa also proves that the Indian merchants imported horses from Kashmir, Bāhlika or Balkh and Greece.[217] According to the *Mahāpurāṇa*, the valuable gems were the main items of the trade, so far as the trade relation with frontier countries is concerned.[218] From the Jain Purāṇas we gather the information

212. *Āvaśyaka Cūrṇi*, 472.
213. *Bṛhatkalpa Bhāṣya*, 1, 2506, also *Āva. Cūr.*, p. 69.
214. *Āva. Cūr.*, II, 197.
215. *QRHS*, XVII, I, p. 49; see also *Kuvalayamālā*, Pts. 1 and II, ed. A.N. Upadhye (Bombay, 1959).
216. *Āvaśyaka Cūrṇi*, p. 424 (a).
217. *Uttara Purāṇa*, 68, 562.
218. *Ādi*, II, 32, 70.

that the merchants used to purchase cotton from Uśiravartadeśa or Uśiravatī (near Puṣkalāvatī in Gāndhāra region) and sell in Tāmralipti.[219]

The ambitious Jain merchants made adventurous journeys to foreign countries. They visited Siṁhala (Ceylon,), Parasa (Persia), Joniya or Javana (Greece), Arabaka (Arabia) and other countries with their merchandise and carried on business. The items which were generally exported from India to foreign countries, include ivory, silk and cotton clothes, sandalwood, conch, diamonds, gems, etc. Silk cloth was also imported from China. Woollen clothes were imported from Central Asia and Balkh in Afghanistan.

While dealing with foreign trade mention may specifically be made of regular commercial intercourse between India and Persia during the Gupta age. From the Jain canon it appears that Indian merchants used to visit Persia by land-routes.[220] The commentatorial tradition of the Jains confirms it that the merchants of Ujjain frequently travelled to Pārasakūla (Persia) with their goods for trade. The commodities which were imported from Persia, include *śaṅkha* (conch), *popphala* (nuts), *candana* (sandalwood), *aguru* (aloe), *mañjittha* (madder), silver, gold, gems, pearls and corals.[221] The items of export from India to Persia include conch, sandalwood, nuts, gems, etc. The Persian merchants visited India with their goods and returned with their ships loaded with Indian goods. It is fairly stated in *Uttarādhyayana* commentary (p. 252a) that the merchants had to pay custom duty on their foreign goods. In case of failure to do so they were subjected to severe punishment. The presence of port-towns like Tāmaralipti, Broach and Sopārā promoted the growth of maritime trade of India with Western and Eastern Asia, Greece, Rome and Egypt in ancient times.

The *Vasudevahiṇḍi* (a non-canonical Prākr̥t Jain work of high antiquity, originally composed by Saṅghadāsagaṇi Vācaka probably in the latter half of the sixth century AD), which is an authentic version of the *Br̥hatkathā* of Guṇādhya, the celebrated court poet of Sātavāhana kings, narrates the story of Cārudatta, a merchant's son, who had set out on his undaunted journey to foreign countries in order to acquire wealth. In connection with the sea-voyage of a trader it is prolixily narrated in the said work that he proceeded form Campā with cotton yarn and reached Tāmralipti and therefrom he set out on sail for other countries. In the course of his journey he visited Suvarṇabhūmi (Lower Burma),

219. *Harivaṁśa*, 21, 75-76; also *Ādi*, II, 46, 145.

220. *Āvaśyaka Cūrṇi*, pp. 448, 507.

221. *Uttarādyayana Ṭīkā*, 3, p, 64a; see also Motichandra, *op. cit.* pp. 168-69; for items of import and export in general see *JISOA*, vol. VIII, 1940, pp. 101 f, 188f.

Kamālapura (Kambuja on the mainland of Indo-China), Yavanadvīpa (Jāvā), Siṁhala (Ceylon), Barbara (Barbaricon — famous harbour on the middle mouth of the Indus and an emporium of coral trade) and Yavana (an island town on the Indus called Alakanda or Alexandria) and earned enough wealth. The Indian merchant is said to have entered into trade relations also with a Central Asia — (the Khasa or Kāśagar, Hūṇas) and China.[222] Not only the Prākṛt Jain narrative literature, but also the Purāṇas[223] testify to the truth that the ambitious sons of traders and merchants travelled to foreign countries to amass wealth and to make their fortunes.

The Jain canonical literature reveals that India imported female slaves from Siṁhala, Pārasa, Palhava, Babbara, Joniya or Greece, Arabaka or Arabia, Bāhali, (Vaṁkṣu, Bāhlika or Balkh in Afghanistan) and many other countries.[224]

The market economy was well controlled and well regulated. The producer and consumer mutually entered into buying and selling in open market-place or exchanged the goods, and the surplus, if any, was dispactched to the trade centres. Campā and other towns contained market complex (*vivaṇi*). Prices were fixed in terms of money which was the chief medium of exchange in India. Coins made of gold, silver and copper were used as means of transaction. *Hiraṇya*, *suvarṇa*, and *dīnāra*, were gold coins. *Ruvagas* or *rūpakas* were used as silver coins. The copper coins include *māsaka* and *kāgini*. The *māsaka* (equal to 5 *rattīs*), *ardha-māsaka* (equal to 2.5 *rattīs*) and *kākaṇi* (equal to 1.25 *rattīs*), like the *kārsāpaṇas* were of gold, silver and copper. They were very popular. The *kapardakas* or cowries were used in buying and selling the goods.[225] So far as weights and measurements are concerned, *māṇa*, *ummāṇa*, *avamāṇa*, *gaṇima* and *paḍimāna* were extensively in use. The rules with regard to weights and measures were laid down by the king, and those, who violated them, were punished.[226]

The canonical and the post-canonical Pāli literature and some Sanskrit Buddhist texts also bear testimony to the fact that both internal and external trade flourished in ancient India during the period from the sixth century BC to the fifth century AD. In the

---

222. *Vasudevahiṇḍi*, Gujarātī tr. by B.L. Sandesaria (Bhāvnagar, 1946), pp. 187-92; see also text, Ātmānand Sabhā, Bhāvnagar, 1930-31; *QRHS*, XVII, 1, p. 47.

223. *Uttara Purāṇa*, 70, 150; *Harivaṁśa*, 21, 78-80; *Padma*, 25, 44.

224. *Antagaḍadasāo*, tr. L.D. Barnett, pp. 28-29.

225. *LAIJC*, pp. 158-61; G.C. Jain, *op. cit.*, p. 195; K.C. Jain, *op. cit.*, p. 282; see also *Padma*, 71, 64; *Harivaṁśa*, 18, 98; *Uttara Purāṇa*, 70, 149.

226. *LAIJC*, pp. 162-63; also *Padma*, 24, 60-62; *Harivaṁśa*, 4, 341; 4, 326; *Uttara Purāṇa*, 61, 71.

Mahādukkhakkhandha Sutta of *Majjhima Nikāya*[227] *vanijja* (trade and commerce) is included in the list of six important professions of the Buddhists.

The trade was carried on both by land-routes and sea-routes. Those merchants and traders who followed land-routes were called *thalapathakammikā*. They were distinguished from *jalapathakammikā* or those who followed water-routes.[228] The merchants transported their goods either up and down the great rivers or along the coasts by boats or right across the country by two-wheeled bullock carts travelling in caravans.[229] The merchants and traders using wagons or bullock-carts and known as caravan merchants or *sātthavāhā* were guided by a land-pilot (*thalaniyāmaka*) in course of their journey.[230] The sailors of boats across the river were called *kaivarttas*.

The early Buddhist literature contains valuable references to the land routes followed by different traders. No satisfactory account thereof is available in the pre-Buddhistic literature. One of the important inland land-routes north to south-west was from Sāvatthi (Śrāvastī)to Patiṭṭhāna (Paithan on the Godāvarī) with six halting places (beginning from the south) namely, Māhissati, Ujjeni, Gonaddha, Vediśa, Kośāmbī and Sāketa.[231] Another route north to south-east was from Sāvatthi to Rājagaha and back (about 300 miles)[232] and also towards borders, i.e., Gāndhāra.[233] The halting places were Setavya, Kapilavastu, Kuśinārā, Pāvā, Hatthi-gāma, Bhaṇḍagāma, Veśāli, Pāṭaliputta and Nālandā.[234] The north-western route or Uttarāpatha extended from Sāvatthi and Kośāmbī to Takkhaśilā (Takṣaśilā or Taxila) via Madhurā across the sandy desert of Rājpūtānā. Further westward the journey was performed overland to Sind from where horses and asses[235] were imported, and to Sauvīra and its ports.[236] Northward the trade route connected India with Central and Western Asia by the way of Taxila in Gāndhāra near Rāwalpiṇḍī and possibly also Sāgala in the Punjab. The extensive land-routes have been

227. Vol. I, pp. 83-90.
228. *Jāt.*, I, p. 121.
229. *Ibid.*, I, p. 194 f.
230. *Ibid.*, I, p. 107.
231. *Sutta-nipāta*, vv. 976-77 and 1011-13; *BI*, p. 103.
232. *Jāt.*, I, 92, 348.
233. *Ibid.*, I, 377 f.
234. *Vinaya Texts*, 1, 81.
235. *Jāt.*, I, 124, 178, 181; II, 31, 287; also Hopkins, *JAOS*, XIII, 257, 372.
236. *Vimānavatthu-aṭṭhakathā* (Comm), p. 336.

referred to in the *Jātaka* as Mahāmagga, Mahāpatha and Rājamagga.[237] The *Jātaka* records are littered with references to the land-routes.[238]

From east to west the trade was carried on largely by rivers. The merchandise was transported by means of country boats. Upwards the rivers were used along the Ganges as far west as Sahajāti,[239] along the Yamunā as far as Kośāmbī[240] and downwards along the Ganges as far as Campā and Tāmalitti. Downwards the boats also went either across or along the coast to Burma.

The *Jātakas* testify to the existence of trade-relations between Benares and Ujjain,[241] Videha and Kāśmira-Gāndhāra,[242] Benares and Sāvatthi,[243] Rājagaha and Sāvatthi.[244] Further, we are told of traders going from Videha to Gāndhāra,[245] from Magadha to Sovira,[246] from Bharukaccha (or Broach) round the coast to Burma,[247] from Benares down the river to its mouth and thence on to Burma[248] and from Campā to the same direction.[249]

While entering into the details or inland trade, as provided in early Buddhist literature, we would first like to make mention of the traders of Aṅga and Magadha who used to visit each other's kingdom for trade purposes.[250] Aṅga was a prosperous country containing many merchants. At the the time of the Buddha its capital Campā was not only a big town but also a centre of trade.[251] It is evident from the *Vimānavatthu* commentary[252]

237. *Jāt.*, I, 196.
238. *Ibid.*, II, 12, 70; I, 211; III, 152; II, 423, 434; see also *Dhammapada-aṭṭhakathā*, II, 31.
239. *Vinaya Texts*, 3, 401.
240. *Ibid.*, 3, 382 cf. *BI*, p. 103.
241. *Jāt.*, II, p. 248.
242. *Ibid.*, III, pp. 363, 365, 369.
243. *Ibid.*, II, p. 294 f.
244. *Sutta-Nipāta*, vv, 1012-13.
245. *Jāt.*, III, 365.
246. *Vimānavatthu-aṭṭhakathā*, pp. 336, 370.
247. *Jāt.*, III, 188.
248. *Ibid.*, IV, 15-17.
249. *Ibid.*, VI, 32-35.
250. *Ibid.*, II, 148.
251. *Vinaya Cullavagga*, p. 337; see also tr. T.W. Rhys Davids and H. Oldenberg in SBE, (Oxford, 1882) vol. XVII, pt. II.
252. P. 332.

that the people of Aṅga used to travel in a caravan with their merchandise to Sindhu-Soviradeśa for trade.

From the canonical Pāli literature it distinctly appears that Benares was one of the most important commercial centres.[253] It was the chief centre of trade in the cotton. The traders of this place were well known for dealing in cotton and silk clothes.[254] The cotton cloth was one of the principal items of merchandise for both internal and external trade. The Pāli commentary also furnishes us with an account which embodies the tradition regarding the trade and commerce carried on at this centre. It is categorically stated in the *Sumaṅgalavilāsinī* (comm. on *Dīgha Nikāya*)[255] that the weavers of Benares produced soft and beautiful garments. From *Mahāparinibbāna Sutta*[256] we learn that Benares was also famous for muslins. We are told that it had direct trade relation with Gāndhāra and Takṣaśilā.[257] The Sanskrit Buddhist texts contain very valuable information about the importance of Benares as a centre of trade. From the *Mahāvastu* we learn that Benares was a great trading centre for the Buddhist traders. Rich merchants of the city used to cross over high seas with ships laden with merchandise. It is said that a wealthy merchant once came to Benares from Takṣaśilā to sel their horses.[258] The *Divyāvadāna* informs us that a caravan trader reached Benares from Uttarāpatha during the reign of king Brahmadatta, who heard him saying thus : "Now I have reached Benares bringing with me articles for sale." He was welcomed by the king who extended to him his royal patronage.[259] The Sanskrit Buddhist text — the *Divyāvadāna*[260] as well as the Pāli canon — the *Jātaka*[261] confirm the truth that the horse-traders from Uttarāpatha frequently travelled to Benares via Sovira[262] with the object of carrying on their trade. The horse traders of Punjab and Afghanistan also used to visit different other parts of India. In the

---

253. *Jāt.*, IV, 405; VI, 77, 144, 154.
254. *Ibid.*, III, 286; VI, 47, 77.
255. Pt. II, p. 563.
256. 5, 16
257. *Dhammapada-Aṭṭhakathā*, I, 123.
258. *Mahāvastu*, ed. E. Senart, II, pp. 166-67; III, p. 268; see also tr. J.J. Jones, SBB, 3 vols (16, 18 & 19, London, 1949-56).
259. *Divyāvadāna*, ed. E.B. Cowell and R.A. Neill, pp. 510 ff.
260. *Ibid.*, p. 22.
261. *Jāt.*, I, 124; II, 122.
262. *Ibid.*, I, 124, 178, 181; II, 31, 287.

Divyāvadāna[263] it is explicitly stated that a trader from Punjab reached as far as Mathurā with 500 horses for trade.

From the *Sumaṅgalavilāsinī*[264] it appears that the kingdom of Gāndhāra was also a trading centre. From some other sources[265] we learn that the red blankets of Gāndhāra also formed the part of the trade. In the *Niddesa*[266] we are told that the people of Taxila earned a lot of money through trade and commerce.

Śrāvastī (Saheta-Maheta, Goṇḍā Dist. U.P.) was another famous trade emporium. The traders from this place travelled up to Campā in Bihar and Tāmralipti in Bengal in the wake of their trade and commerce. The distance from Śrāvastī to Taxila was 192 *yojana*.[267] The importance of Mithilā city as a centre of trade is highlighted in the *Mahaummaga Jātaka*. The city is said to have contained several market complex.[268]

Within the country, all kinds of produce were brought to markets for sale. There were *āpana*s or shops were commodities were displayed for sale.[269] The commodities sold in these *āpana*s were textile fabrics, groceries and oil, green-groceries, grain, perfumes and flowers, articles of gold and jewellery, carriages, arrows, etc.[270] Prices were note fixed and there was competition by which the dealers wanted to prevail upon the purchasers. On the part of the buyers there was the haggling of price.[271] The prices of the commodities were fixed only for the royal household by officer known as *aggahakāraka*. All native and foreign goods imported into the city were assessed and a duty was levied upon them.

Coins appear to have been the chief medium of exchange, but the more primitive barter system was also not unknown. Barter was not, however, the usual practice. Among the coins of different denominations mention may be made of some of the popular copper coins like *kahāpaṇa* (weighing about 146 grains), *addhakahāpaṇa*, *kākaṇika*,

---

263. pp. 26, 353.
264. Pt. II, p. 389; B.C. Law, *HPL*, vol. II, p. 434.
265. *Jāt*., VI, 47; *Vinaya Mahāvagga*, 8, I, 36.
266. *PTS*, vol. I, p. 154.
267. Rāhul Sānkṛtyāyana, *Purātattva Nivandhāvali*, pp. 33-35.
268. *Jāt*., VI, 330.
269. *Ibid*., II, 267; IV, 488; VI, 29; *Vinaya*, IV, 248; *Cullavagga*, V. X, 10, 4; *Majjhima*, I, 359, 447.
270. *Jāt*., I, 290f; x, 411; II, 267; IV, 82, 228; VI, 336; *VinayaTexts*, III, 343; *Vinaya*, IV, 248-50.
271. *Jāt*., I, 111f; for details or prices see Mrs. Rhys Davids, *JRAS*, 1901, pp. 875-82.

māsaka, *addhamāsaka*, *pāda* and *addhapāda*,[272] which served as standard currency and were used for carrying on transactions. Silver coins do not appear to have been in use and the utility of ancient gold coins like *nikkha* (*niṣka*)[273] or *suvaṇṇa* is doubtful. There is mention also of cowry shells (*sippikāni*),[274] but they were probably not used as currency.

Both Jain and Buddhist tradition affirm that in those days there were neither banks nor banking facilities. However, loans could be taken. Money-lending was done by professional money-lenders who took it as an honest calling, but this had, unfortunately, given rise to profit-mongering.

It is worthy of note that the freedom of initiative and mobility in trade went a long way in encouraging the traders and merchants to carry on their professions for the economic prosperity of the people at large. The Jain and Buddhist traders, professedly, made significant contributions to the growth of material culture in early India.

Foreign trade was carried on largely by sea and partly by land. The Pāli canon as well as Sanskrit Buddhist texts furnish accounts of sea-voyages undertaken by the Indian merchants with the help of their ships in connection with their trade and commerce with the outside world. The *Suppāraka Jātaka* relates the voyage undertaken by sea-going merchants of Bharukaccha or Broach. It is stated therein that a merchant ship carrying six hundred passengers from this port town sailed across the six seas for about four months.[275] On the basis of the indication given in the *Jātaka* concerned it has been established by K.P. Jayaswal that they followed the sea-routes from Broach to Mediterranean and in course of their journey they visited south-east Arabian and African countries.[276] The *Saṅkha-Jātaka* offers us an account of the wreck of a ship of a brāhmaṇa merchant of Benares, who was on his way to Suvaṇṇabhūmi (Suvarṇadvīpa or the Gold coast, i.e., at Thaton in Burma).[277] The *Sīlānīsaṁsa Jātaka* narrates the story of the wreck of another merchant ship in the midst of the ocean.[278] The *Samuddavānija Jātaka*

---

272. For details see *Jāt.*, I, 129; III, 448; B.C. Law (ed.), *Buddhistic Studies*, chap. XV; *CHI*, vol. I, p. 194; *BI*, p. 100. *JRAS*, 1901, pp. 874f, D.R. Bhandarkar, Carmichael Lectures, 1921, pp. 53, 62.

273. *CHI*, vol. I, p. 194; D.R. Bhandarkar, *op. cit.* pp. 53, 62-64; Pran Nath, *A Study of the Economic Conditions of Ancient India*, p. 85 f.

274. *Jāt.*, I, 425f.

275. *Ibid.*, IV (no. 463), 138-42.

276. For details see *JBORS*, vol. VI, p. 195.

277. *Jāt.*, IV, (no. 442), 10, 15-17.

278. *Ibid.*, II (no. 190), 112f.

narrates the story of the arrival of a large ship carrying thousand families of carpenters at an island in the sea.[279] The *Mahājanaka Jātaka* illustrates the truth concerning visit of prince Mahājanaka to Suvaṇṇabhūmi from Videha or Campā in a ship with seven hundred caravans.[280] The *Valāhassa Jātaka* relates the story of the arrival of five hundred ship-wrecked merchants from Benares at the town of Sirisavatthu in Tambapaṇṇidīpa (Ratnadvīpa, i.e., Siṁhaladeśa or Ceylon), the inhabitants of which were mostly sea-going merchants.[281] The *Bāveru Jātaka* speaks of India's maritime intercourse with Babylonia or Baveru in early Buddhist days. From this *Jātaka* it appears that some traders of Benares went on sea-voyage up to Babylon.[282] The journey was performed through Arabian sea and Persian-Gulf. The *Vinaya* relates the story of how Mahinda travelled by water-routes from Pāṭaliputra to Tāmralipti and on to Ceylon.[283] The Pāli *Nikāyas* mention long voyages lasting even for six months.[284] The Sanskrit Buddhist text abounds in references to India's sea borne trade in early times.[285] The *Avadānaśataka*[286] contains an incidental allustion to the visit of sea-faring merchants of Rājagaha (Rājagṛha) to the countries outside India. According to the *Jātaka*, the course of the ships was steered by the *Niyyāmaka* or water-pilot.[287] Rhys Davids further observes that "later texts, of about the third century BC, speak of voyages down the Ganges from Benares to the mouth of the river and thence across the Indian ocean to the opposite coast of Burma and even from Bharukaccha (Broach) round Cape Comorin to the same destination".[288]

The existence of three important port towns, Bharukaccha, Suppāraka and Sovira

---

279. *Jāt.*, IV (no. 466), 65-67.
280. *Ibid.*, VI (no. 539), 34-36.
281. *Ibid.*, II, 127 f.
282. *Ibid.*, III (no. 339), 126 f.
283. *Vinaya*, II, 338.
284. *Dīgha*, I, 222 (tr. in *Dialogues of the Buddha*, I, 283); *Saṁyutta*, III, 155; V, 51; *Aṅguttara*, III, 368; IV, 127.
285. *Divyāvadāna*, pp. 4f, 26f, 40f, 112f, 229-32, 376f.
286. Ed. J.S. Speyer, I, p. 129.
287. *Jāt.*, IV, 137-38.
288. *BI.*, p. 96.

(near Surāṣṭra) on the western sea-coast[289] and that of Tāmralipti facilitated the growth of both internal and external commercial intercourse in early times.

The *Jātaka* records testify to the trade relations between Bharukaccha, Banāras and Campā, on the one hand, and Suvaṇṇabhūmi, on the other.[290] According to the *Manorathapūrani* (a commentary on the *Aṅguttara Nikāya*) and *Apadāna* (Pāli canonical text), there was regular trade between Bharukaccha, Suppāraka and Suvaṇṇabhūmi.[291]

The *Apadāna* explicitly mentions the visit of traders and merchants from Soṇṇabhūmi (Suvaṇṇabhūmi), Malaya (Malay peninusula) and the distant land of Cina or Cinaraṭṭha (China) to India.[292] The another Pāli text, *Niddesa*, speaks of India's commerce by sea with Yona (Ionia, i.e., Greece) and Paramayona (which may be either located in western Asia or identified with some Greek island in the Mediterranean, if not with Ionia proper). The text further mentions that the Indian sea-going merchants visited twenty-four countries, including Suvaṇṇabhūmi, Kālamukha, Tambapaṇṇi, Jāvā, Vesuṅga, Verāpatha, Tamali and Takkola towards the east, and followed ten difficult land-routes after reaching the harbour.[293] Of all the places mentioned above, we may first speak of Suvaṇṇabhūmi (Suvarṇabhūmi) which is generally applied to the vast region stretching from Burma to Indonesia but actually it is identical with Lower Burma[294] (Pegu and Moulmein districts). This has also been identified with Sudhammanagore,[295] i.e., Thaton (the Gold Coast or "the Gold Country") at the mouth of the Sittaung river. It was formerly styled as Sonaparānta (golden frontier), the possessor of mines of gold, silver, rubies, amber, etc. This may be distinguished from Suvarṇadvīpa (Malay Peninsula, Jāvā, Sumātrā, Bāli, Borneo, and other islands of the East Indies),[296] which was also famous for trade in gold besides spices. The desire to acquire immense gold and other minerals provided stimulus to the Indian traders to sail to these regions of south-east Asia. Kālalmukha may be identified with the Arakan coast. Tambapaṇṇi and Jāvā are no other than Ceylon and

289. *Jāt.*, III, 126-28, 180, 188, 470; IV, 137-48.

290. *Jāt.*, III, 188; IV, 15-17; VI, 34.

291. Cf. *DPPN*, II, p. 1223; also *Avadāna*, II, p. 476, vs. 13ff.

292. *Apadāna*, I, p. 2; II, p. 357 cf. Law, *IETBJ*, pp. 177-78, 188.

293. *Mahāniddesa*, eds. L.D. La, V. Poussin and E.J. Thomas, I, pp. 154-55; II, pp. 414-5; see also Law, *op. cit.*, pp. 187-88; Sylvain Levi, *Étude Asiatique*, II (Paris, 1925), pp. 1-55.

294. R.C. Majumdar, *Ancient Indian Colonies in the Far East*, vol. II, *Suvarṇadvīpa*, pt. I, p. 56f.

295. *Śāsanavaṁsa*, pp. 10, 12 cf. Law, *GEB*, p. 70; *BI*, 104, note I.

296. Majumdar, *op. cit.*, p. 37.

the island of Jāvā in Indonesia respectively. Vesuṅga and Verāpatha nearly correspond to Ptolemy's Besyngeitai (a mart) and Berabai (a city of port town)[297] which have been placed by G.E. Gerini in Burma.[298] Tamali is identical with Tāmraliṅga in Malay peninsula (known to Ptolemy as the "Golden Khersonese").[299] On the combined testimony of Ptolemy,[300] Gerini[301] and some authorities on the history and culture of south-east Asia,[302] Takkola (a mart or port town) can be easily identified with modern Takūa-pā on the west coast of the Isthmus of Kra in Malay Peninsula. It may perhaps be modern port of Trang. It was the first landing stage of the Indian traders and colonists. On the weight of the evidence adduced above B.C. Law's identification of Takkola with "an ancient seaport near Thaton in Lower Burma"[303] can be disposed of. Some other scholars have also mistakenly identified Takkola with Rangoon, Burman Talaing Taikkula, etc.[304] It is striking to note that a fourth-century AD pillar inscription of the Buddhist sea-captain or Mahānāvika, Buddhagupta, of Raktamṛttikā (modern Rangamati in Murshidabad district, Bengal) has been discovered in the Wellesley district of the Malay peninsula.[305]

With the dawn of the first century AD the objective of carrying on sea-borne trade underwent some changes, as evidenced by the post-canonical Pāli text (also called an extra canonical text). The text not only makes mention of some important trading centres like Bharukaccha, Madhurā (Mathurā), Sāgala, Sovira, Suraṭṭho (modern Sūrat), Vārāṇasī and Alasanda (an island town on the Indus called Alakanda or Alexandria) but also points to India's commercial intercourse with Suvaṇṇabhūmi, Cina (China) and Takkola. It is stated in the text that "As a shipowner who has become wealthy by constantly levying freight in some seaport town will be able to traverse the high seas, and go to

297. *MAIT*, VII, 2, 4, pp. 196-97.

298. *RTGEA*, pp. 64-84.

299. R. Le May, *The Culture of South-East Asia*, pp. 74-76; Levi, *op. cit.*, pp. 40-55.

300. *MAIT*, VII, 2, 5, pp. 197-99.

301. *Op. cit.*, pp. 85-87.

302. J.F. Cady, *South-East Asia: Its Historical Development*, p. 30, note 17; May, *op. cit.*, p. 76; H.G.Q. Wales, *The Making of Greater India: A Study in South-East Asian Cultural Change*, pp. 7ff; also his "Archaeological Researches on Ancient Indian Colonization in Malaya", *JRASMB*, vol. XXVIII (1940), pp. 5-40.

303. *HPL*, II, p. 369.

304. *MAIT*, p. 198 and note 27, p. 449, Appendix 7.

305. Kern's *Verspreide Geschriften*, III, (1915), p. 255, quoted in *MAIT*, p. 389, note.

Vaṅga, Takkola, Surat, Sovira, China, Alasandadipa, the Cormondal Coast, further India or any other palce where ship do congregate".[306] The text also refers to visit of traders and merchants from various countries and places to India.[307]

We were handicapped by the absence of details of the articles which the sea merchants exported and imported. The *Suppāraka Jātaka* reveals that they made their fortune by collecting gems, corals, etc., from the seas.[308] Silks, muslins, the finer sorts of cloth, cutlery and armour, brocades, embroideries and rugs, perfumes, drugs, ivory and ivory work, jewellery and gold are said to have been the main articles in which the merchants dealt.[309] Various kinds of plain and dyed cloth, cotton and silk clothes and muslins were exported from Vārāṇasī, Bengal and other places.[310] The best quality of sandalwood was imported from Malaysia by the Indian merchants.[311] Different kinds of precious gems, etc., were imported from Siṁhala or Ceylon and other countries.[312] In course of the sea-borne trade, the Indian merchants obtained perfumed wood, gold, precious stones, spices and other condiments from south-east Asia which in return got high quality cotton textiles from India. Silk cloth was generally imported from China. Clothes, spices, etc., formed the part of trade which was carried on between India and Indonesia. The other items like woollen clothes and blankets of different variety were imported from Central Asia. In the age of the Kuṣāṇas, the Buddhist traders had maintained their trade relation with the Roman empire. In the *Milindapañha*,[313] the city of Sāgala or Sākala (modern Siālkoṭa) has been mentioned as a *putabhedana*, i.e., trade emporium, where the seals of bales of goods coming from different parts of the country were broken and the goods were sold to the traders.

The Jain and Buddhist traditions fairly attest to the fact that internal and external trades flourished side by side in ancient India. The Hindu, Jain and Buddhist merchants

---

306. *Milindapañha*, ed. V. Trenckner, pp. 359, also 127, 327; see also tr. by T.W. Rhys Davids, SBE, XXXVI (II), p. 269.
307. *Milindapañha*, p. 331.
308. *Jāt.*, IV, 21, 139-41.
309. *BI*, p. 98f.
310. *Mahāvastu*, I, 235-36.
311. *Vinayavastu*, Gilgit Manuscript, vol. III, pt. II, p. 64.
312. *Cullavagga*, 9, 1, 3.
313. Cf. Rāhula Sāṅkṛtyāyana, *Pāli Sāhitya kā Itihāsa*, p. 183.

of the pre- and post-Christian era contributed not only to the material prosperity of the country but also to the expansion of Indian culture in both neighbouring and far-off Asian countries through external trade relations with them. The trade with Malay Peninsula, the Indonesian islands, Indo-China (Campā or south Annam = modern Vietnam, and Kambuja called by the Chinese Fu-nan = modern Cambodia) and Brahmadeśa or Burma in south-east Asia was carried on largely by sea-routes and partly by land-routes.[314] The trade with Siṁhaladeśa or Ceylon, the neighbouring south Asian country, was carried on only by sea-route. The so-called Greater or further India and Indian Archipelago were colonised by the Hindu and Buddhist merchants in a very remote age.[315] There were several routes from Bāhlika (modern Balkh in Afghanistan) towards central Asia and China on the east. The land route between China and India passed through Balkh, and Kashagar in central Asia. The sea-borne trade was also carried on between India and China. The land-route between India and south-west Asia (Persia) passed through Afghanistan. The maritime trade in particular carried on in the early centuries of the Christian era led to the diffusion of Indian culture in different countries and islands of south-east Asia which further gave fillip to India's politico-cultural contacts with them.[316]

---

314. See May, *op. cit.*, p. 224f (for map of Asia showing sea-routes between India and the South-East Asia, and between India and the Indo-Chinese Peninsula).

315. *JGIS*, vol. IX, po. 62ff.

316. For details see G.P. Singh, "Trade and Commerce in Ancient India in the light of Jain and Buddhist traditions bearing on its economic and cultural contacts with the Asian Countries", *Studies in History and Culture* (Journal of the post-Graduate Department of History, Berhampur University, Orissa), vol. IV, no. I, 1996, pp. 1-8.

4

Social and Economic Formations in the Latter Half of the First Millennium BC

THE formations of classes, castes, associations and institutions in socio-economic milieu in early India in the latter half of the first millennium BC form very important parts of the subject of our study. The study as a whole is based on the data available in early Buddhist literature — the Pāli Canon (fifth to first century BC), the Jain *Sūtras* (*c.* 500-100 BC), the *Aṣṭādhyāyī* of Pāṇini (*c.* 500-400 BC), the *Arthaśāstra* of Kauṭilya (*c.* 300 BC), the *Dharmaśāstra* — the *Manu-Smṛti* (*c.* 200-100 BC), the *Dharmasūtras* (*c.* 600-200 BC) and the *Mahābhāṣya* of Patañjali (*c.* 184-148 BC).

The brāhmaṇical concepts of *varṇa* and *jāti* (class and caste respectively) of the later Vedic period had tremendous impact on the social system of post-Vedic times. The trends of social formation in the latter half of the first millennium BC were almost identical with that of the Vedic age. The class formation was essentially based on the traditional *varṇa* system. In order to maintain the traditional *varṇa* order or social order the brāhmaṇa scholars of both the pre- and post-Buddhist period unheld the validity of the division of Āryan society into four *varṇa*s based on occupations and functions and advocated the social superiority of the brāhmaṇas. The brāhmaṇical social order was meant for social equilibrium. From Pāṇini to Manu all were the followers of Vedic tradition in respect of *varṇa* organisation. Pāṇini,[1] Patañjali,[2] Kauṭilya,[3] Manu,[4] and

1. *Aṣṭādhyāyī*, II, 4, 10; III, 1, 103; IV, 1, 172; V, 1, 7; VI, 4, 171; also V.S. Agrawala, *India as known to Pāṇini*, pp. 78-80.
2. *Mahābhāṣya*, I, 1, 39; II, 2, 16-17; also B.N. Puri, *India in the time of Patañjali*, p. 83.
3. *Arthaśāstra*, ed. with Hindi tr. by Vācaspati Gairola, I, chs. 2 & 3, pp. 10-13; see also N.M. Upādhyāya, 'Kautilya on social Legislation', *JIH*, LVI, II (1978), p. 237.
4. *Manu-Smṛti*, I, 87-93; X, 4, 75-80; XII, 97.

Āpastamba (one of the authors of the *Dharmasūtras*)[5] — all refer to the four social classes represented by the brāhmaṇa, kṣatriya, vaiśya and śūdra.

It was the age of the Buddha (*c*. 563-483 BC) which marked the fundamental departure from the brāhmaṇical tradition of *varṇa* and *jāti*. The order of the first two *varṇa*s was reversed from the point of view of social grades with the result that the *khattiyas* (kṣatriyas) came to be placed first and the brāhmaṇas just next to them. The other two classes were represented by the *vessas* and *suddas* as evidenced by the Pāli canon.[6] The four classes have also been enumerated in the Jain *Sūtras*[7] perfectly in the same order. The Jains and Buddhists contended for the precedence of the *khattiyas* over the brāhmaṇas from the point of view of social status. The former two, however, represented the two upper classes and the latter two the lower classes. The polarisation of society into privileged and unprivileged classes accentuated the social differentiation. Here it should made clear that the division of the Jain society into four classes was fundamentally based on occupations and not birth or *jāti*. They did not strictly follow the *varṇa* rules before the dawn of the early medieval period. The four-fold divisions of the Buddhist society was also based on the theoretical concept. The *varṇa* distinction was not strictly followed by the people in the early phase of Buddhism. There is striking parallelism between the Hindu, Buddhist and Jain traditions so far as the functional aspects are concerned. The brāhmaṇas belonged to the priestly class, the kṣatriyas to a class of warriors, princes or nobles, the vaiśyas to a class of agriculturists, cattle-breeders, traders and merchants and the śūdras to a servile class and low caste. The persistent attempts on the part of the Brāhmaṇist to give hereditary character to occupational distinctions by birth-right led to the formation of castes and castes within castes in early Indian society. The Jains and Buddhists, of course, did not maintain such distinctions on the basis of birth, but they also could not check the formation of castes and sub-castes in their society.

A comparative picture of class and caste formations in the Hindu, Buddhist and Jain society can be drawn on the basis of all the available evidences. Pāṇini associates the

5. *Āp. Dh. S.*, cf. F. Max Muller, *HASL*, p. 184.

6. *Aṅguttara Nikāya*, ed. R. Morris and E. Hardy, III, p. 214; *Sutta-Nipāta* (Part of the *Khuddaka Nikāya*) ed. Rāhul Sānkṛtyāyana, 1, 7; III, 9; also T.W. Rhys Davids, *BI*, pp. 53-54; B.C. Law, *HPL*, 1, pp. 87-88; *IETBJ*, pp. 139-40; see also G.P. Singh, 'The Concepts of *varṇa* and *jāti* in the Jain and Buddhist Traditions', *Adhyayan*, JBIAS, VII, 1 & 2, (1997), pp. 45-57.

7. *Uttarādhyayana Sūtra*, ed. J. Charpentier, 25, 31-33; *Ācārāṅga*, tr. H. Jacobi, SBE, XXII (Oxford, 1884), 19, 27.

class of brāhmaṇa with the caste (VI, 4, 171).[8] In the social organism, the brāhmaṇas, according to him, formed the highest caste on the basis of birth. Patañjali in his *Mahābhāṣya* makes it clear that even if a brāhmaṇa failed to perform the duties assigned to him, birth alone entitled him a place in his soical group.[9] He occupied the highest position in the society.[10] Pāṇini has mentioned the kṣatriya caste in different perspective. Members of the ruling families also belonged to this class.[11] The vaiśyas, according to him, were given the title *ārya* in order to indicate their social status.[12] Pāṇini in his *sūtra* (II, 4, 10) has referred to different classes of the śūdras : (1) those who were living within the pale of the Āryan society and (2) those (probably the aboriginal peoples), who were considered outside thereof. As illustrations of first group of śūdras, Pāṇini mentions the cowherds (cattle-rearers), barbers, goldsmiths, potters, wood-carvers, balcksmiths Bhillas, fishermen, etc. There was another class of śūdras who were entrusted with some specific duties connected with *yajña*s or sacrifices, such as carpenters (*takṣā*), metal-workders (*ayaskāra*), washermen (*rajaka*) and weavers (*tantuvāya*). The latter class comprised those śūdras who were untouchables or pariahs and had separate settlements of their own in a village or town within the confines of Āryan colonies. The *cāṇḍāla*s who were of the lowest grades, *mr̥t-apa*s and the *haḍḍipa*s are cited as illustrations of this class.[13] In sharp contrast to the homogeneous character of three upper *varṇa*s the śūdras represent the heterogeneous group.[14]

Kauṭilya has laid emphasis on the point that all the four *varṇa*s should strictly adhere to their respective occupations promote to welfare of the people.[15]

Manu has mentioned the three upper *varṇa*s, viz., brāhmaṇa, kṣatriya and vaiśya as *dvijāti*s and the śūdras as *ekajāti* who formed the part of society in Āryāvartta.[16] The brāhmaṇa, according to him, on the basis of his superior origin or birth, knowledge of the Vedas, and the high degree of culture that he followed, represented the highest

---

8. V.S. Agrawala, *op. cit.*, p. 78.
9. *Mahābhāṣya*, V, 1, 115; also B.N. Puri, *op. cit.*, p. 83.
10. *Ibid.*, VI, 2, 36.
11. V.S. Agrawala, *op. cit.*, p. 79.
12. Pāṇini, III, 1, 103.
13. V.S. Agrawala, *op. cit.*, pp. 80-81.
14. R.S. Sharma, *Śūdras in Ancient India*, p. 280 f.
15. *Arth.*, 1, 2.
16. *Manu*, X, 4.

caste.[17] He, on the one hand, has condemned those brāhmaṇas who deviated from their prescribed duties, occupations and professions,[18] but, on the other, maintains that they must be honoured in the society.[19] This is a dichotomy between his Catholic outlook and dogmatic approach. His emphasis on pure lineage in case of kṣatriya *varṇa* contributed towards the formation of subdivisions within its fold. The śūdras, who represented the lowest social order, were treated contemptuously in the contemporary society.[20]

The compositional periods of the *Dharmasūtras* and *Manu-Smṛti* witnessed the gradual hardening of the caste system in general and the deterioration of the position of the vaiśyas and śūdras in particular. According to *Baudhāyana Dharmasūtra*, a brāhmaṇa if compelled by the situation could adopt the profession of a warrior.[21] It seems that integrity of caste was not seriously maintained. According to *Gautama Dharma Sūtra*, brāhmaṇas could take food in need even given by a śūdra.[22] The opinion of authors of the *Dharmasūtras* appears to be paradoxical probably because of variations in local customs and conditions.

In the Buddhistic tradition, no hard and fast line was drawn or the basis of birth in respect of choosing the occupations. The process of class and caste formations went on in the Buddhist society too. There were various classes of brāhmaṇas including those who followed the pursuits of agriculturists, craftsmen, tradesmen and soldiers; those who acted like servants and those who lived as low-caste hunters and trappers.[23] The kṣatriyas, of course, belonged to the ruling class and the class of warriors *par excellence*. But there are some instances from the *Jātakas* to show that a kṣatriya prince adopted the occupations of a potter, a basket-maker, trader, etc.[24] The vaiśyas, *gahapatis* or *seṭṭhis* controlled the whole of trade and commerce, agriculture and industry. There was hardly any social group which did not participate in production, distribution and commercial activities. So on the basis of occupation alone it is difficult to ascertain as to

17. *Manu.*, 1, 93.
18. *Ibid.*, III, 150-67.
19. *Ibid.*, IX, 319.
20. *Ibid.*, II, 31; III, 241; X, 126.
21. *Bau. Dh. S.*, 1, 1, 17 f.
22. *Gau. Dh. S.*, XVII, 1, f.
23. *Sutta-Nipāta*, p. 122; *Aṅguttara Nik.*, III, p. 223 f; *Jāt.*, II, pp. 15, 165, 200; III, p. 162; IV, pp. 207, 276; V, p. 471; VI, 170; also R. Fick, *The Social Organisation in North-East India in Buddha's time*, p. 221 f.
24. *Jāt.*, II, 5, 290; IV, 84, 169.

what extent social distinctions were maintained. The *Jātaka*[25] bears witness to the fact that a *seṭṭhi* worked as a tailor and as a potter retaining the respect of his community. The social status of the śūdras in the Buddhist society remained more or less the same what it was in the Hindu society. They were treated like slaves.

The terms *varṇa* and *jāti* were used in comprehensive sense in the context of ancient Indian system of social stratification. The term *varṇa* was used not only in the sense of distinctive colour or complexion but also in the sense of class and caste, order and status group, and *jāti* in that of distinctive mode of birth, pedigree or relationship and caste. Pāṇini twice uses the term *varṇa* in the sense of caste (V, 2, 132; VI, 3, 84).[26] Kātyāyana (fourth century BC) in his *Vārttika* on Pāṇini mentions the four *varṇa*s as four castes (V, 1, 124) in their order of status (II, 2, 34).[27] According to Rhys Davids, *varṇa* stands for colours and not castes and *jāti* for birth which had nothing to do with the building up of caste prejudices.[28] But in Pāli and other contemporary Indian texts these two terms appear as synonyms.[29] The concepts of *varṇa* and *jāti* have generated a lot of controversy among the scholars. They have provided different interpretations of these two terms within the conceptual framework.[30] Whatever may be the fact it is undeniable that *varṇa* and *jāti* formed the basis of social distinctions. No clear-cut demarcation line was drawn between the two terms.

The prevalence of the system of intermarriages among the four castes resulted in the formation of many new castes or mixed castes. The system, no doubt, quickened the process of caste formations. According to Manu, both *anuloma* (where husband's caste

---

25. *Jāt.*, VI, 372.
26. V.S. Agrawala, *op. cit.*, p. 77.
27. *Ibid.*
28. *BI*, p. 62.
29. B.C. Law, *IETBJ*, p. 143; *Concepts of Buddhism*, Ch. III. p. 11.
30. N. Wagle (*Society in the time of the Buddha*, pp. 122f, 121) is of the view that *varṇa* was order and not caste or class. The *varṇa* and *jāti* denoted status in the time of the Buddha; Max Weber (*Religion of India*: *The Sociology of Hinduism and Buddhism*, New York, 1968) associates *varṇa* with status group and not class. See also R.S. Sharma, 'Problems of Social Formations in Early India' General President's Address, Indian History Congress, 36th Session, Aligarh, 1975 for both classes and castes; see also his 'Class formation and its material basis in the upper Gangetic basin (*c.* 1000-500 BC)', *IHR*, II, I, (1975), pp. 1-13 for the origin of the *varṇa* system in the later Vedic age; Lallanji Gopal (*JIH*, 43, 1965, p. 771) has correctly stated that the traditional Indian caste structure was based on occupations. Each Section was entrusted with the work of which they had natural aptitude.

was higher than that of the wife) and *pratiloma* (where the husband's caste was lower than that of the wife) types of marriages were prevalent.[31] The offspring from the union between a brāhmaṇa father and a vaiśya mother was known as Ambaṣṭha, from brāhmaṇa father and śūdra mother as Niṣāda or Pāraśava[32] and from kṣatriya father and śūdra mother as Ugra.[33] These are the examples of the former type of marriage. The examples of the latter type of marriages are the following. The offspring of the kṣatriya father and brāhmaṇa mother was called Sūta, the vaiśya father and kṣatriya mother Māgadha, vaiśya father and brāhmaṇa mother Vaideha,[34] śūdra father and vaiśya mother Āyogava, śūdra father and kṣatriya mother Kṣatta and śūdra father and brāhmaṇa mother *cāṇḍāla*.[35] The *Vaśiṣṭha Dharmasūtra* also makes a mention of *caṇḍāla* of mixed parentage who was treated as outcaste.[36] The progeny of a Niṣāda father and a śūdra mother was called Pukkasa.[37] Most of them attained the śūdra status. In their case the caste was marked by the occupations they followed and occupation was determined by the caste they belonged to. The society consisted of many *jāti*s which traced their origin to common ancestors and the *gotra*s of many families. Marriage was forbidden within the *gotra*, but not oustside the *jāti*. Many new groups were adjusted within the caste hierarchy, which was based on the notion of purity and impurity. By the end of the first millennium BC quite a good number of mixed castes had emerged.

Pāṇini also refers to the terms *anuloma* and *pratiloma* (V, 4, 75) — the two different types of marriage which led to the formations of mixed castes. A class of people called *udakahāra* (or *udabhāra*, VI, 3, 60), i.e., drawer of water of low caste, was known to him. Kātyāyana speaks of *mahāśūdra* who belonged to a special caste or *jāti*.[38] Members of the same caste or *varṇa* have been mentioned by him as *savarṇa* (VI, 3, 85). Next to caste in importance was *gotra* which denoted the ancestral family from which its members traced their descent. Pāṇini is said to have prescribed elaborate rules for the formation of *gotra* names, e.g., Garga, father, Gārgī, son, Gārgya, grandson, etc.[39]

31. *Manu*, X, 25, 46.
32. *Ibid.*, X, 8.
33. *Ibid.*, X, 9.
34. *Ibid.*, X, 11.
35. *Ibid.*, X, 12.
36. *Vas. Dh. S.*, XVIII, 1.
37. *Manu*, X, 18.
38. V.S. Agrawala, *op. cit.*, p. 82.
39. *Ibid.*, p. 94.

Patañjali mentions 'Vr̥śalas',[40] 'Varudas',[41] 'Ugras',[42] 'Niṣādas',[43] 'Cāṇḍālas',[144] and 'Mr̥tapas'.[45] The 'Cāṇḍālas' and 'Niṣādas' belonged to despised castes and were engaged in very low processions. They are believed to have represented non-Āryan tribal group. The 'Varudas' and 'Ugras' belonged to the mixed castes. The former belonged to one of the seven low castes called *antyaja*. The 'Mr̥tapa' belonged to a class of outcastes. It has been rightly pointed out that the incorporation of non-Āryan social group of tribal origin into the expanding 'Indo-Aryan' *varṇa* system widened the scope for using the word *jāti* in the sense of caste.[46]

The institution of family (*kula*), which constituted the nucleus of society in ancient India, also comes within the gamut of social formation. The family though formed the smaller unit, it had practical importance in context of determining the soical status of an individual and in respect of judging the relative purity or impurity of men and women on the basis of marriages.

The system of inter-marriage (connubium) was also prevalent among the Buddhists and Jains. The members of two upper classes, the brāhmaṇas and kṣatriyas, enjoyed the privileges of marrying the girls from the vaiśya and śūdra families, but the vaiśyas, śūdras and outcastes could not aspire to marry the girls of families of upper classes. The members of two lower grades married within their own class (*samāna jāti* and *samāna gotta*).[47] They followed the custom of endogamy. The intermingling of various classes and consequent upon it the formation of mixed castes are also the notable features of Buddhist and Jain society. In the Buddhist society in particular distinctions and restrictions were also based upon *kula* or family and *gotta*, which stands for ancestral lineage. The term *gotta* was employed more in the sense of agnate than cognate. I take the liberty to differ from N. Wagle who holds that endogamy, one of the chief

40. I, 1, 7.
41. IV, 1, 97.
42. IV, 1, 14.
43. V, 4, 36.
44. II, 4. 10.
45. *Ibid.*
46. D.C. Sircar, *Studies in the Society and Administration of Ancient and Medieval India*, vol. I, pp. 103-5.
47. *IETBJ*, pp. 166-67, 174-75, 180; also *Jāt.*, I, 257 f, 477 f; J.C. Jain, *LAIJC* (Delhi, 1984), pp. 206-7.

characteristics of the modern caste system, was conspicuously absent in early Indian society at the time of the Buddha.[48]

The existence of many despised classes, untouchables and low caste professional groups below the four recognised social grades of kṣatriya, brāhmaṇa, vaiśya and śūdra in the Jain and Buddhist society can also be proved on the basis of evidences recorded in the relevant sources.

In the Jain sources the 'Pāṇas', the 'Ḍombas' and 'Morattiyas' have been referred to as condemned castes. The 'Pāṇas' correspond to the *caṇḍāla*s who were living outside the village. They were employed to carry corpses. The 'Ḍombas' were outcaste people. The 'Mātaṅgas' and 'Morattiyas' belonged to the same group. The professional group of low castes included peacock-tamers, hunters, butchers, cobblers, barbers, washermen, etc.[49] The Jain *Sūtra*s mention *cāṇḍāla*s and 'Pukkusas' together as despised castes.[50]

In contradistinction to the upper grades, the canonical Pāli texts enumerates the five *hīna jāti*s (despised castes or low tribes) as the 'Cāṇḍāla', 'Veṇa', 'Niṣāda', 'Rathakāra' or 'Cammakāra' and 'Pukkusa'. The *cāṇḍāla*s are distinguished from the Pukkusas as corpse-throwers. The *veṇa*s were the workers in bamboo, the *cammakāra* the workers in leather and the *niṣāda*s the hunter.[51] Rhys Davids has described them as aboriginal tribes.[52] Their social status was low not only because of low profession but also due to their cultural backwardness.[53]

The available data leads us to warrant the belief that caste distinctions were maintained in the Hindu, Buddhist and Jain society at some points of time on the basis of birth or lineage, social status and occupations. The evidence furnished in the Jain *Sūtra*s creates an impression that intially the Jains opposed the caste system.[54] The Pāli canon also bears testimony to the fact that the Buddha himself denounced the caste system.[55] But it cannot be denied that their social structure subsequently underwent

48. *Op. cit.*, pp. 132-33.
49. J.C. Jain, *op. cit.*, pp. 192-93.
50. H. Jacobi (tr.), *Jain Sūtras, Sūtrakṛtāṅga*, I, 3, 9, in SBE, XLV, II, p. 301; see also BI, p. 55.
51. *Aṅguttara Nik*, I, pp. 107, 162; II, p. 85; III, p. 214; *Saṁytta Nik.*, ed. M.L. Feer and Mrs. Rhys Davids, V, p. 161; R. Fick, *op. cit.*, p. 27 f.
52. *BI*, p. 55.
53. R.S. Sharma, *Śūdras in Ancient India*, pp. 142-43.
54. *Uttarādhyayana*, 12, 37; 25. 29 f; *Ācārāṅga*. 2(3), 49.
55. *Sutta-Nipāta* (Vāseṭṭha Sutta), cf. *HPL*, I, p. 88.

metamorphosis as a result of which the gap between the high castes and low castes was widened and it took long time to bridge them up. The Buddha failed to weed out casteism and untouchability. However, it is a fact to be reckoned with that the caste structure had lot of flexibility and was free from rigidity. Rhys Davids' view that at the time of Buddha the caste system was not in existence[56] may be accepted. But his statement that this system in the exact use of the term did not exist till long afterwards[57] can be disposed of. E.W. Hopkins has correctly observed that 'In the point of fact, even the Buddhist writings recognise the formal castes'.[58] D.D. Kosambi, while dealing with 'the Buddha and his society', has also pointed out that 'caste might exist as a social distinction; it had no permanence, no inner justification'.[59] Romila Thapar's observation that the Buddhists were against the institution of caste, but 'in the routine working of the society there were bound to be social distinctions. . .'[60] stands to logic and reality.

The formation of classes of slaves can be discussed in the contemporary socio-economic set-up. The existence of slaves in the days of Manu can irrefutably be proved by his own description of seven types thereof : (1) those who were made captives in war (*dhvajāhr̥taḥ*), (2) those who offered their sevices for his daily food or for receiving sustenance (*bhaktadāsa*), (3) son of a female slave or *dāsī* (*gr̥haja*), (4) one who was bought (*kr̥ta*), (5) one who was given by another in gift or so (*datrima*), (6) hereditary slave (*paitr̥ka*) and (7) those who accepted slavery because of non-payment of his debts.[61] He has also mentioned a separate category of śūdra slaves.[62] The practice of employing the domestic servants (both male and female) by the rich people was widely prevalent during the period concerned. Pāṇini (*Niyukta*, IV, 4, 65)[63] and Patañjali have also referred to this category of slave who had śūdra status.[64] The slavery was also in existence during the time of Kauṭilya, for he exhaustively deals with the subject. According to him, the

---

56. *BI*, p. 62.
57. *Ibid.*
58. E.J. Rapson (ed.), *CHI*, vol. I, *Ancient India*, p. 198.
59. *The Culture and Civilisation of Ancient India in Historical Outline*, p. 113; see also his 'Early Stages of the Caste System in Northern India', *JBBRAS*, New Series, XXII (1946), p. 38.
60. 'Society and Law in the Hindu and Buddhist Traditions' in *AISH*, p. 32.
61. *Manu*, VIII, 415.
62. *Manu.*, 414.
63. V.S. Agrawala, *op. cit.*, p. 114.
64. B.N. Puri, *op. cit.*, p. 110.

members of the four *varṇa*s of the Āryan society were not made slaves except when they were captives or had fallen into the grip of catastrophy. The *mleccha*s could sell their sons as slaves. Those, who accepted slavery of their own accord and thereafter absconded, could be enslaved for whole life. Those, who made any of the four *varṇa*s their slaves, were punished. He has referred to female slaves too. A slave could regain his freedom if he paid for it. Kauṭilya has described slavery as one of the social evils, and that is why he laid down some rules to eradicate it.[65]

The Jain[66] and Buddhist sources[67] also make mention of different classes of slaves which include male and female slaves who were employed by the master of the family as domestic servants; those who were born of slave parents; those who were purchased by kings and rich people; those who were captured in raids or taken as prisoners of war; those who accepted slavery under compulsion; those who were deprived of their freedom as a judicial punishment of certain crime; those who were made slaves because of non-payment of debts, etc. It seems that slavery had almost assumed the character of a soical institution.

The classes of artisans and craftsmen, who followed economic pursuits to cater to the needs of the whole village community and to promote the growth of material culture, also deserve mention here. The prominent among them were the potters (Skt. and Pāli — *kumbhakāra* and *kumbhakāra* respectively), carpenters (Skt. *takṣā*; Pāli *tacchakā*), weavers (Skt. *tantuvāya*; Pāli *pesakārā*), leather-workers (Skt. *carmakāra*; Pāli *cammakāra*), blacksmiths (Skt. *karmāra*; Pāli *kammāra*), goldsmiths (Skt. *suvarṇakāra*), jewellers (Pāli *manikāra*), dyers (Skt. *rañjaka*; Pāli *rajakāra*), washermen (Skt. *rajaka*), tailors (Skt. and Pāli *tunnavāya* and *tunnavāya* respectively), ivory-workers, basket-makers, workers in cane and bamboo and bow and arrow makers. Besides these, there were many other groups who were engaged in different occupations and professions. They functioned either as producers, manufacturers, suppliers or sellers. The above list

65. *Arth.*, *op. cit.*, 3, 13, 1-20; *JIH*, LVI, II (1978), p. 242.
66. J.C. Jain, *op. cit.*, pp. 140-42.
67. *Jāt.*, I, 200; III, 343; IV, 220; VI, 135, 486, 521, 577; *Dīgha Nikāya*, ed. T.W. Rhys Davids and J.E. Carpenter, I, 72; *Majjhima Nik.*, ed. V. Trenckner and R. Chalmers, II, 149.

is based on the information supplied in the works of Pāṇini,[68] Patañjali,[69] and Kauṭilya,[70] and in the *Manu-Smṛti*,[71] Pāli canon[72] and Jain *Sūtras*.[73]

Each class of artisans, craftsmen, traders and merchants, and other occupational and professional groups formed their respective associations or guilds (*seṇis*, *pūgas*) in the age of the Buddha with a view to consolidating their position, safeguarding their interest and protecting their rights. The members of each guild mutually agreed to be governed by their own laws and customs. Each guild was a autonomous body or self-governing economic institution. The guilds were invested with the powers of framing their own laws to regulate and control the whole affairs. The guilds played very important role as an economic institution in the contemporary society.[74] The guild formation became a prominent feature of the commercial life in ancient India from *c*. 500 BC onwards. It is worthy of remark that owing to strict adherence of the followers of common profession to the rules of marriage and eating within their own class or group the guilds were being hardened into castes. The social process was further complicated by the general tendency to segregate one class of workers from another within the same profession. It further resulted in the formations of several working groups with unhealthy competition which adversely affected the soical order and economic system in the country during the period.

---

68. V.S. Agrawala, *op. cit*., pp. 229-34.
69. B.N. Puri, *op. cit*., pp. 108-10.
70. *Arth*., IV, 1, 1-30.
71. *Manu*., III, 160; IV, 214-16; VIII, 327, 397; IX, 292; X, 36, 48-49.
72. *Jāt*., I, 320, 356; II, 18, 197, 405; III, 281, 376; IV, 81, 159, 207; VI, 7; *Dīgha Nik*. (*Sāmaññaphala Sutta*), 1, pp. 47-86; *Apadāna*, II, p. 357 f; *BI*, pp. 88-96; See also R.S. Sharma, *Material Culture and Social Formations in Ancient India*, Ch. 7.
73. J.C. Jain, *op. cit*., pp. 127-37.
74. *Jāt*., I, 267, 314; III, 281; IV, 411; VI, 22, 427; *BI*, pp. 90-96; *IETBJ*, p. 179; Mrs. C.A.F. Rhys Davids, 'Notes on Early Economic conditions in Northern India', *JRAS*, October 1901, pp. 863-72; *LAIJC*, pp. 143-44.

5

Ancient Indian Economy as Described by Manu
(*c.* 200-100 BC)

MANU'S description of science and art of economics finds reflection in the use of a technical term *vārttā*,[1] which comprised agriculture (*kṛṣi*),[2] cattle rearing (*paśūnāṁ parivardhanam*),[3] arts and crafts (*vividhāni ca śilpāni*),[4] indigenous industry including the manufactures (*karmayoga*),[5] labour (*bhṛti* and *bhṛtyāḥ*),[6] trade (*kraya-vikraya*)[7] and commerce (*vāṇijya*)[8] taxation system (taxes on trade and industry, tariff and octroi or *śulka*),[9] currency, weights and measures (*tulāyoga*, *mānayoga*),[10] money-lending and banking (*dravyavṛddhi* and *prayoga*),[11] profits and loss (*lābhālābhaṁ ca paṇyānāṁ*),[12] etc. It was one of the principal duties of the king to have a thorough knowledge of the art of the *vārttā* and to keep a watchful eye on its application to the practical life of the people.[13] The study of the subject is purely based on the original source.

Agricultural activities, cattle rearing, trade and commerce were the sole concern of the vaiśyas and not of the brāhmaṇas and kṣatriyas. In this regard, Manu has categorically stated that only the vaiśyas are meant for economic pursuits and no other class of the

---

1. *Manu.*, IX, 326; X, 80.
2. *Ibid.*, I, 90; X, 79 and 82.
3. *Ibid.*, I, 90; IX, 326, 328 and 331; X, 79 and 82.
4. *Ibid.*, II, 240.
5. *Ibid.*, X, 115.
6. *Ibid.*, IX, 332.
7. *Ibid.*
8. *Ibid.*, X, 79.
9. *Ibid.*, VII, 127, 128, 131-32, 138.
10. *Ibid.*, IX, 330.
11. *Ibid.*, IX, 333; X, 115.
12. *Ibid.*, IX, 331.
13. *Ibid.*, VII, 43.

society.[14] It was the bounden duty of the vaiśyas to make all possible efforts in their respective spheres of activities to promote the economic growth of the country.

Agriculture was taken as the most honourable economic profession during the times of Manu. This can be fairly substantiated by the following evidence:

kr̥ṣiṁ sādhviti manyante sā vr̥ttiḥ sadvigarhitā.[15]

It was the duty of the vaiśya to enquire about the different varieties of seeds and methods of sowing them and to ensure the fertility of the soil and productivity of the fields.[16] The production and distribution system and land ownership have also been referred to by Manu. The wooden plough tipped with iron (*ayomukha-kāṣṭha*) was used for cultivating the fields.[17] Attempts were also made to make waste or barren lands worthy of agricultural purposes. The ownership of such land vested in him who first redeemed it from its waste condition.[18] The fields were prepared for cultivation by the farmers. In a well-cultivated and irrigated fields, seeds were sown by them at the proper season, and the production of plants depended very much on the qualities of seeds.[19] Various kinds of seeds were sold in the market. Those, who were found guilty of selling barren seeds or mixing inferior quality of seeds with superior one, were severely punished by the king.[20] Fields were divided into different small parts (*kṣetra*, or *kedara*s) and seeds were sown accordingly.[21] The crops were of different kinds, viz., rice, wheat, barley, cotton, mudga beans, sesame, sugar-cane, and vegetables.[22] The harvest seasons were spring and autumn.[23]

The owners generally engaged servants, mostly the śūdra cultivators, to do the work in the fields.[24] The etymology of the word *ārdhika* suggests that they also got share in the produce of the fields of their masters. There is positive evidence to show that the

14. *Manu.*, IX, 326-33; X, 79-80, 82-84.
15. *Ibid.*, X, 84.
16. *Ibid.*, IX, 330.
17. *Ibid.*, X, 84.
18. *Ibid.*, IX, 44.
19. *Ibid.*, IX, 36-40.
20. *Ibid.*, IX, 291.
21. *Ibid.*, IX, 37-38.
22. *Ibid.*, IX, 39.
23. *Ibid.*, VI, 11.
24. *Ibid.*, IV, 253.

owner of the field and the cultivator used to divide the produce between themselves. As per their mutual agreement the cultivator had to supply seeds in addition to labour for claiming half of share in produce of the land.[25] Herein we find to a limited extent the reflection 'bataidari system'. But, on the other hand, we also find that in absence of any clear-cut terms and agreements or contracts between the owner of the land (*kṣetra*) and the cultivator, the produce belonged to the former only and the latter was not entitled to anything.[26] Thus, from the analysis of the data concerned it appears that both the systems were in vogue in ancient India during the period concerned. They obviously formed parts of the agricultural system operating during the times of Manu.

Royal share of the produce was 1/6th, 1/8th and 1/12th portion of the corn, of course, according to qualities and advantages of the soil.

As the king received his revenue in kind, it was his duty to see that harvests did not suffer either by the negligence of the cultivator or because of the carelessness of his servants. In the former case fine was ten times and in the latter only five times of the royal dues.[27]

Cattles like buffaloes, cows, sheep and goat were reared. They were taken to pasture grounds by the herdsmen, who were also responsible for their protection from wild beasts and thieves. If the cattles damaged the crops in presence of their keepers, the latters were fined by the king.[28] Sheep rearing seems to have been very popular in the hilly regions of the north. Manu specifically refers to sheep dealers (*aurabhr̥ka*).[29] The word *kutapa*, as used by him, has been explained by the commentator of the text as Nepal blanket.[30]

There were several occupational groups including artisans, craftsmen, traders, merchants, mechanics, gold-smith, black-smith, dyer, carpenter, oiler, weaver, tailor, potter, leather-worker, cane and bamboo worker, etc.

The arts and crafts constituted the bases of rich economic life of the country. The status of artisans (*śilpī*), craftsmen (*kāruka*) and mechanics (*yantra-pravartaka*)[31] was

25. *Manu.*, IX, 53.
26. *Ibid.*, IX, 52; see also IX, 51 & 54.
27. *Ibid.*, VIII, 243.
28. For details see *ibid.*, VIII, 232-44.
29. *Ibid.*, III, 166.
30. *Ibid.*, III, 234-35.
31. *Ibid.*, X, 99-100; XI, 63.

considerably higher than that of the śūdras in the society. The king colonised bands of artisans in the metropolis or cities and made them work for himself for at least one day in the month.[32]

Manu has categorically referred to worker in gold (*hemakāra*),[33] gem-driller (*maṇīnāṁvedhakaḥ*),[34] dyer (*rañjaka*),[35] blacksmith (*karmāra*),[36] who smelted rods in the furnace and prepared several articles like agricultural implements — plough (*sitā*) and spade (*kārṣṇāyasī abhri*), and double-pointed spear (*riṣṭi*), spikes (*śakti*), iron-staff (*āyasa-daṇḍa*), weapons (*āyudha, śastrāstra*), long nails (*daśāṅgulaśaṅku*), iron-balls (*ayoguḍa*), hollow iron-image (*sūrmi*) and iron-bed (*āyasa-śayana*),[37] carpenter (*tvaṣṭi*),[38] oiler (*tailika*),[39] tailor (*tunnavāya*),[40] weaver (*tantuvāya*),[41] who ginned cotton and separated the seed (*kārpāsthi*), then spun yarn (*sūtra-tantu*), and wove it into cloth of cotton, silk, linen and wool; prepared some precious clothes of fine variety (*uttamavāsasām*), noted for export markets, and supplied eleven *palas* of cloth in exchange for ten *palas* of yarn,[42] potter (*bhāṇḍika*), who prepared earthenware (*mr̥ṇmaya-bhaṇḍa*),[43] workers in cane and bamboo (*veṇavaidalabhāṇḍakāraka*),[44] makers of bow and arrow (*dhauḥśarāṇāṁ-kartā*),[45] brick-killer (*iṣṭakāpāka*),[46] leather-worker (*carmakāra*),[47] (who manufactured bags, shoes, etc)[48] and other working group. They all added to the enrichment of socio-economic life of the people.

32. *Manu*, VII, 75 & 138.
33. *Ibid.*, IX, 292; also IV, 215.
34. *Ibid.*, IX, 296.
35. *Ibid.*, IV, 215-16.
36. *Ibid.*, IV, 215.
37. *Ibid.*, II, 133; VIII, 271, 315, 372; IX, 293; X, 79; XI, 103, 133.
38. *Ibid.*, X, 48.
39. *Ibid.*, III, 158; IV, 85.
40. *Ibid.*, IV, 214.
41. *Ibid.*, VIII, 397.
42. *Ibid.*, IV, 78, VIII, 321 & 397.
43. *Ibid.*, VIII, 327.
44. *Ibid.*
45. *Ibid.*, III, 160.
46. *Ibid.*, VIII, 259.
47. *Ibid.*, X, 36 & 49.
48. *Ibid.*, VIII, 369.

The traders, artisans, merchants and other working group formed different organisations called *kulas*, *pūgas*, *śreṇīs*, and *gaṇas*[49] for safeguarding their respective interests with little information about their constitution, powers and functions. However, *kulas* were more or less like families whose legislative autonomy were vested in the eldest male members.[50] The *pūgas* were traders' associations. The *śreṇīs* were guild organisations of artisans and workmen whose rules were binding upon courts. *Gaṇas* were as sort of merchant association of corporations. *Saṁgha* was both a commercial and religious organisation. It has been pointed out that 'one should in no case break his contract once entered into with Saṅghas and Grāmas'.[51] The later constitutional writers and political thinkers devoted more attention to the organisation of these various bodies.

The wage earners were called *bhṛtaka*. It was the duty of the vaiśya to acquaint himself with the customary wages of all workmen.[52] Women and menial servants employed in king's service used to receive their wages per day in accordance with their position and work.[53] The lower grade of servants engaged in daily works received one *paṇa* = (*paisā* in copper coin) and higher grade of servants received six *paṇas* per day as their wages. Every month they received one *droṇa* weight of corn (1/2 kilo) from the king.[54] Non-payment of wages was a cognisable offence. If a servant not being ill left the work incompleted, he was fined eight *kṛṣṇalas* and got nothing for the work done. But after his recovery from the illness if he completed his work, he was entitled to receive full dues.[55]

The trade and commerce were in a very flourishing stage. The market system was well-organised. There were various kinds of shops composing the market (*vipāni* = shop).[56] Articles exposed for sale in different shops were the high standard and pure quality.[57] The large variety of saleable commodities, as mentioned in the *Smṛti*, were jewels, pearls, corals, costly clothes, dyed clothes, clothes made of silk, cotton, wool and linen,

---

49. *Manu*, 1, 118; 111, 151, 164; VIII, 41.
50. *Ibid.*, VIII, 46.
51. *Ibid.*, VIII, 219.
52. *Ibid.*, VI, 45; IX, 332.
53. *Ibid.*, VII, 125.
54. *Ibid.*, VII, 126 (see also VIII, 136).
55. *Ibid.*, VIII, 215-17.
56. *Ibid.*, X, 116.
57. *Ibid.*, V, 129.

yarn, horn, ivory, bones, conches and shells, skins, blankets, drugs, medicines, honey, butter, milk, curd, corn, molasses, poison, *soma*, cooked food, vegetables, sweets, condiments, salt, oil, tallow, meat, wine, birds, fish, indigo, lac, cane-articles, earthenware, bamboo ware, leather, bronze, copper, silver, iron, stones and weapons.[58] These bear testimony to the richness of market-places. Sale and purchase generally took place in coins. The market rates were fixed by the king every fortnight or every after five days in counsultation with the chief traders.[59] It was the duty of the king to take into consideration the distance of the places concerned with import (*āgama*) and export (*nirgama*), the position of demand and supply, etc., before fixing the prices of the commodities and making declaration about their sale and purchase.[60] According to Kullūka (commentator on the text), the articles were purchased and sold in the market before *kulas* signifying body of merchants.[61]

The state and the merchant organisations formulated several rules to maintain high degree of business morality so far as the market transaction is concerned. Adulteration in the market-place was strictly forbidden.[62] The sellers were not allowed to keep low quality of goods in their shops.[63] Those, who were found guilty of using false weights and measures and cheating the honest customers by charging higher prices than the fixed one by any fraudulent means, were fined by the king in proportion to the prices of goods or nature of the crime. Generally the punishment equivalent to *prathama sāhasa* (250 *paṇa*) or *madhyama sāhasa* (500 *paṇa*) was imposed on the culprits.[64] It was the duty of the vaiśya to collect information about the fluctuation in prices of the market commodities.[65] The market economy was largely based on the rules framed by the government.

Both internal and external trade system flourished. The commerce was carried on by both land and sea-routes, as evidenced by the use of the word *vanikpatham* and the explanation given by Kullūka thereof as *sthalajalādinā vāṇijyam*.[66] The inland trade-

58. *Manu*, IX, 329; X, 85-89.
59. *Ibid.*, VIII, 402.
60. *Ibid.*, VIII, 401.
61. *Ibid.*, VIII, 201.
62. *Ibid.*, VIII, 203; IX, 332.
63. *Ibid.*, VIII, 203; IX, 286.
64. *Ibid.*, IX, 287.
65. *Ibid.*, IX, 329.
66. *Ibid.*, 1, 90.

routes led through forests, marshes and jungles.[67] Wheeled carts (*yanani*)[68] and sometimes even animals and men were used for transport of merchandise. Navigable rivers also served as channels of transport. Boat-fare for long distances in rivers was fixed according to the time and distance.[69] While the charges of boats were ascertainable to some extent, those of ships in the sea could not be so determined.[70] The boats or ships belonged to the boatmen (*kaivarta* or *dāsa*)[71] who engaged themselves in the business of shipping transport (*naukarmajīvī*).[72]

The government kept strict control over the imports and exports of the country in the days of Manu. The merchants were not at liberty to export the items of their choice. The king reserved the right to confiscate the whole of the property of a trader who out of greed exported those goods over which the king had a monopoly or the export of which was forbidden.[73] Those products which were very valuable and rare like costly clothes, precious gems and for state use, were not made the articles of commerce. The export of foodgrains to other countries during famines was forbidden. As a matter of fact, there were famines during Manu's time.[74] Manu does not throw any light on the articles which were exported to other countries. However, there are some indications to this effect on the basis of which some tentative inferences can be drawn. The early traditions of an extensive commerce carried on by India within her own borders as well as with distant countries of the world outside are very well substantiated by the evidence furnished in *Manu-Smr̥ti*.

Mineral resources of the country were very rich. The mineral wealth consisted of gold (*suvarṇa* or *hema*),[75] silver (*rajata*),[76] copper (*tāmra*), bronze (*kāṁsya*), lead (*sīsā* or *saisaka*), iron (*ayas*), pewter (*raitya*), etc.[77] Different methods were applied for purification

67. *Manu*, VII, 185.
68. *Ibid.*, VIII, 405.
69. *Ibid.*, VIII, 406.
70. *Ibid.*
71. *Ibid.*, X, 34.
72. *Ibid.*
73. *Ibid.*, VIII, 399.
74. *Ibid.*, VIII, 22.
75. *Ibid.*, IV, 215; IX, 292.
76. *Ibid.*, V, 112; V, 113.
77. *Ibid.*, V, 114, also XI, 133; XI, 167.

of these metals. Manu has prescribed very stringent punishment for dishonest goldsmith. Those, who were found guilty of mixing the inferior quality of metal with the superior one or stealing gold or silver, were cut to pieces by the king.[78]

The origin of iron is said to be from stone (*aśmano lohamutthitam*).[79] This is, undoubtedly, indication towards availability of iron from mines located in rocky areas of granite stone. The code refers to various articles made out of stone, gold, silver, pearls, iron, bronze, diamond and other precious jewels.[80] It seems that slabs were obtained from quarries of stratified stone, which has been referred to as stone-slabs (*upalānānāṁ steyam*). Gems like diamond, etc., were dug from their respective mines in abundance and sold in the market. Pearls and corals were water-born gems, which were obtained probably from sea near the mouth of the Tāmraparṇī many centuries before the Christ.

The ownership of the mines belonged to the king and it was necessary to seek his permission for undertaking the mining operations.[81] The king being the master of the soil usually exercised his righ to receive half of what was obtained from different mines.[82] All encouragements were provided by the state to miners. Someone, from amongst the ministers was appointed by the king to supervise the working of the mines, particularly, the gold mines and to collect the royal share of income.[83]

The duties, called *śulka* and different kinds of taxes (*kara*) collected from traders and merchants increased the resources of the state.

The king adopted the enlightened policy of taxation. The king first used to ascertain the buying and selling rates (*krayavikrayaṁ*), distance of passage, pricipal and subsidiary charges borne in importing the article, expenditure incurred on its safety, and profits and loss in transit, and then asked the tradesmen to pay the royal taxes.[84] The king used to fix the taxation policy of the state in such a manner that both he as well as the tradesmen should receive their respective share of profit.[85] The duties were fixed and

---

78. *Manu*, IX, 292.
79. *Ibid.*, IX, 321.
80. *Ibid.*, V, 111; VIII, 100; X, 86; XI, 167.
81. *Ibid.*, XI, 63.
82. *Ibid.*, VIII, 39.
83. *Ibid.*, VII, 62.
84. *Ibid.*, VII, 127.
85. *Ibid.*, VII, 128.

the price schedule was drawn up by the king through his octroi superintendents in consultation with the merchant representatives. The king realised one — twentieth of the profits accrued on the trade by land and sea and on the selling of the commodities in the market according to the fixed price as duties or his royal dues.[86] Custom houses were set-up on all vulnerable trade-routes to check the quality and quantity of goods carried by the traders and to collect the duties from them. Custom officers well-trained in the art of tariff management and well equipped with the knowledge of the prices of all commodities were posted at each check-post. The traders passing through the trade-routes other than those with check-posts while carrying the goods or evading the check-posts with a motive to hood-wink the officers or doing the transactions at night time or secretly or by adopting any unfair means or violating the custom rules had to pay a fine eight times the duty, which they were supposed to pay indeed.[87] The king used to receive one-sixth (part) of honey, ghee, meat, perfumes, herbs or medicines, salt, fruits, vegetables, skins, earthen ware, stone-objects, etc., as tax.[88]

There is nothing to show that the king ever applied high-handed policy in collecting taxes and dues from traders, merchants and common people. Nor is there any evidence to prove that the taxpayers were ever subjected to harassment or any torture. Rather, we find that the sense of justice was highly applied in collection of either royal share or dues.

Arrangements were also made to provide banking facilities to the traders and merchants in order to promote the growth of trade and commerce as well as to the needy persons as general case.

It was the business of the vaiśya class exclusively to invest the money for earning interest. Brāhmaṇas and kṣatriyas were not allowed to lend the money only for getting interest but for the sake of *dharma* (for trade, agricultural works, etc.). They could give loan on little interest. The earning of money through interest (*prayoga*) was one of those seven means of accumulating the wealth, which were held legal in the eyes of law or *dharma*. The vaiśyas were not only supposed to grow maximum crops but also to increase the resources of the state through trade, agriculture (*karmayoga*), investment of money on legal rates of interest, etc.[89]

---

86. *Manu*, VIII, 398.
87. *Ibid.*, VIII, 400.
88. *Ibid.*, VII, 131-32.
89. For details see *ibid.*, IX, 33; X, 115 and 117.

Manu seems to have followed the rate of interest as prescribed by Vasiṣṭha as is evident from his own statement. While referring to the name of Vasiṣṭha in this regard, it has been stated that the creditor or persons enagaged in money-lending business should charge 1/80 or one rupee twenty-five paisā (or 1¼) per cent interest per month from the debtor.[90] The statement of Vasiṣṭha[91] goes well in accord with that of Manu.

The money-lenders were also allowed to charge two per cent (or two rupees per hundred) interest per month, as sanctioned by law.[92] The rates of interest were also fixed according to the *varṇas*. Brāhmaṇas had to pay 2 per cent, kṣatriyas 3 per cent, vaiśyas 4 per cent and śūdras 5 per cent interest per month.[93] The amount of interest charged in no case could be more than double of the capital invested.[94] As for example, if hundred rupees were the capital the interest could not exceed tow hundred rupees. The creditors and debtors had to settle the accounts at least once in a year. It was binding on the parts of debtors to clear the interest of one year. The creditors were not allowed to charge the interest of more than one year at a time or to charge more than what prescribed in *Dharmaśāstra*, or to take *cakravṛddhi* (compound interest), *kālavṛddhi* (interest accumulating more than the capital itself), *kāritā* (by forcing the debtors to pay more interest), etc.[95] The debtors unable to pay the interest in time and further willing to take loan had to execute a new agreement (a kind of of handnote) with the creditor or to sign a new bond agreeing to pay either only interest or capital with outstanding interest and the interest to be accrued thereon.[96]

The gold, silver and copper coins were the standard currency through which the normal business was transacted.[97] Manu has not only mentioned the names of different coins but also shown the different methods for fixing their relative value.

The standard gold coin was *suvarṇa* which was equal to 80 *kṛṣṇalas* (*rattīs*) in weight (= one rupee). This has been explained in different other ways. *Kṛṣṇala* was equivalent to *rattī*; 5 *kṛṣṇala*s = 1 *māsā* or 1 *ānnā*; 16 *māsā*s = 16 *ānnā*s =1 *suvarṇa* or one rupee =

---

90. *Manu*, VIII, 140.
91. *Vasiṣṭha-Smṛti*, III, 51.
92. *Manu*, VIII, 141.
93. *Ibid.*, VIII, 142.
94. *Ibid.*, VIII, 151.
95. *Ibid.*, VIII, 153.
96. *Ibid.*, VIII, 154, 155.
97. *Ibid.*, VIII, 131.

rattīs.[98] The scale of silver weight was different from that of gold. It was like this — 2 *kṛṣṇala* = 1 *raupya māsā*; 16 *māṣaka* = 1 *dharaṇa* and 10 *dharaṇa* = 1 *rajata* or silver (*śatamāna*).[99] Copper *kārṣāpana* (*paisā*) was known as *karṣa* or *paṇa*. It was 80 *kṛṣṇalas* in weight (= 150 grs). Four *suvarṇas* were equivalent to one *niṣka* (*aśarfī*).

The golden *māsā* was much superior to silver *māsā* in value.[100] Six *niṣkas* of gold were superior to 100 copper *karṣas* or 1500 grains of copper. Coins equal in value to 1/8th of a *kārṣāpaṇa* were also current. The value of a *paṇa* may be judged by the fact that 'menial servants received one *paṇa* and higher servants six *paṇas* as daily wages by the king.'[101] Gold and silver coins weight were also used for weighing gold, diamond and other precious jewels.[102]

The government maintained strict supervision over the standards of weights and measures applied in the market. Different scales used for weighing the articles and the measurements system were known as *tulāmān pratimāna and tarāju*. They were checked by the government officials every after six months.[103] Those, who charged the higher price or used false weights and measures at the time of selling gold, clothes, etc., were treated as theives and punished by the king according to nature of crime.[104] It was also the duty of the vaiśyas to ascertain the correct use of measurement system.[105]

From the foregoing description it can be gathered that a well-balanced economic system was maintained in ancient India during the times of Manu. The economic conditions of the people were by and large very satisfactory. The availability of all economic facilities and necessary infrastructure resulted in the economic prosperity of the people as well as the country.

---

98. *Manu*, VIII, 134.
99. *Ibid.*, VIII, 135-37.
100. *Ibid.*, VIII, 392-93.
101. *Ibid.*, VII, 126.
102. *Ibid.*, VIII, 321-22.
103. *Ibid.*, VIII, 403.
104. *Ibid.*, IX, 257.
105. *Ibid.*, IX, 330.

6

Ancient Indian Religious System in the Times of Manu and Patañjali* (*c.* 200-100 BC)

ANCIENT Indian religious system in the times of Manu and Patañjali was more or less based on the Vedic and Brāhmaṇical traditions in respect of sacrifices, *yajñas*, rituals, priesthood, pantheism and other popular religious beliefs. But in respect of idols' worship in the temples the period concerned marked the fundamental departure from the earlier traditions. Patañjali's time (the first half of the second century BC) is particularly marked by the co-existence of Brāhmaṇism, Buddhism and Jainism. His time also witnessed the growth of Śaiva and Bhāgavata cults of Hinduism and other minor religious cults. The system, as a whole, prevailing in the second century BC, which synchronises with their times, appears to be analogous to that of the Vedic and post-Vedic times. The paper is primarily based on the data contained in the Vedic literature, the *Manu-Smṛti*, the *Mahābhāṣya* of Patañjali, the Sanskrit Buddhist text and the epigraphic records.

Both *smṛtikāra* (Manu) and *bhāṣyakāra* (Patañjali) mention different types of sacrifices, offerings and *yajñas*, including some of those which were very popular in the Vedic age. The most popular Vedic *yajñas* known as *agniṣṭoma*, *rājasūya* and *vājapeya*, as distinctly mentioned in the *Athārvaveda*[1] and partly described in the three Saṁhitās

---

*From *ABORI*, LXXV, 1994, pp. 81-90.

1. XI, 4, 7, 7.

of Black and White *Yajurveda* (*Taittirīya*, *Maitrāyaṇī* and *Vājasaneyī*) and other *Brāhmaṇas*,[2] have been referred to by Patañjali in his work.[3]

Manu (ascribed to the second century BC) calls these Vedic *yajñas* by the name *vidhiyajñas*.[4] *Agniṣṭoma* was the most common form of *yajña* in which the animals including goat were sacrificed and offered to Agni.[5] The royal consecration ceremony known as *rājasūya-yajña* was performed in connection with the proclamation of kingship. It was a kind of inauguration ceremony on the occasion of *abhiṣeka* or crowning of a king. The *vājapeya-yajña* was performed primarily for celebrating the victory as well as for establishing the supremacy.[6] The *aśvamedha* sacrifices, as referred to by Manu and Patañjali, were performed in India for different purposes. According to Manu, the *yajña*, which was jointly attended by kings and brāhmaṇas, was meant for those who after committing any sin (*brahmahatyā*) wanted to get purified after taking the final bath (*avabhṛta*).[7] Patañjali refers to *aśvamedha* sacrifice performed by his contemporary Brāhmaṇical Śuṅga emperor, Puṣyamitra (*c*. 185-149 BC).[8] The epigraphic evidence[9] also confirms this truth. In all likelihood, this sacrifice might have been performed by him after slaying his master, the last Mauryan ruler, Bṛhadratha, for vindicating his sovereignty and stabilising his imperial position. The revival of this sacrifice was no doubt the antithesis of the doctrines propounded by Aśoka.

One of the *yajñas* which was popular in the time of Patañjali was known as the *yūpas* in which the wooden pillars were set-up for binding the sacrificial animals.[10] Several stone *yūpas*, a prototype of those used in the second century BC, were later discovered in

---

2. *Ait. Br.*, III, 41-43; *Śat. Br.*, III, 7, 1, 13.
3. *Mahābhāṣya*, IV, 3, 66; VI, 1, 84; also Kielhorn, "Notes on the *Mahābhāṣya*", *Ind. Ant.* XV, pp. 80f, 203f, 228f; XVI, pp. 101f, 178f, 244f; R.G. Bhandarkar, "Patañjali's *Mahābhāṣya*", *Ind. Ant.*, II, pp. 69f; P.C. Chakravartty (tr.), *Mahābhāṣya, IHQ*, II, pp. 67f, 262f, 464f. 738f.
4. *Manu-Smṛti*, II, 86; IV, 26.
5. A.B. Keith, *The Religion and Philosophy of the Veda and Upanishads*, p. 327; SBE, XLI, p. xiii.
6. Keith, *op. cit.*, p. 340; Macdonell and Keith, *Vedic Index*, II, pp. 25f.
7. XI, 82.
8. *Mahābhāṣya*, I, 1, 1; 1, 4, 9; III, 1, 85; III, 2, 123; III, 1, 26; VII, 1, 39.
9. Ayodhyā inscription of Dhanadeva, *JBORS*, X, 203, 2; *Ep. Ind.*, XX, 54.
10. *Mahābhāṣya*, I, 1, 1; II, 1, 36.

northern India, which is represented by one used during the time of Kuṣāṇa ruler Vasiṣka.[11]

The domestic or *gṛhya* sacrifices (domestic purification combined with temporal duties and customs) were also in vogue during the period concerned. Both Manu[12] and Patañjali[13] mention *pāka-yajña*. The former refers to four different kinds of this *yajña*. The same *yajña* figures in the *sūtra* literature (*c*. 600-200 BC) too but with little variation. The *Āśvalāyana Gṛhyasūtra* refers to three kinds of *pāka-yajña*, which include the offering or sacrifice over the fire, feeding of the brāhmaṇas, etc.[14] Gautama mentions seven forms of this *yajña* which were performed on the new and full moon days on the occasion of funeral oblations, etc.[15] According to the *Āpastamba Gṛhyasūtra*, this *yajña* stands for the ceremonies intimately connected with worldly life.[16] But Max Müller holds that the general name of the sacrifice performed according to *Gṛhyasūtra* is *pāka-yajña* which is not in the sense of cooking but signifies either small or good or excellent or perfect because "these ceremonies impart to every man that peculiar fitness without which he would be excluded from the sacrifices and from all the benefits of his religion".[17]

The importance of *pañca-mahā-yajña* has also been focussed by Manu,[18] Yājñavalkya[19] and Patañjali.[20] It was sacred duty of every householder to observe this ceremony. The five daily *mahāyajña*s were *brahma* (the study of the Vedas), *deva* (the sacrifices offered to Goda), *pitṛ* (the offering of water), *bhūta* (the sacrifice offered to the *bhūta*s) and *nṛyajña* or *atithiyajña* (the hospitable reception of guests).[21] Actually, the period concerned marked the revival of sacrificial religion. The necessity of a definite and authoritative ritual was felt, because the sacrifices had been out of use for a long time.

---

11. J. Vogel, *Catalogue of the Mathura Museum*, no. Q. 13.
12. II, 86.
13. IV, 2, 35.
14. 1, 1, 23.
15. V, 1; VIII, 18.
16. 1, 9, 26.
17. *HASL*, pp. 180-81. For details see E.J. Rapson (ed.), *CHI*, vol. I. *Ant. Ind.*, pp. 204-8.
18. III, 69, 70.
19. 1, 20.
20. IV, 1, 33.
21. *Manu.*, III, 70.

The true knowledge of *yajñaśāstra* was absolutely necessary.[22] That is why, an allusion to *jñaña-yajña* has been explicitly made in the *Manu-Smṛti*.[23]

Equally important was the *soma-yajña*s which were performed in India according to established norms. According to Manu, only those who had enough stock of food to maintain their families and dependents for three years or so, were entitled to perform this particular *yajña*.[24]This kind of practice was followed probably to ascertain the economic prosperity of an individual in the society. This can be further corroborated by the statement of *bhāṣyakāra*. He has also stated that the privilege of drinking *soma* was granted to only those in whose family "no one had suffered social degradation during the preceding three generations".[25]

Manu has strongly defended the animal sacrifices performed in the Vedic tradition. His basics philosophy is this that the God has created animals for sacrifices; such sacrifices or *yajña*s are performed for the material prosperity of the world and, therefore, the slaughter of animals is not tantamount to any sin.[26] The ordinance of meat-eating or killing animals in those days was restrictive and not injunctive. The society vigorously pursued the Vedic system of sacrifices and *karmakāṇḍa*. That is why, M. Elphinstone observed that "the religion of Manu is that of Vedas".[27] Manu has equated Āryāvartta with *yajñīyadeśa* — "country distinguished for its sacrifices". Further, he has referred to Mlecchadeśa — country not known for *yajña*.[28]

The observance of penances (*prāyaścitta*) for non-performance of sacrifices had become customary in India in the time of Manu. "There was no sharp division of secular and religious law in archaic system of jurisprudence, and hence they prescribed religious penances even for secular offences. The sinner emancipates himself from sin by honest confessions and cordial repentance for his past action. . . ."[29]

---

22. *Manu*, IV, 22.
23. IV, 24.
24. XI, 7-8.
25. B.N. Puri, *India in the Time of Patañjali*, p. 163; *Mahābhāṣya*, IV, 1, 93.
26. 5, 3, 9.
27. "The Age of Manu and the Vedas", in *Ancient India* (Vārāṇasī, 1983), p. 3.
28. II, 23, See also V.S. Agrawala, *India as described by Manu*, pp. 32-33.
29. V.S. Agrawala, *op. cit.*, p. 33.

Manu has provided a long list of sins for the expiation of which one had to undergo different forms of penances. It covers a much wider range than crimes punishable by Courts.[30] There is remarkable similarity in the details furnished in the *Manu Saṁhitā* and the *Baudhāyana Dharmasūtra* about the penances. The importance of penances gradually began to decline, as it appears from the absence of details in the *Mahābhāṣya*.

The duration of sacrifices varied from time to time, and the sacrificial rituals were too elaborate and complicated to satisfy the common people. However, the priests used to play very conspicuous role in the successful completion of the ceremonies. During the time of Manu, the sixteen priests and the five sacrificial fire-pits[31] were indispensable for the performances of different *yajña*s discussed above. The priests used to perform their duties on the principle of partnership, which is an example of corporate actions.[32] "The respective share of each in the dakshina or sacrificial fee was pre-determined, and disputes concerning its division were settled in the law courts."[33] The sacrifices were sometimes managed by common funds on behalf of corporations (*pūga-yajña*), villages (*grāmayājaka*), and the *gaṇās* (*gaṇānām caiva yājakaḥ*).[34]

The priestly functions were manifold. They were supposed to build the altar, to prepare sacrificial vessels, to fetch water and wood, to kindle the fire, to offer oblations, to recite the *mantra*s and to bring the animals to the sacrificial post and to sacrifice them. The duties and functions of the priests and the rituals described in the *Mahābhāṣya*[35] go well in accord with what we find in the Vedic literature.[36] This shows that there was not much difference between the Vedic system of religion and the system, which had evolved during the times of Manu and Patañjali.

The deities of Vedic pantheon were worshipped along with the new gods and goddesses during their times. The Vedic deities, like Indra, Varuṇa, Agni, Māruta, Prajāpati and Soma were propitiated during the times of both. But at the same time the worship of

30. *Manu.*, XI, 54-66, 165, 194 and 227.
31. *Ibid.*, II, 231; VI, 9; VIII, 210.
32. *Ibid.*, VIII, 4.
33. *Ibid.*, VII, 206-10. Patañjali (*Mahābhāṣya*, VI, 2, 38) also mentions the amount of *dakṣiṇā* given to brāhmaṇas.
34. *Ibid.*, III, 151; III, 164, IV, 205; V.S. Agrawala, *op. cit.*, pp. 33
35. I, 1, 1; II, 2, 49.
36. *R̥gveda*, 1, 15, 3; II, 1, 2; 1, 94, 6; II, 5, 2; X, 41, 3; *Ait. Br.*, VI, 3.,10; VI, 10; 7. 16, etc. *Śat. Br.*, III, 8, 2, 1; IV, 3, 4, 22; IV, 6, 66 etc.; *Taitt. Saṁ.*, 1, 8, 18, 1; III, 3, 1; *Taitt. Br.*, 1, 8, 2, 3; *Vāj. Saṁ*, X, 21.

some new deities were also introduced. During the time of Manu, Antaka or Yama, Indu, Viśvadeva, Brahmā, Kuhu, Dhanvantari, Anumati, Śrī, Bhadrakālī, Vāstoṣpati, Divacara, etc., were also worshipped.[37] By the time of Patañjali the worship of Vāyu, Sūrya, Rudra, Āditya, Viṣṇu, Śiva (under different names), the Sun and the Moon, Brahmaprajāpati, Kṛṣṇa, Lakṣmī, etc., had become very popular.[38] Patañjali also refers to the festive gatherings, which were held at that time in the temples of Rāma and Keśava (identified with Balarāma and Kṛṣṇa).[39]

One of the notable features of the Indian religious system of that time was the construction of temples and installation of images therein for the worship. Manu refers to the temples dedicated to gods. According to him, any damage caused either to a temple or to an idol was considered to be a cognisable offence. The new temples were erected under the care of king. The people used to worship the gods especially on festive occasions. It is curious to note that the "Brāhmaṇas employed in the worship of gods in temples were disqualified from havya and kavya ceremonies". It also appears that the devotees were not so particular about the maintenance of the temples which is substantiated by the reference to temples left in a deserted conditions.[40]

The worship of the images in the temples continued unabated up to the time of Patañjali. The selling of images was strictly prohibited. The worship of the divinities — "Śivaḥ", "Skandaḥ", "Viśākhaḥ" in the temples can very well be confirmed by other evidence too. Kauṭilya also refers to the installation of images of Śiva and Vaiśravana in temples.[41] The reference to the Mauryas selling objects of worship for obtaining gold in the *Mahābhāṣya* (*mauryair hiraṇyārthibhir arcaḥ prakalpitaḥ*) points to the worship of images and the quality of metal used for making these images.[42]

The people also used to worship the demi-gods or semi-divine beings because of fear of their destructive power. These gods include *sādhyas*, *pitṛs*, *apsarās*, *gandharvas*, *yakṣas*, *rākṣasas*, *piśācas*, *guhyakas* and *vaimānikas*.[43] The worship of *yakṣas* and the

---

37. *Manu.*, III, 87; III, 88; III, 90; III, 194-99; III, 217.
38. 1, 2, 45; 1, 1, 1; VI, 3, 26; 1, 1, 39; 1, 1, 4; 1, 2, 45; 1, 1, 1; II, 2, 11; 4, 4, 10; VI, 1, 108; III, 2, 207; VIII, 3, 82; III, 134; III, 2, 15; VI, 4, 77; VI, 1, 7; VI, 2, 7, etc.
39. II, 2, 34.
40. III, 285; IV, 152-53; IV, 46; VIII, 248; IX, 290.
41. II, 4.
42. V, 3, 99.
43. *Manu.*, XII, 47-48.

nāgas remained popular for a considerable period of time. The carvings of such demi-gods on the Bhārhut gateway and in the railings of Sāñcī and the findings of numerous statues bearing inscriptions testify to the popularity of this minor religious cult. The worship of particularly the *yakṣas* became associated with images, temples, offerings, etc. Later, they were worshipped together with the *nāgas* and goddesses. Such practice became finally based on the cult of *bhakti*.

The ancestor worship constitutes an important aspect of the popular religious life of the *Smṛti* period. This finds reflection in the form of *pitṛ-yajña*, which was more important *ṛta* than that of the worship of gods.[44]

India in the time of Patañjali witnessed the growth of the two popular religious cults (the Śaiva and the Vaiṣṇava) of Hinduism. There is a clear indication in the *Mahābhāṣya* to the prevalence of "Śaivism" at that time. The popularity of the cult of Śaiva is well attested to by the presence of two different categories of devotees of Śiva, known as "Śiva Bhāgavata" and "Śiva-Vaiśravaṇau". The members of the former group used to carry an iron lance signifying trident or *triśūla*, which is still a popular emblem of this deity. They also had faith in practising penance. But, on the other hand, the devotees of other group propitiated the deity simply by offerings.[45] It seems that phallic worship was not at all popular at that time. Patañjali in his commentary on Pāṇini's *Aṣṭādhyāyī* (IV, 1, 49; IV, 1, 112; V, 3, 99) refers to Rudra, Bhava, Sarva and Śiva. He describes Śiva as a *laukika-devatā* (folk-god) exactly like that of Skanda-Viśākha. His interpretations of Pāṇini's *Sūtra* (V, 3, 99) prove beyond doubt that the worship of Śiva was more popular than that of his phallic emblem among the common people.

The Bhāgavata cult whose antiquity goes back to much earlier period also flourished during the time of Patañjali. Viṣṇu, the well-known Vedic deity, was identified with Vāsudeva, Nārāyaṇa and Kṛṣṇa generally called by the name of Vāsudeva-Bhāgavata cult, which clearly denotes the existence of Vaiṣṇavism. Viṣṇu enjoyed a very high position amongst votaries of the Bhāgavata cult. Vāsudeva was associated with Baladeva and the Vṛṣṇis. Actually, the sense applied by Patañjali is different. Here he takes them as sons of Vāsudeva and Baladeva. He also mentions the names of Kṛṣṇa and Janārdana as synonyms of Vāsudeva. He further refers to festive gatherings held in the temples of Keśava (Vāsudeva) and Rāma (Balarāma). The frequent allusion to the names of Viṣṇu, Vāsudeva and Kṛṣṇa in the *Mahābhāṣya* are indicative of the prevalence of worship of

44. *Manu.*, III, 203.

45. V, 2, 76; *Ind. Ant.*, XLI, p. 272, also B.N. Puri, *op. cit.*, p. 176.

Viṣṇu in various menifestations. Actually, the Vedic god Viṣṇu later became synonym of Vāsudeva.[46] The identification of Vāsudeva and Kṛṣṇa with Viṣṇu has also been supported by Keith.[47] Pāṇini as a *sūtrakāra* also refers to Vāsudeva and Kṛṣṇa.[48] As a matter of fact, the concept of Bhāgavatism was nothing new to this period. The religious concept of the epic and Purāṇic ages associated with the *bhakti* cult culminated in the time of Patañjali. R.G. Bhandarkar[49] has referred to two popular religious movements in this connection, one in the east and other in western India.

The archaeological evidence also confirms the popularity of the Bhāgavata cult in the second century BC. The Ghasundi Stone Slab found about four miles north-east of Nāgarī in the Udaipur State of Rajasthan bearing inscription in Brāhmī characters of the second century BC bears witness to the erection of a stone enclosure of worship for Bhāgavata Saṁkarṣana and Vāsudeva.[50]

Along with Śaivism and Vaiṣṇavism the Buddhism and Jainism also flourished in the second century BC. The famous *stūpa*s at Bhārhūt and Sāñcī, the former with its railing and *toraṇa*s and the latter with railing alone, bear testimony to uninterrupted growth of Buddhism and unhampered activities of the Buddhists who were noted for their endowments during the period concerned. On the basis of the evidence furnished in the Buddhist text[51] about the persecution of the Buddhists and the destruction of the earlier Sāñcī *stūpa* and other monuments by the brāhmaṇa rulers of the Śuṅga dynasty, the co-existence of Buddhism and Brāhmaṇism during the period concerned became debatable subject. The anti-Buddhist attitude of Brāhmaṇical Śuṅga monarch, Puṣyamitra, was highlighted in various sources. The purpose behind incorporation of such facts in the Buddhist literature was possibly to create an impression that the first Śuṅga monarch followed the policy of religious persecution against the doctrine of Buddhism propounded by Aśoka only for raising the status of brāhmaṇas. But we do not find any positive evidence to confirm this hypothetical belief. The Brāhmaṇical Śuṅga rulers were extending the liberal patronage to the Buddhists.

---

46. *Mahābhāṣya*, IV, I, 114; V, 1, 144; VI, 3, 5; III, 1, 26; B.N. Puri, *op. cit.*, pp. 172-73.
47. *JRAS*, (1908), pp. 169f.
48. IV, 3, 98, VI, 2, 148.
49. *Vaishnavism, Saivism and Minor Religious Systems* (Strassburg, 1913), pp. 9f. See also his article, "Allusions to Kṛṣṇa in Patañjali's *Mahābhāsya*", *Ind. Ant.*, III, pp. 14f.
50. H. Luders, "List of Brāhmī Inscriptions from the earliest times to the Second Century AD", *Ep. Ind.*, X (Calcutta, 1910), App. N.6.
51. *Divyāvadāna* (ed. by E.B. Cowell and R.A. Neil, Cambridge, 1896), pp. XXIX, 433.3.

The reference to *ācārīyakula* ("a Buddhist school") and *ānnācārīyakula* ("the other school") in one of the inscriptions on the railing of the Sāñcī *stūpa*[52] proves the existence of different schools of religion in India in the second century BC. Kern has rightly observed that "in the three centuries which elapsed between the death of Asok and the reign of Kanishka, Buddhism was steadily on the increase in the North, flourishing in the domains of the Bactrian Greeks".[53]

The Hāthigumphā inscription of king Khārvela of Kaliṅga[54] reveals the flourishing state of Jainism in the middle of the second century BC. The followers of this school of religion enjoyed the patronage of king Khārvela and other donors. During the period concerned the ascetic orders also flourished some of which figure in the *Mahābhāṣya*. Mathurā was another important centre of Jainism.

From the preceding discussion it is quite evident that the Vedic system of religion continued up to the middle of the second century BC so far as the sacrifices, *yajña*s, rituals, priesthood and pantheism are concerned. Actually, the period concerned witnessed the revival of the Vedic tradition in the field of religious practices. This also shows the impact of the Vedic culture on the contemporary Indian society. There is hardly any contradiction in the statements of Manu and Patañjali so far as the above aspects are concerned, rather both have highlighted the basic philosophy of religion more or less in the same fashion. The introduction of image-worship and the construction and preservation of Hindu temples were essential features of the religious system which continued from the time of Manu to Patañjali. During the time of Patañjali in particular, Śaivism and Bhāgavatism also flourished. One of the notable developments in the second century BC was the co-existence of Hinduism. Buddhism and Jainism. The period under review was no doubt eventful in the cultural history of ancient India. It constitutes the synthesis of the religious systems of both the Vedic and post-Vedic times.

---

52. *JBORS*, III, pp. 425f; B.N. Puri, *op. cit.*, p. 183.

53. *Manual of Indian Buddhism*, p. 48, cf. B.N. Puri, *op. cit.*, p. 183.

54. *JBORS*, III, pp. 425f; B.M. Baura, *Old Brāhmi inscriptions in the Udaigiri and Khandagiri caves*, pp. 28f. See also J.G. Buhler, "Sañcī Votive Inscriptions", *Ep. Ind.*, II, pp. 88 ff. The earliest inscription found and ed. by Buhler has been assigned to the middle of the second century BC.

PART III
Political History : Some Landmarks

7

Pre-Persian Foreign Expeditions of North-western India

THE foreign expeditions of north-western India successively undertaken by the Egyptians under Sesostris and the Assyrians under Semiramis before the time of Cyrus (*c.* BC. 558-530), king of Persia, still go unrecorded in ancient history of India. As a matter of fact, they are enveloped in haziness because of manifold reasons. The primary reason for this may precisely be attributed to conflicting, confusing and contradictory accounts of the classical geographers and historians alluding to the subject under discussion. The history and mythology or facts and fictions have been jumbled up to such an extent that sometimes we are led to doubt the value of even credible and faithful accounts presented with minuteness, accuracy and precision. The classical scholars had some sort of tradition of accusing each other as liar. Some of them are stigmatised as fabulist writers. It is also remarkable that some considerable portions of the original classical texts in general have been lost for unknown reasons. That is why, some missing links in the classical description of India are generally found.

It is further striking to note that some classical writers in an attempt to glorify the Hellenistic Age, to magnify the success of the Macedonians and to minify or belittle the achivements of Pre-Persian as well as the Persian monarchs went to such an extent of distorting the historical truth that whole picture of the subject appears to be dim and topsy-turvey. Thomas Maurice[1] has also dealt with this aspect of the subject. The avowed objective behind such exercise was to highlight the glorious deeds of the Macedonians and to push into background the success of invaders of Pre-Alexanderian period. As for

1. *Indian Antiquities or Dissertations of Hindostan*, vol. I, pp. 138-39.

instance, both Megasthenes[2] and Arrian[3] tried to create an impression that before the Macedonaian invasions led by Alexander India was neither invaded nor conquered by any foreign power except Hercules and Dionysos. The Egyptian, the Assyrian and the Persian rulers could not execute their imperialistic designs. No great conqueror approached Indian borders which is far enough from the truth. This is not only an inconsistent approach but also deliberate distortion and falsification of historical truth on the part of the both Megasthenes and Arrian. Eratosthenes[4] considers them incredible and fabulous. Both Hercules and Dionysos, purely mythical figures, have been misunderstood as historical personages. Even well-proven fact that Cyrus launched his campaign in Baluchistan (Gedrosia), conquered Bactria and some portions of Kābul valley (Archosia) in north-western India including Kapisa city (Kapisa-Kanti mentioned in the Bahistun Inscription of Darius *c.* 522-486 BC) and Gāndhāra[5] has not been given due recognition which will suffice to reflect the lack of their perfect historical sense. Megasthenes also tried to impress upon our mind that we should not repose our faith in the ancient history of India which is really very obnoxious. This is also ridiculous that at one stage or the other they deny the same statement which they affirm. E.J. Rapson's[6] view that there is no evidence to show that any foreign powers of western Asia extended their political sway to the east as far as India until the time of Cyrus is also misleading to some extent. Max Müller's[7] statement that Sesostris and Semiramis, who were the conquerors of great antiquity, did not disturb the peace of the Āryan settlers in north-western India also lacks clarity of thought. It does not help us much to make out anything positive of it in this context.

These are possibly the reasons because of which the subject under review attracted the attention of very few scholars, oriental as well as occidental. However, distortions and confusions should not be allowed to mar the prospect of historical reconstruction

---

2. Bk. IV, Fragm. XLVI (Epit. 23.6) cf. *MAIMA*, pp. 4-5, 107-9; See also Strabo, *Geogr.*, XV, 1.6-8, pp. 686-88; E.J. Rapson (ed.), *CHI*, vol. I, *Ancient India*, pp. 296-97.
3. *Indika*, Pt. I, Ch. V, cf. *MAIMA*, pp. 194-95; See also *Indika*, V, 4-7; IX, 10 cf. *CHI*, vol. I, p. 297.
4. Cf. *MAIMA*, pp. 109-10.
5. J. Gilmore (ed.), *Fragments of Ctesias" Persica*, Bk. X, Fragm. 37, pp. 133-35; Xenophon's *Cyropaedia*, ed. & tr. W. Miller, I. 1.4; 6, 20, 21; O. Hude (ed.), *Herodotus' History*, III, 88; I, 177; Rennell *GSH*, vol. I, pp. 303-5.
6. *Ancient India from the Earliest Times to the first century AD*, p. 43.
7. *The Vedas*, p. 3.

wherever it may be deemed necessary. Any way, the classical accounts of the subject concerned as supplemented and confirmed by other interested scholars of great eminence are no doubt worthy of our credence to a considerable extent. Hence we find ample scope for making fresh attempt to deal with the subject in a very objective and dispassionate manner by placing our reliance on the statements furnished by Nearchos (*c.* 325 BC) in his *Journal of Voyage*, Magasthenes (*c.* 321-297 BC), Arrian (second century AD), Strabo (*c.* 64 BC- AD 21), Diodorus Siculus (first century BC), Pliny (*c.* AD 23-79) and other collateral evidence. All possible attempt has been made to analyse the available data and critically examine the historical validity of varying statements.

Sesostris, the greatest of the early kings of Egypt, extended his conquests to different parts of the world even to the land of the Ganges and to Skythia. Diodorus in his Universal History named *Bibliotheke* or *Bibliotheca Historica* calls him Sysoosis and observes that "he first conquered the Ethiopians and made them tributary and then he sent forth a fleet of 400 ships into the Red Sea, by the help of which he gained all its islands and subdued the neighbouring nations as far as to India, while marching by land route he conquered all Asia. He not only invaded all those nations which Alexander (the Macedonian) afterwards subdued, but even others whose territories he entered with great difficulties. He passed over the river Ganges and likewise pierced through all India to the main ocean and subdued the Skythians as far as the Tanais which divides Europe from Asia".[8]

In order to test the credibility of this classical tradition we shall also have to ascertain the views of those scholars who have dealt with the subject to a considerable degree.

R. Montgomery Martin,[9] while supporting the statement as recorded by Diodorus Sicilus, has clearly stated that Sesostris' expedition of India was successful and disastrous. All the countries stretching along the Erythrean or Arabian Sea to India were subjugated by his commercial people with help of naval power. He himself led his army through Asia and being everywhere crowned with victory crossed the Ganges and advanced to the Indian Ocean. He spent nine years in this expedition and exacted no other tokens of submission from the conquered nations except the tribute, which were being sent annually to Egypt. The primary purpose behind this expedition of India was an extension of Maritime commerce. But his success proved to be contrary to his expectation.

---

8. Bk. I, C. 4, pp. 62-64; also *MAICL*, p. 11, fn. 1.
9. *The History of the Indian Empire*, vol. I, p. 19.

Henry Beveridge, while proving Diodorus, account as preserved in his *Bibliotheca* very valuable and authentic, confirms his statement. He has further elaborated that Sesostris was invader of indefatigable industry and unflinching courage and high ambition. Immediately after having ascended the throne in 1500 BC he collected an army consisting of 6,00,000. Infantry, 24,000 cavalry, 27,000 war chariots and a fleet of 1,000 ships and resolved to conquer the different parts of world. He continued his voyage as far as India and his victorious army reached eastward not only to the frontier of India but beyond the Ganges. On his return he installed pillars in various places with inscriptions attesting to his victories.[10] Herodotus, (II, 102-11) account concerning both the maritime and land expeditions of Sesostris bears strong testimony in favour of Diodorus. In fact, he confirms his statement. A.K. Majumdar[11] has also corroborated this classical account of India.

It ought to be observed that the above narrative, which Diodorus admits to be very reliable of all the accounts circulated in Egypt, has been contradicted by the classical writers as well as other scholars because of some palpable discrepancy and extravagence on the face of it. Strabo[12] and Arrian[13] do not give any credence to this account as recorded by Diodorus. Robertson[14] has discredited it as an invention of the Egyptian priests. According to him, the whole account of Sesostris expedition of India is fabulous. In other sorce[15] he has been considered as a legendary figure in the history of Egypt. On the other hand, Henry Beveridge remarks that "To reject a statement thus supported because some flaws may be picked in particular parts of it, is to strike at the foundation of human testimony, and countenance the captious quibbling process under which all ancient history, sacred as well as profane runs some risk of being converted into a myth. The fair conclusion concerning the Indian expedition of Sesostris seems to be that they really took place, but that in the accounts given of them, both the means which he employed and the extent of country which he subdued or traversed are exaggerated".[16]

---

10. *A Comprehensive History of India*, vol. I, pp. 22-24.
11. *Early Hindu India : A Dynastic Study*, vol. I, p. 29.
12. *Geogr.*, XV, I, 6, cf. *MAICL*, p. 11.
13. Cf. *MAIMA*, p. 195.
14. *An Historical Disquisition concerning Ancient India*, pp. 6, and 289-91, App. Note I.
15. *En. Br.*, 1768, vol. 20, p. 262.
16. *Op. cit.*, p. 24.

It has been further observed that "such vague traditions probably represent a racial memory of actual historical events, distorted, of course, as to all details".[17]

The problems relating to identification of Sesostris and the antiquity of his Indian expedition must be dealt with for the sake of judging the historical authenticity of the classical accounts. He has been generally identified with Ramses the Great, the third king of the nineteenth dynasty of Manetho, the son of Seti and the father of Menephthah (the pharaoh). Lep-Sius, however, from the study of the Tablet of Rameses II found at Abydos in Egypt (now in British Museum) has identified him with the Sesortasen or Osirtasen of the great 12th dynasty.[18] According to Wilkinson, Ramses II ruled between 1311 and 1245 BC.[19] An epigraphic evidence further testifies to his existence as a historical personage. In an Egyptian inscription in the tomb of Khnumhotep II at Benihasen, Sesostris II is ascirbed to 1900 BC.[20]

George Rawlinson also describes him as a "great conqueror, who traversed the whole continent of Asia. The pillars erected by him in the conquered countries for the most part disappeared". He has referred to him as the first king of the 12th dynasty but, on the other hand, also connects him with the 19th dynasty.[21]

The plausible conclusion which we can derive from the above account is that Sesostris expedition of India is not absolutely unfounded. It may be one of the mysteries of history. But it is very difficult to determine the location which was conquered and year in which the event took place.

The history of Indian expedition of the great Assyrian queen Semiramis (wife of king Ninus) has been fairly illustrated by Diodorus (ii, 16-20) on the authority of the *Assyriaka* of Ktesias the Knidian (*c.* 416-398 BC). Having learned that India was the greatest and richest country in the world and was ruled by a powerful monarch called Staurobates or Stratobates who was well equipped with innumerable hostes of soldiers and a great number of well-trained elephant, she resolved to attempt the subjugation of India in order to prove her prowess and majesty. It is stated that she set out on her Indian expedition from Bactria or Balkh (dependency of the Assyro-Persic empire) and

17. Henry Smith Williams (ed.), *HHW*, vol. I, p. 146.
18. *RPICO*, p. 44; *MAICL*, p. 11, fn. 1; *MAIMA*, pp. 108-9; Baveridge, *op. cit.*, p. 22.
19. *American Cyclopedia*, vol. XIV, p. 521 cf. B.N. Puri, *India as Described by Early Greek Writers*, p. 2, fn. 3.
20. *Periplus*, pp. 51 and 192.
21. *History of Herodotus*, vol. II, pp. 143, 145, 148 & 151.

on reaching the Indus defeated Staurobates, the Indian king, in a naval engagement fought on the bank of that river. It is also stated that the king of India built four thousand boats of reeds, which grew about the river Indus. However, she was less succeesful when fighting on land and was eventually compelled to return to Bactria after losing two-thirds of her vast army.[22] Actually, she took three years in assembling and immense army drawn from all the provinces of her extensive empire. The country west of the Indus was already subject to her power. But in order to cross that mighty river an immense number of ships were necessary. She brought shipbuilders from Phoenicia, Syria and Persia and asked them to sent to frontier of the Indus 2000 ships, which were put in array against the naval force of the Indian. Everything being ready she marched from Bactria with large number of troops. Diodorus quoting Ctesias as his authority states the fabulous number of 30,00,000 infantry, 5,00,000 cavalry and 1,00,000 war chariots and 1,00,000 camels. Because of having fear of elephants of Indian king she had recourse to a singular stratagem. The camels were made to resemble elephants being covered with the skins of oxen. This device was employed to delude the Indians into the belief that invading forces are superior to them in this respect. Further, by this device she hoped that the Indians would be terror struck on seeing themselves opposed to this force.

However, Staurobates, the king of the countries bordering the Indus, on receiving the intelligence of the intended invasion assembled his troops. Besides a land force scarcely less numerous that of Semiramis and headed by a formidable array of elephants, his fleet composed of 4,000 vessels constructed out of reeds or bamboos covered the river. On the eastern bank of the Indus the first encounter took place and a great naval battle was fought. The victory was long undecided but at length it went in favour of the warlike queen possibly because of superior naval skill of the Phoenician and Cypriot sailors. The Indian Staurobates with the loss of a large portion of his fleet and an immense carnage of his soldiers was obliged to withdraw and leave the passage of the river free. The queen Semiramis immediately caused a bridge of boats to be constructed and crossing with her whole army hastened forward with the hope of soon completing the conquest which she had so successfully begun. Staurobates, however, had no idea of tendering his submission before the invader and stood prepared for her approach. At first in the general engagement which ensued, the Indians were greatly disconcerted at the appearance of the fictitious elephants and a king of panic took place. In fact, the counterfeit elephants

22. *MAICL*, p. 10, fn. 4 and pp. 59-60, fn. 4; See also Eng. tr. of Diodorus' work by C.H. Oldfather, Leeb. Classical Library, London, 1933; *MAIT*, *CAP*, 11, p. 271.

marched in the front and created great alarm. But this trick and deceptive device was soon revealed by some deserters from the camp. Thereafter the Indians recovered their spirits. A fierce contest ensued in which the Assyrians had at first some advantage but were eventually totally overthrown. Most of her army perished in the field or in attempting to regain the right bank of the Indus river. She herself being severely wounded during a personal encounter with Staurobates made her escape with shattered dream and humbled pride accompanied by a handful of troops to her own dominion. Thus notwithstanding the enormous extent of her preparation her expedition against India terminated in her discomfiture and she dreamed no more of crowning her fame by an another conquest of India.[23]

As Diodorus borrowed the account from Ctesias, who is said to have extracted it from Persian records, it is not improbable that its basis of fact has been overlaid with the embellishment which usually adorn a Persian tale. Some exaggeration is, of course, apparent in some parts of the narrative particularly in case of enormous army of the Queen. That is why, Walter Raleigh[24] regards the strength of her army more fictitious than real. Sometimes grave doubts have been raised as to the individual existence of Semiramis because she is erroneously believed to have been a creation of Assyrian mythology. However, it is impossible to doubt that the whole account of the Indian expedition of Semiramis as highly coloured. Actually, the kernel of attested fact with later accretion of fabulous history created lot of confusion. With regard to Semiramis recent discoveries of ruins and decipherment of inscription have proved her existence as a historical personage beyond doubt.

Apart from Diodorus other classical authors have also presented trustworthy account of this expedition. Nearchos (Admiral of Alexander) who is generally acknowledged as the most scrupulous and honest in depicting the result of his exploration is a pirncipal authority on the subject. His memoirs have been lost but their contents have been in great measures preserved in the works of Strabo and Arrian.

Nearchos maintains that the far famed Assyrian Queen Semiramis and the Persian king Cyrus led expeditions against the Indians through Gedrosia (Baluchistan) but both had been forced to retreat the former escaping with twenty men and the latter with only seven. This fact was related to Alexander by the inhabitants of the Gedrosia which he

23. H. Beveridge, *op. cit.*, pp. 24-25; See also Trotter's *History of India*, pp. 28-29.

24. *History of the World*, p. 125.

was planning to march through it. He was told that "no one had ever before escaped with an army by this route excepting Semiramis on her flight from India".[25] Alexander having felt inspired by the exploits of his predecessors thought that it would be a glorious achievement if he led his victorious army through those countries and nations where Semiramis and Cyrus had suffered such great disasters.

The account of Nearchos has been strongly supported by Arrian.[26] Justin[27] has also emphatically asserted that "no one invaded India except Semiramis and Alexander". E.A. Schwanbeck[28] Corroborates this statement. Arrian in another faithful account expressely states that the Indians between the river Indus and the river Cophen or Kābul were in ancient times subject to the Assyrians, the Persians and Macedonians. It is indeed a fact that the country on the right bank of upper Indus was subject to Assyrian rule and paid tribute to them. According to him, the two Indian tribes the Astakenoi and Assakenoi — (Aśvakas) dwelling in the regions beyondthe Indus river on the west extending up to Kābul in ancient times acknowledged the sovereignty of the Assyrians.[29]

Arrian's statement contains some substratum of truth. Because these tribes had been living in this region since time immemorial. The mention of Aśvakas in the *Mahābhārata*, the Purāṇas and Pāṇini's *Grammar* (Aśvakānāmvataḥ II, 2, 31) amply substantiate the primaeval antiquity of this group of tribes of north-west India. The numismatic evidence[30] also confirm the existence of these tribes in the north-west India. It may reasonably be suggested that these tribes might have played some role in repulsing the invasion of the Assyrian Queen, Semiramis, under the leadership of their king Staurobates, who has not yet been properly identified. A.K. Majumdar has identified him with Sthavarpati[31] which seems to be a hypothetical one. But he has no doubt

---

25. Cf. Strabo, *Geogr.*, XV, I, 5; XV, II, 5, *MAICL*, pp. 10-11 and 84 respectively; H.C. Hamilton and W. Falconer (trs.), Strabo's *Geography*, pp. 686-722; See also J.W. McCrindle, *CNES*, pp. 153-54, 186-87.
26. *Anabasis* (Eng. tr. by E.J. Chinnock, VI, 24, 2, 3; *Indika*, Pt. I, C. 5.4; Pt. II, Chs. XVIII ff; See also *CHI*, vol. I, p. 296; B.N. Puri, *op.cit.*, p. 3, fn. 1.
27. F. Ruehl (ed.), Justin's *Historiae Philippicae*, I, 29 cf. *CHI*. I, p. 297.
28. *Megasthenis' Indika*, p. 13. He quotes a passage from Justinus (I, ii,10) in support of his contention; See *MAIMA*, p. 11.
29. *Indika*, Pt. I, Ch. I, cf. *MAIMA*, p. 179 and *CHI*, vol. I, p. 297.
30. A. Cunningham, *Co. An. Ind.*, p. 61, pl. II.17; V.A. Smith, *CCIM*, vol. I, p. 157.
31. *Op. cit.*, vol. II, pp. 367-68; See also *HHW*, vol. II.

supported the statement of the classical authors. M. Elphinstone[32] also confirms the account of Arrian.

The classical accounts concerning the Indians expedition of Assyrian Queen Semiramis has been further supported be many competent authorities like Henry Beveridge,[33] Montgomery Martin,[34] H.H. Wilson[35] and A.H.L. Heeren.[36]

We have also an archaeological evidence to prove the historical authenticity of this account. According to Pliny, Arachotus, a celebrated city, was founded by Semiramis[37] the remains of which, M. Court says, are to be seen on the Arghasan river, four farsangs from Kandahār, on the road to Shikarpur.[38]

St. Martin at his first instance thought that Diodorus Siculus' (II, 16-19) account of the expedition of Semiramis has almost the character of a legend abounding with peculiarities and entirely destitute of those geographical details which stamp events with reality but further on the basis of epigraphic record he was constrained to change his judgement. The Cuneiform Inscription of Niveveh throws so much unexpected light on the ancient history of Asia. The positive chronology drawn from this inscription fully confirms the indication given by Herodotus as to epoch of Semiramis (a celebrated Assyrian queen) which is the eighth century BC.[39]

The eighth century BC may undoubtedly be considered as an epochmaking event in the ancient history of north-western India. This epoch is quite in harmony with the data which we possess from other sources regarding the condition of north-west India in the post-Vedic period. The classical accounts of this expedition is interwoven in the oriental tradition of the east. Whatever be the real historical character of the expeditions of Semiramis and Cyrus, it is certain that their conquests of the Indus were only temporary acquisitions.

---

32. "The Greek Accounts of India", rept. from his *The History of India*, ed. by E.B. Cowell, 9th edn. (London, 1911) in *Ancient India* (Delhi, 1983), Ch.III, p. 13, see also pp. 11-12, note 3.
33. *Op. cit.*, pp. 24-27.
34. *Op. cit.*, vol.I, p. 19.
35. *Ar. Ant.*, pp. 126-27.
36. *Historical Researches*, vol. I, *Asiatic Nations*, p. 424; vol. II, p. 211; vol. III, p. 387 (He has clearly mentioned Semiramis' conquest of Bāhlika or Bactria in N.W. India); See also H.H. Wilson, *op. cit.*, p. 163.
37. *Nat. Hist.*, VI, 25.
38. Cf. H.H. Wilson, *op. cit.*, p. 157, fn. 2.
39. *Etude.*, p. 14, cf. *MAIMA*, pp. 107-8.

Thus on the weight of evidence adduced here the conventional explanation submitted by Megasthenes, that Semiramis meditated on an expedition against India but died before the necessary preparation were made,[40] can be outrightly rejected. Arrian reproduced the whole mendacious account of Megasthenes[41] without showing any meticulous regard for the truth. But later on he corrected his statement already discussed above. Even Strabo who is well known for his critical faculty, judicious and reasonable approach and sound judgement appears to be hypocritical in his assessment of this expedition. He quoting Magasthenes enjoins us not to place any confidence in the account of the subject concerned. Semiramis and Cyrus, according to him, did not invade India but only approached its frontier.[42] His view is absolutely unbelievable.

The statement of Sir Halford J. Mackinder that "Indian expeditions of Semiramis and Cyrus through Mekran-barren region lying along the coast of Baluchistan may or may not be historical"[43] seems to be bit confusing. However, this confusion has been set at rest.

McCrindle's view that "the invasions of India by Semiramis and Cyrus are as mythical as those which had been ascribed to Dionysos and Herakles"[44] is neither a convincing analogy nor is it based on sound reasoning. Hence this view can be dismissed without any hesitation. Actually, his judgement is based on the impression that Diodorus had taken the legend from Kleitarchos, who accompanied Alexander in India, modified the narratives of Ktsias (Contemporary of Xenophon) and finally harmonised the both with his better knowledge of the country. Even if it is accepted, we are sure that it will not cast any shadow on the historical character of the narratives.

Duncker being influenced by the fictitious account of classical writers concerned questioned the validity of narratives of Diodorus without exhibiting any sound reasoning. But he has honestly admitted that the Assyrians extended their conquests to Ariana.[45] After a thorough investigation of the details about its geography one can obtain the result that greater portion of Ariana formed part of the Bhāratavarṣa before its occupation by the Persians.

---

40. *MAIMA*, p. 109.
41. *Indika*, Pt. I, Ch. V, cf. *MAIMA*, p. 195.
42. *Geogr.*, XV, I, 6 cf. *MAICL*, pp. 11-12.
43. *CHI*, I, p. 26.
44. *MAICL*, p. 10, fn. 4.
45. *HA*, vol. IV, pp. 375-84.

According to J.B. Bury, S.A. Cook and F.E. Adcock, the name of Semiramis is associated with classical imagination. It was Sammuramnat who was the real figure.[46] But this view is not supported by any authority. Hence this can be disposed of.

To sum up: The two aforesaid expeditions of the north-west are not the figments of classical imagination. The Assyrian expedition of north-western India undertaken in the eighth century BC. was really an epoch-making event. Some parts of Gedrosia (Baluchistan), Archosia (Afghanistan) and the regions between the Indus and Kabul were subjugated. It was a fight against the tribal people of north-western region. The Astakonoi or Assakemoi tribes acknowledged the political sway of Assyrians.

The portion of India lying along the right or west bank of the Indus formed the part of the Assyrian empire which was later on overthrown by Cyrus the great. As a sequel to this event, this portion figures as a Satrapy or province of the Persian empire. The Assyrian empire was overthrown by the Persian empire in the same manner as the latter was overthrown by the Macedonian empire. This discovery should not be made an object of doubt. Greater doubt may reasonably be entertained about the historicity of Egyptian invasion of India but the Assyrian expedition of north-west must be given due place in the pages of ancient history of India.[47]

---

46. Ed., *CAH*, vol. III, p. 27; See also D.D. Luckenbill (ed.), *ARAB*, vol. I, pp. 731-45; *En. Br.*, vol. 20, pp. 207-8.
47. See G.P. Singh, "An Analytical and Critical Study of the Classical Accounts of Foreign Expeditions of North-Western India before the Time of Cyrus (*c.* 558-530 BC) of Persia", *Research Journal (Humanities & Social Sciences)* of Manipur University, Imphal, vol. IV, no.1, 1987, p. 7.

8

Assam in the Gupta Age (*c.* AD 335-594) A Reappraisal in Ancient Indian Historical Perspecive

ASSAM known to Vālmīki, Vyāsa, Kālidāsa and *purāṇakāras* as Prāgjyotiṣa or Kāmarūpa (interchangeably) for the first time distinctly appeared on the political map of ancient India in the classical age during the time of Samudragupta (*c.* AD 335-80). The statement made by M. Arokiaswamy that the kingdom of Kāmarūpa or Assam formed part of the Maurya empire during the time of Aśoka[1] amounts to a perceptional distortion of the historical fact.

The frequent attempts made by the imperial and later Gupta monarchs to extend their political sway over the eastern kingdoms of Kāmarūpa (then under the rule of Varman dynasty) and Bengal (northern and eastern) during the period under review resulted in the transformation of the political status of former which can be proved with the help of contemporary epigraphic records and other reliable sources. Before we proceed further to throw light on this particular aspect of the subject, here it will be worthwhile to discuss two very vital questions as to which Varman ruler of Kāmarūpa was the contemporary of Samudragupta ? and whether he was defeated by the latter and his kingdom was annexed to the Gupta Empire ?

Attempts have, of course, been made by other scholars too in the past to deal with the questions concerned, but we do not find the answers given by them fully satisfactory. The divergent views expressed by them have made the confusion worse confounded. Hence, there is an imperative need to re-examine them in the light of the fresh evidence.

---

1. "The Gupta Dynasty and the Early Pallavas of Kanchi", *JIH*, vol. LVI, 1978, pt. I, p. 108.

R.G. Basak[2] and H.C. Ray[3] are of the opinion that Samudravarman (Puṣyavarman's son) was the contemporary of Samudragupta, whereas, on the other hand, R.G. Bhandarkar[4] and K.N. Dixshit[5] hold that it was Balavarman (Puṣyavarman's grandson) who was his contemporary. N.N. Vasu by placing Puṣyavarman between AD 275-300 has tried to prove that Samudragupta inflicted defeat on Balavarman.[6] N.K. Bhattasali by placing Puṣyavarman between AD 310-30 and his grandson Balavarman between AD 360-90 has also attempted to establish the contemporaneity of the latter with Samudragupta.[7] J.F. Fleet, while going a step further, has contended that Balavarman, one of the nine kings of Āryāvartta as mentioned in the Allahabad Pillar Inscription of Samudragupta and exterminated by the latter, was successor of Puṣyavarman of Kāmarūpa.[8]

None of the above views is tenable because there is no evidence on the basis of which the contemporaneity of Samudragupta either with Samudravarman or Balavarman can be conclusively proved.

As a matter of fact, it was Puṣyavarman who was the contemporary of Samudragupta. He founded the Varman dynasty under Guptan aegis in *c.* AD 355. This can be irrefutably proved with the help of an evidence furnished in *A Historical Atlas of South Asia*[9] through cartographic illustration of the subject. the fact brought to light here can also be supported by the statements of other scholars. D.C. Sircar has rightly pointed out that Puṣyavarman, the contemporary of Samudragupta, accepted the Gupta hegemony maintaining the relation that of a vassal and an overlord.[10] It has been further observed by B.M. Barua that "Puṣyavarman was the first Indo-Aryan ruler, who was set up by Samudragupta over the two territories of Kāmarūpa and Devaka, unified into a single kingdom".[11] But they have not substantiated their viewpoints on the chronological ground. K.L. Barua

2. *The History of North-Eastern India* (extending from the foundation of the Gupta Empire to the rise of the Pāla dynasty of Bengal, *c.* AD 320-760), pp. 33, 267.
3. *The Dynastic History of Northern India*, vol. I, p. 238.
4. *A Peep into the Early History of India*, p. 48.
5. *Proceedings of the 1st Oriental Conference* (Pune, 1919), 1920, vol. I, p.cxxiv.
6. *Social History of Kāmarūpa*, vol. I, p. 141.
7. *IHQ*, vol. XXI, 1945, pp. 19f; also *Ep. Ind.*, vol. XXVII, 1947, pp. 18-23.
8. *CII*, vol. III, I, p. 11, Lines 20-21.
9. Ed. by J.E. Schwartzbeg, p. 25 (Map pl. III, D.1 — "South Asia in the Gupta Vākāṭaka Age, *c.* 300-550)".
10. *IHQ*, vol. XXI, 1945, pp. 143-45; *JARS*, vol. X, pp. 63-64; *Ep. Ind.*, vol. XXX, no. 47, p. 292.
11. B.M. Baura, *IHQ*, vol. XXIII, 1947, pp. 200ff.

has also referred to the defeat of Puṣyavarman at the hands of Samudragupta in about AD 380.[12] The correctness of the date is not beyond question. However, it will not be anachronistic to show Puṣyavarman as a contemporary of Samudragupta on the basic of the evidence adduced above.

Further, we do not find any historical basis to support the identification of Balavarman of the inscription of Samudragupta with that of the Varman dynasty of Kāmarūpa. Because Balavarman was one of those nine kings of Āryāvartta or the Gangetic plain who were exterminated by Samudragupta. Assam at that time was not a part of Āryāvartta but a frontier state. Kāmarūpa has been separately mentioned in his inscription as one of the five frontier subordinate states. Samudragupta also did not follow the policy of ruthless annexation towards Kāmarūpa as he did in case of the kingdoms of rulers of Āryāvartta. Moreover, there was a separate Varman family ruling over western Mālwā. Thus, in all probability Balavarman of the inscription concerned was a ruler of the kingdom other than Kāmarūpa. This can be confirmed by the statements of of H.C. Raychaudhuri.[13] K.P. Jayaswal has identified Balavarman of the Allahabad Pillar Inscription with Kalyāṇavarman of Pāṭaliputra[14] whose exactitude is difficult to be ascertained. Nor is it corroborated by epigraphy or any other source.

The Allahabad Pillar Inscription bears testimony to the fact that Kāmarūpa was one of those five frontier (*pratyanta*) kingdoms (the other four being Samataṭa or south-eastern Bengal, Devaka, Nepal and Kartripur) in the north-east whose kings submitted to the mighty Gupta emperor, Samudragupta, and gratified his imperious commands by paying all kinds of taxes and obeying his orders.[15] He is also believed to have entered into a subordinate alliance with him. It goes without saying that the king of Kāmarūpa concerned was none other than Puṣyavarman. Here it must be made clear that the kingdom of Kāmarūpa which was split up at that time into a number of petty principalities was not annexed to the Gupta empire nor was it governed by vassals of the Gupta

---

12. *Early History of Kāmarūpa* (Shillong, 1933), pp. 42-43, 53.
13. *PHAI*, pp. 534-35.
14. *JBORS*, March-June, 1933, p. 142.
15. See Fleet, *CII*, III, I, p. 11, Lines 22-23; D.C. Sircar (ed.), *SI*, vol. 1 (from the sixth century BC to the sixth century AD), pp. 265-66, Lines 22, note 4; J.E. Schwartzberg, *op. cit.*, pp. 25 & 179; R.G. Basak, *op. cit.*, pp. 26-27, 33, 267; R.S. Tripathi, *History of Ancient India*, p. 244; Romila Thapar, *A History of India*, vol. I, p. 137; B.C. Law, *The Magadhas in Ancient India*, p. 20.

emperor. It merely remained within the geographical limits of the Gupta empire for sometime maintaining its subordinate status. V.A. Smith has correctly stated that "His (Samudragupta's) empire in the middle of the 4th century AD extended from the Brahmaputra on the east to the Yamunā and Chambal on the west and from the foot of the Himālayas on the north to the Narmadā on the South. Beyond these wide limits the frontier kingdoms of Assam and the Gangetic delta (Samatata) were attached to the empire by bonds of subordinate alliance".[16]

There is no doubt about the fact that the seven generations of Kāmarūpa kings from Puṣyavarman to Nārāyaṇavarman remained as subsidiary allies of the contemporary imperial Gupta monarchs from Samudragupta to Bhānugupta which covers the period *c.* AD 335-510. But the decline of the Gupta power in the middle of the sixth century AD provided an opportunity to Bhūtivarman, a contemporary of the later Gupta ruler of Magadha Kumāragupta III (who is generally place between *c.* AD 510-54), to refurbish the tarnished image of his family by conquering the territories ruled by the Guptas and placing them under his political hegemony. He ultimately succeeded in occupying Puṇḍravardhanabhukti or northern Bengal (which remained an intergral part of the Gupta empire from *c.* AD 443 to 544), southern and eastern Bengal (Samataṭa) and the neighbouring kingdoms sometime between *c.* AD 545-54. In fact, it was he who for the first time by putting an end to the long political influence of the Guptas over Kāmarūpa raised its status from a subordinate state to an independent state. After breaking off the subordinate alliance of the Guptas he performed as *aśvamedha* sacrifice to assume an imperial status.[17] Barganga Rock Inscription of Bhūtivarman also testifies to the fact that he performed a horse-sacrifice and assumed the royal title *Paramadaivatā* and *Paramabhaṭṭāraka*[18] which exactly conforms to the Gupta tradition. Dubi Copper Plates

---

16. *The Early History of India* (4th rev. edn. by S.M. Edwards, p. 303. See also *Jour.* & *Procee.* of A.S.B., 1910, p. 144.

17. D.C. Sircar, *IHQ*, vol. XXVI, 1950, pp. 241-46; *JARS*, vol. X, pp. 63-77; N.K. Bhattasali, *Ep. Ind.*, vol. XXVII, 1947, pp. 18-23; *JRAS*, vol. VIII, 1941, no. 4, pp. 138-49; N.N. Dasgupta, *Indian Cullture*, vol. II, pp. 37-45; R.G. Basak, *op. cit.*, pp. 269-70; Bhandarkar (*Ind. Ant.*, vol. LXVI, pp. 41-55, 61-72) denies the extension of the boundary of the kingdom of Bhūtivarman to north Bengal on the ground that at that time the imperial Guptas had hold over those regions. But the available evidences go to contradict his views.

18. M.M. Sharma, *Inscriptions of Ancient Assam*, p. 5f (text of four lines with Eng. tr.); D. Sarma (ed.), *Kāmarūpaśāsanāvalī*, pt. II, texts, p. 4; pt. III, tr. p. 150; N.K. Bhattasali, *Ep. Ind.*, XXVII, pp. 18-23; *JARS*, VIII, 1941, pp. 138-39; D.C. Sircar, *Ep. Ind.*, XXX, pp. 62-67.

of Bhāṣkarvarman (first quarter of the seventh century AD) explicitly mentions his victory over his enemies (kings of northern and eastern Bengal), his kingship over the paternal kingdom which he received after getting crownded with victory, etc.[19] His conquest stemmed the tide of the rising power of the Guptas in north Bengal and struck a severe blow to the declining later Guptas.

After an interregnum of more than three decades Mahāsena Gupta (Dāmodar- gupta's son), the most illustrious among the later Gupta rulers of Magadha, invaded Kāmarūpa and attained glorious victory over Susthitavarman (father of Bhāṣkaravarman) in the battle which was fought on the bank of the Lauhitya or Brahmaputra sometime between *c.* AD 590-94 which can be confirmed by the Aphsad (Gayā district, Bihar) stone inscription of Ādityasena (*c.* AD 660-75).[20] The political relations between the Magadhan Gupta and the Varmans of Kāmarūpa became strained. Mahāsenagupta strengthened his position and reoccupied the territories in north Bengal and thereby restored the fallen fortunes of his dynasty. The Varman ruler concerned became his subordinate ally. The status of Kāmarūpa was once again reduced to a subordiante state. But Bhāṣkarvarman (*c.* AD 594-650) in the early part of the seventh century by recapturing all the lost territories raised the kingdom of Kāmarūpa to a height of glory.

The vicissitude of fortunes of Kāmarūpa was no doubt always linked up with that of the Guptas during the period concerned.

---

19. M.M. Sharma, *op. cit.*, text, vv. 28-31, p. 14, tr. pp. 22-23; D. Sarma, op. *cit.*, II, texts, p. 12, III, tr. p. 154.

20. Fleet, *CII*, vol. III, no. 42, p. 203, Lines 13-14, also pp. 204-08; see also D.C. Sircar (ed.), *SI*, vol. II, p. 44; *Ep. Ind.*, vol. XXXVII, pp. 183ff; R.G. Basak, *op. cit.*, p. 146; H.C. Raychaudhuri, *op. cit.*, pp. 606-7; R.S. Tripathi, *op. cit.*, pp. 286-87.

    Ādityasena, son of Mādhavagupta, was placed by Harṣa in Magadha as his feudatory or Viceroy and as bulwark against the aggressions of Śasāṅka.

    The Aphsad inscription of Ādityasena and Deo-Baranark (Śāhābād dist.) inscription of Jīvitagupta II (the last ruler of Magadha) throw light on the genealogy of Later Guptas of Magadha.

General Bibliography

General Bibliography

Original Sources: Texts, Translations and Commentaries

Literary Sources

THE VEDAS

Atharvaveda Saṁhitā, ed, with Sāyaṇa's comm. by S.P. Pandit, Bombay, 1895-98; trans. with comm. by R.T.H. Griffith (*The Hymns of the Atharvaveda*), 2 vols., Vārāṇasī, 1896-97, rept. 1968; trans. by W.D. Whitney (*On the Vedas*), HOS, Cambridge, 1905, 2nd Indian rept., Delhi 1971, Calcutta, 1972; text with Hindi trans. and comm. by Dayānanda Sarasvatī, Dayānanda Saṁsthān, Delhi, vs 2032; ed. with Hindi trans. based on Sāyaṇa's comm. by R. Sharma Ācārya, 2 vols., Bareli, 1973, 1975.

Ṛgveda Saṁhitā, ed. with Sāyaṇa's comm. by F. Max Müller, 2nd edn., London, 1890-92; trans. by R.T.H. Griffith, Benares, 1896-97; trans. by H.H. Wilson, 6 vols., London, 1866-88; ed. with Hindi trans. based on Sāyaṇa' comm. by R. Sharma Ācārya, 4 vols., Bareli, 1974-75.

Yajurveda, Maitrāyaṇī Saṁhitā, ed. by L.V. Schroeder, Leipzig, 1888.

———, *Taittirīya Saṁhitā*, ed. by Mahādev Śāstrī, Mysore, 1884; trans. by A.B. Keith, *The Veda of the Black Yajus School*, HOS (ed. C.R. Lanman), vols. XVIII and XIX, Cambridge, Mass 1914, rept. Delhi, 1967; ed. with the comm. of Mādhava, Calcutta, 1854-99.

———, *Vājasaneyi Saṁhitā* (of the Śukla *Yajurveda*), ed. with Mahīdhara's comm. by A. Weber, London, 1852; ed. by Lakṣmaṇa Śāstrī, Bombay, 1894; trans. by A.B. Keith, Cambridge, Mass. 1914.

———, trans. with a popular comm. by R.T.H. Griffith, *The Texts of the White Yajurveda*, Banaras, 1899, rept. Vārāṇasī, 1976.

THE BRĀHMAṆAS

Aitareya Brāhmaṇa, ed. and trans. by M. Haug, 2 vols., Vārāṇasi, 1976-77; trans. by A.B. Keith, HOS, vol. XXV, Cambridge, Mass. 1920, 1st Indian rept. Delhi, 1971; ed. and trans. with Sāyaṇa's comm. by U.S. Sharma, Vārāṇasī, 1963.

Śatapatha Brāhmaṇa, ed. by A. Chinnaswami Śāstrī, P. Śāstrī and R.N. Dikshita, 2nd edn., Vārāṇasī, 1984; trans. by J. Eggeling, in SBE, XII, I, Bks. I-II, Oxford, 1882, rept. Delhi, 1972; XXVI, II, Bks. III-IV Oxford, 1885, rept. Delhi, 1972; XLI, III, Bks. V-VII, Oxford, 1894, rept. Delhi, 1972; XLIII, IV, Bks. VIII-X, Oxford, 1897, rept. Delhi, 1972; XLIV, V, Bks. XI-XIV, Oxford, 1900, rept. Delhi, 1972.

Taittirīya Brāhmaṇa, ed. with Sāyaṇa's comm. by R. Mitra, 3 vols., BIS, Calcutta, 1855-70; ed. by N. Godabole, Poona, 1898; ed. by R. Shamaśāstrī, Mysore, 1921.

Tāṇḍya Brāhmaṇa, ed. by Caland, BIS, Calcutta, 1932.

THE ĀRAṆYAKA

Taittirīya Āraṇyaka, ed. by H.N. Apte, Poona, 1898.

THE SŪTRAS

Dharma-sūtras

Āpastamba Dharmasūtra, ed. by G. Bühler, Bombay Sanskrit Series, 1892, 1894; ed. by Mahādeva Śāstrī, Mysore, 1893; trans. by G. Bühler, in SBE, *The Sacred Laws of the Āryas*, vol. II, pt. I, Oxford, 1879, rept. Delhi, 1969.

Baudhāyana Dharmasūtra, ed. by A. Chinnaswami Śāstrī, Banaras, 1934; trans. by G. Bühler, in SBE, XIV, II, Oxford, 1882, rept. Delhi, 1969.

Gautama Dharmasūtra, ed. by Śrīnivasācārya, Mysore, 1917; trans. by G. Bühler, in SBE, II, I, Oxford, 1879, rept. Delhi, 1969.

Vasiṣṭha Dharmasūtra, ed. by A.A. Führer, Bombay, 1916; trans. by G. Bühler, in SBE, XIV, II, Oxford, 1882, rept. Delhi, 1969.

Gṛhya-sūtras

Āpastamba Gṛhyasūtra, ed. A. Chinnaswami Śāstrī, Banaras, 1928; trans. by H. Oldenberg, in SBE, XXX, II, Oxford, 1892, rept. Delhi, 1964.

Āśvalāyana Gṛhyasūtra, with the comm. of Gārgya Nārāyaṇa, Calcutta, 1893; trans. by H. Oldenberg, in SBE, XXIX, I, Oxford, 1886, rept. Delhi, 1964.

THE DHARMAŚĀSTRAS

Manu-Smṛti (*Mānava Dharmaśāstra*), ed. with Hindi trans. and the *Manvartha-Muktāvalī* comm. of Kullūka Bhaṭṭa and the *Maṇiprabhā* Hindi comm. of H.G. Śāstrī by Gopāla Śāstrī Nene, Vārāṇasī, 1970; Eng. trans. G. Bühler, *The Laws of Manu*, with Extracts from seven commentaries, SBE, vol. XXV, Oxford, 1886, rept. Delhi, 964; A.C. Burnell, *The Ordinances of Manu*, completed and ed. by E.W. Hopkins, London, 1884, 2nd edn., Delhi 1971.

Vasiṣṭha-Smṛti, in *Dharmaśāstra Saṁgraha*, ed. by J. Vidyāsāgara, Calcutta, 1876; *Twenty Smṛtis,* ed. with Hindi trans. by R. Sharma Ācārya, 2 vols., Bareli, 1979-80.

Yājñavalkya-Smṛti, ed. by H. Apte, Ānandāśrama Skt. Series, Poona, 1903; with Mitākṣarā comm. of Vijñāneśvara, 4th ed. Bombay, 1936.

THE EPICS

Mahābhārata, ed. with Hindi trans. by S. Dāmodar Śatavalekar and Śrutiśīla Śarmā, Pāradi (Gujarat):

Āraṇyaka Parva, 2 vols., 1969.

Bhīṣma Parva, 1972.

Sabhā Parva, 1982.

Śalya Parva, 1973.

Śānti Parva, 2 vols., 1979-80.

Udyoga Parva, 1969.

Vālmikī-Rāmāyaṇa, ed. by D.R. Mankad, Oriental Research Institute, Baroda, 1965; trans. by R.T.H. Griffith, London, 1870.

Kiṣkindhā Kāṇḍa, ed. with Hindi trans. by Akhilānanda, Amritsar, vs 2021.

PURĀṆAS

Agni Purāṇa, ed. R.L. Mitra, Calcutta, 1873-79; trans. by M.N. Dutt, 2 vols., Cacutta, 1903-04; text with Hindi trans. of T. Jha and G.S. Tripāṭhī, Prayāg, 1986.

Bhāgavata Purāṇa, text with Hindi trans. and annotation, 2 vols., 8th edn. Gorakhpur, Samvat, 2040; ed. with Eng. trans. by C.L. Goswami, 2 pts. 2nd edn., Gorakhpur, 1982.

Bhaviṣya Purāṇa, Veṅkaṭeśvara Press, Bombay, 1910; ed. with Hindi trans. by R. Sharma Ācārya, 2 vols., Bareli, 1978.

Brahma Purāṇa, ed. by H.N. Apte, Ānandāśrama Skt. Series, Poona, 1895; text with Hindi trans. of T. Jha, Prayāg, 1976.

Brahmāṇḍa Purāṇa, Veṅkaṭeśvara Press, Bombay, 1913; ed. with Hindi trans. by R. Sharma Ācārya, 2 vols., Bareli, 1988.

Harivaṁśa Purāṇa, ed. by N. Mukhopādhyāya, ASB, Calcutta, 1858; R. Kinjawadekar, Poona, 1936; text with Hindi trans. and comm., 4th edn., Gorakhpur, Samvat, 2044.

Kūrma Purāṇa, ed. with Hindi trans. of Shree Chaudhari Shree Nārāyaṇa Singh by Ānandasvarūpa Gupta, Vārāṇasī, 1972.

Liṅga Purāṇa, Veṅkaṭeśvara Press, Bombay, 1927.

Mārkaṇḍeya Purāṇa, ed. by K.M. Banerjee, BIS, ASB, Calcutta, 1862; ed. with Hindi trans. by Dharmendra Nath Śastrī, Meerut, 1983; trans. by F.E. Pargiter, BIS, ASB, Calcutta, 1904.

Matrsya Purāṇa, Ānandāśrama Skt. Series, Poona, 1907; text with Hindi trans., 2 vols., Gorakhpur, 1985; ed. with trans. of various oriental scholars and notes of B.C. Majumdar, S.C, Vasu, H.H. Wilson, Bentley, Wilford and others by J.D. Akhtar, vol. I, SBA, Delhi, 1972.

Padma Purāṇa, ed. by V.N. Mandalika, Ānandāśrama Skt. Series, Poona, 1893-94; *Svargakhaṇda*, ed. by Aśoka Chatterjee Śāstrī, Vārāṇasī, 1972.

Vāmana Purāṇa, ed. with Hindi trens. of G.C. Vedānta Śāstrī, Shree Chaudhari Shree Nārāyaṇa Singh and G.S. Rai by Ānandasvarūpa Gupta, Vārāṇasī, 1968.

Vāyu Purāṇa, Ānandāśrama Skt. Series, Poona, 1905; ed. by R.L. Mitra, 2 vols., BIS, ASB, Calcutta, 1880-88; text with Hindi trans of R.P. Tripāṭhī Śāstrī, Prayāg, 1987.

Viṣṇu Purāṇa, ed. by J. Vidyāsāgara, Calcutta, 1882; text with Hindi trans. of Muni Lal Gupta, 9th edn., Gorakhpur Samvat, 2041; trans. by M.N. Dutt, Calcutta, 1894, and H.H. Wilson, Calcutta, 1961.

OTHER LITERARY WORKS

Amarakośa of Amara Siṁha, text with the *Maṇiprabhā* Hindi comm. of H.G. Śāstrī, Vārāṇasī, 1957.

Arthaśāstra of Kauṭilya, ed. by R. Shamasastrī, Mysore, 1909; trans. by R. Shamaśāstrī, Bangalore, 1915; ed. with Hindi trans. by Vachaspati Gairola, Vārāṇasī, 1984.

Aṣṭādhyāyī of Pāṇini (*Sūtrapāṭha* with *Gaṇas* and *Vārttikas*), ed. by S.C. Śāstrī, Trichinopoly, 1912; ed.

with Eng. trans. by S.C. Vasu, 7 vols., Allahabad 1891-98, rept. 1929; ed. with comm. by Brahmandatta Jijñāsu, pt. I, 1st edn., Amritsar, vs 2021, pt. II, 2nd edn., Amritsar, vs 2031.

Bṛhat Saṁhitā of Varāhamihira, ed. by H. Kern, BIS, ASB, Calcutta, 1865; ed. with Hindi trans. and comm. by B.P. Mishra, Bombay, 1952.

Mahābhāṣya of Patañjali, ed. by F. Kielhorn, 3 vols., Bombay Skt. Series, Bombay, 1880-85.

BUDDHIST WORKS

Aṅguttara Nikāya, ed. by R. Morris and E. Hardy, 5 vols., PTS, London, 1885-1900.

Apadāna (part of the *Khuddaka Nikāya*), not yet edited.

Avadānaśataka, ed. by J.S. Speyer, 2 vols., St. Petersburg, 1906.

Cullaniddesa (part of the *Khuddaka Nikāya*).

Dhammapada (part of the *Khuddaka Nikāya*), ed., by S.S. Thera, PTS, London 1914; trans. from Pāli by F. Max Müller, SBE, vol. X, pt. I, Oxford, 1881, rept. Delhi, 1973; ed. with Sanskrit and Hindi trans. by Rāhul Sāṅkṛtyāyana, Sāranātha, 1933, 2nd edn., Lucknow, 1957; *aṭṭhakathā* or comm. (*Dhammapada-aṭṭhakathā*), by Buddhaghoṣa, ed. by H.C. Norman and L.S. Tailang, 5 vols (in 6 pts), London, 1906-15.

Dīgha Nikāya, ed. by T.W. Rhys Davids and J.E. Carpenter, 3 vols., PTS, London, 1890-1911, rept. 1947-60; trans. by T.W. and C.A.F. Rhys Davids, *The Dialogues of the Buddha*, 3 vols., PTS, London, 1899-1921, rept. 1959; comm. (*Sumaṅgalavilāsinī*), by Buddhaghoṣa, ed. by Rhys Davids and J.E. Carpenter, 3 vols., PTS, London, 1886-1932.

Divyāvadāna, ed. by E.B. Cowell and R.A. Neil, Cambridge, 1886, rept. 1976; ed. by P.L. Vaidya, Delhi, 1959.

Jātaka (part of the *Khuddaka Nikāya*), ed. by V. Fausböll, 6 vols., London, 1877-97; trans. by various scholars under the editorship of E.B. Cowell, 7 vols., Cambridge, 1895-1913.

Mahāniddesa (part of the *Kuddaka Nikāya*), ed. by L.D. La, V. Poussin and E.J. Thomas, 2 vols., London, 1938.

Mahāvastu, ed. by E. Senart, 3 vols., Paris, 1882-97; trans. by J.J. Jones, SBB, XVI, XVIII and XIX, London, 1949-56.

Majjhima Nikāya, ed. by V. Trenckner and R. Chalmers, 3 vols., PTS, London, 1888-99; comm. (*Papañcasūdanī*), by Buddhaghoṣa, ed. by J.H. Woods, D. Kosambi and I.B. Horner, 5 vols., London, 1922-38.

Milindapañha, ed. by V. Trenckner, London 1880; R.D. Vadekar, Bombay, 1940; trans from Pāli by T.W. Rhys Davids, *The Questions of King Milinda*, SBE, vols., XXXV, pt. I, Oxford, 1890, rept. Delhi, 1969; XXXVI, pt. II, Oxford, 1894, rept. Delhi, 1969.

Petavatthu (part of the *Khuddaka Nikāya*), ed. by Minayef, PTS, London 1888; comm. (*Paramatthadīpanī*), by Dhammapāla, ed. by E. Hardy, PTS, London, 1901.

Saṁyutta Nikāya, ed. by M.L. Feer and Mrs. Rhys Davids, 5 vols., PTS, London, 1884-1904; comm. (*Sāratthappakāsinī*), by Buddhaghoṣa, 3 vols., PTS, London, 1929-37.

Sāsanavaṁsa

Suttanipāta (one of the 15 Books of *Khuddaka Nikāya*), ed. by D. Andersen and H. Smith, PTS, London, 1913; ed by Rāhul Sāṅkṛtyāyana, Rangoon, 1937; trans. from Pāli by V. Fausböll, *A Collection of*

Discourses, SBE, X, II, Oxford, 1881, rept. Delhi, 1973; comm. (*Paramatthajotikā*) by Buddhaghoṣa, ed. by H. Smith, 4 vols. (in 2), London, 1916-18.

Theragāthā (part of the *Khuddaka Nikāya*), ed. by H. Oldenberg, PTS, London, 1883; Rāhul Sāṅkṛtyāyana, Rangoon, 1937; trans. *Psalms of the Brethren*, by Mrs. Rhys Davids, PTS, London, 1913; comm. (*Paramatthadīpanī*), by Dhammapāla ed. by F.L. Woodward, 2 vols., London, 1940.

Therigāthā (part of the *Khuddaka Nikāya*), ed. by R. Pischel, PTS, London, 1883; Rāhul Sāṅkṛtyāyana, Rangoon, 1937; trans. *Psalms of the Sisters*, by Mrs. Rhys Davids, PTS, London, 1909; comm. (*Paramatthadīpanī*), by Dhammapāla, ed. by E. Müller, PTS, London, 1893.

Vimānavatthu (part of the *Khuddaka Nikāya*), ed. by E.R. Goonaratne, PTS, London, 1886.

Vinayapiṭaka, ed. by H. Oldenberg, 5 vols., London, 1879-83; comm. (*Sāmantapāsādikā*) by Buddhaghoṣa, ed. J. Takakusu and M. Nagai, 4 vols., PTS, London, 1924-38.

Vinaya Texts: *Mahāvagga*, ed. by B.J. Kashyapa, Nalanda Devanāgarī Pāli Series, Nālandā, 1956; trans. from Pāli by T.W. Rhys Davids and H. Oldenberg, in SBE, XIII, I (I-IV) and XVII, II (V-X), Oxford, 1882, rept. Delhi, 1974; *Cullavagga*, ed. by B.J. Kashyapa, Nālandā, 1956; trans. from Pāli by T.W. Rhys Davids and H. Oldenberg, in SBE, XVII and XX.

Vinayavastu, Gilgit Manuscript, vol. III, pt. 2. Srinagar, 1942.

JAIN WORKS

Canonical

Ācārāṅga Sūtra, ed. W.S. Schubring, Leipzig, 1910; trans. from Prākṛt by H. Jacobi, in SBE, XXII, I, Oxford, 1884, rept. Delhi, 1973; *Niryukti,* Bhadrabāhu; *Cūrṇi,* Jinadāsagaṇi Mahattara, Ratlam, 1941; comm. Śilāṅka, Sūrat, 1935.

Antagaḍadasāo, ed. P.L. Vaidya, Poona, 1932; trans. L.D. Barnett, London, 1907; comm. Abhayadeva, ed. M.C. Modi, Ahmedabad, 1932.

Āvaśyaka, *Niryukti*, Bhadrabāhu; *Cūrṇi,* Jinadāsagṇi Mahattara, Ratlam, 1928; comm. Haribhadra, Bombay, 1916.

Bṛhaṭkalpa Sūtra Bhāṣya, ed. Muni Punyavijaya, Vārāṇasī, 1933.

Jambuddīvapaṇṇati, comm. Śānticandra, Bombay, 1920.

Kalpasūtra of Bhadrabāhu, ed. H. Jacobi, Leipzig, 1879; ed. Muni Punyavijaya, Bombay, 1952; trans. from Prākṛt by H. Jacobi, in SBE, XXII, I, Oxford, 1884, rept. Delhi, 1973; comm. Samayasundaragaṇi, Bombay, 1939.

Nāyādhammakahāo, ed. N.V. Vaidya, Poona, 1940; comm. Abhayadeva, Bombay, 1919.

Niśītha, Bhāṣya, Cūrṇi, Jinadāsagaṇi Mahattara, ed. Upādhyāya Kavi Amar Muni and Muni Kanhaiyālāl, Agra, 1957-60.

Ovāiya, comm. Abhayadeva, 2nd edn., Sūrat, vs 1914.

Sūtrakṛtāṅga Sūtra, trans. from Prākṛt by H. Jacobi, in SBE, XLV, II, Oxford, 1895, rept. Delhi, 1973.

Uttarādhyayana Sūtra, ed. J. Charpentier, Uppasala, 1922; trans. from Prākṛt by H. Jacobi, in SBE, XLV, II, Oxford, 1895, rept. Delhi, 1973; *Ṭīkā*, Śāntisūri, Bombay, 1916; Nemicandra, Bombay, 1937.

Uvāsagadasāo, ed. P.L. Vaidya, Poona, 1930; trans. A.F.R. Hoernle, Calcutta, 1888.

Vavahāra Bhāṣya, comm. Malayagiri, Bhavnagar, 1926.

Non-Canonical

Ādi Purāna of Jinasena III, ed. Pannālāl Jain, Ist edn., BGP, Kāśī, 1951.

Aṅgavijjā, ed. Muni Punyavijaya, Prākṛt Jain Text Society, Vārāṇasī, 1957.

Harivaniśa Purāṇa of Jinasena II, ed. Pannālāl Jain, BGP, Kāśī, 1962; MDJG, edn., Bombay, 1930.

Kuvalayamālā of Udyotana Suri, pts. I & II, ed. A.N. Upadhye, Bombay, 1959, revd. edn., 1970.

Padma Purāṇa of Raviṣena, ed. Pannālāl Jain, 3 vols., BGP, Kāśī, 1958-59; also MDJG, edn., Bombay, 1928-29.

Tilakamañjarī of Dhanapāla, ed. Bhavadatta Śāstrī, 2nd edn., Bombay, 1938.

Tiloyapaṇṇati of Yativṛṣabha, ed. A.N. Upadhye and H.L. Jain, Sholapur, 1951.

Uttara Purāṇa of Guṇabhadra, ed. Pannālāl Jain, revd. edn., BGP, Kāśī, 1954.

Vasudevahiṇḍi of Saṁghadāsa, Bhavnagar, 1930-31; Gujarātī trans. by B.L. Sandesaria, Bhavnagar, 1946; *The Vasudevahiṇḍi — An Authentic Jain Version of the Bṛhatkathā*, by J.C. Jain, Ahmedabad, 1977.

Yaśastilakacampu of Somadeva Sūri, ed. Sivadatta and K.P. Parab, Bombay, 1901-03.

CLASSICAL (GREEK AND LATIN) SOURCES

Greek and Roman Authors and their works (ed. & trans.)

Arrian, *Anabasis*, ed. by A.G. Roos, Leipzig, 1907.

——, *Indika, Arriani Scripta Minora*, pp. 1-55, ed. R. Hercher, 2nd edn., Leipzig, 1885; *Indika*, pt. I chaps. I-XVII, Leipzig, 1867; pt. II, chaps. XVIII-XLIII, *The Voyage of Nearkhos* from the Mouth of the Indus to the Head of the Persian Gulf, copied from the *Journal of the Voyage* written by Nearkhos himself, Eng. trans from C. Müller's edn. as given in the *Geographi Graeci Minores* (Paris, 1855), by J.W. McCrindle, 1st edn., London, 1879, rept. Calcutta, 1973, Patna, 1987.

——, *Anabasis* and *Indika*, Eng. trans. of both by E.J. Chinnock, London, 1893.

Diodoros Siculus, *Bibliotheca Historica*, Eng. trans. by C.H, Oldfather, London, 1933.

Herodotus, *Historica* (History), ed. by O. Hude, 2nd edn., Oxford, 1913-14; Eng. trans. by G. Rawlinson, vol. II, London, 1862; Eng. trans. by G.C. Macaulay, London, 1904; Eng. trans. by J.E. Powell, Oxford, 1939; Eng. trans. by A.D. Godley, 4 vols., revd. and rept. London, 1946.

Justinus (Justin), *Historiae Philippicae*, ed. by F. Ruehl, Leipzig, 1886.

Ktēsias, *Indika,* Eng. trans. of its abridgement by Phōtios, and of the *Fragments* of that work preserved in other writers, by J.W. McCrindle, *Ancient India as Described by Ktēsias the Knidian* (rept. with additions from the *Ind. Ant.*, 1881), London, 1882, rept. Delhi, 1973.

——, *Persica* (*History of Persia*), its *Fragments* ed. by J. Gilmore, London, 1888.

——, *Fragments* of the *Indika* and of the *Persica*, ed. by C. Müller, in Dindorf's *Herodotus*, Paris, 1844.

Megasthenes, *Indika*, its *Fragments* collected and ed. by E.A. Schwanbeck and pub. in his book, *Megasthenis Indica,* Bonn, 1846.

Periplus Maris Erythraei (Travel and Trade in the Indian Ocean), by an anonymous writer (a Greek merchant of the first century AD), ed. by B. Fabricius, Leipzig, 1883; Eng. trans. (with comm.) by J.W. McCrindle, *The Commerce and Navigation of the Erythraean Sea* (trans. from the text as given in the *Geographi Graeci Minores,* ed. by C. Müller, Paris, 1855), 1st edn., London, 1879, rept. Calcutta, 1973; also McCrindle's trans. in *Ind. Ant.*, vol. VIII, 1879, pp. 108-51; trans. from the Greek and annotated by W.H. Schoff, *The Periplus of the Erythraean Sea*, London, 1912.

Pliny, *Naturalis Historia* (*Natural History*), ed. by C. Mayhoff, Leipzig, 1892-1909; Eng. trans. by B. Riley, London, 1962.

Ptolemy, *Geographica*, ed. by C.F.A. Nobbe, 3 vols., Leipzig, 1898-1902; Eng. trans. by E.L. Stevenson, *The Geography of Claudius Ptolemy*, New York, 1932.

Strabo, *Geographica*, ed. by A. Meineke, Leipzig, 1866-67; Eng. trans. by H.C. Hamilton and W. Falconer, 3 vols., London, 1854-57, Eng. trans. by H.L. Jones and John R.S. Sterrett, *The Geography of Strabo*, 8 vols., New York and Cambridge, Mass. 1917-32, rept. London, 1949.

Xenophon, *Cyropaedia*, ed. and trans. by W. Miller, London and New York, 1914.

Translated Works

Majumdar, R.C., *The Classical Accounts of India* (a compilation of the English translations of the accounts of ancient Greek and Roman writers bearing on Indian history and culture), Calcutta, 1960, rept. 1981.

McCrindle, J.W., *Ancient India as Described by Megasthenes and Arrian* (trans. of the *Fragments* of the *Indika* of Megasthenes and of the first part of the *Indika* of Arrian) 1st edn., London, 1877; the same work ed. with conculturuum, appendices, notes, etc. by R.C. Jain, Delhi, 1972, rept. 1984; McCrindle's trans. of the *Fragments* of the *Indika* of Megasthenes also in *Ind. Ant.*, vol. VI, 1877.

——, *Ancient India as Described by Ptolemy*, Eng. trans. (with annotations) of Ptolemy's *Geography of India and Central and Eastern Asia*, 1st edn., London, 1885 (rept. with additions from the *Ind. Ant.*, 1884); ed. with notes by S.N. Majumdar Śāstrī, Calcutta 1927; ed. with conculturuum, appendices, etc. by R.C. Jain, Delhi, 1973-74.

——, *The Invasion of India by Alexander the Great as Described by Arrian, Q. Curtius Diodoros, Plutarch and Justin*, 2nd edn., Westminster 1896, new edn., Patna, 1989.

——, *Ancient India as Described in Classical Literature* (a collection of ancient Greek and Latin texts relating to India, translated into English, with notes), 1st edn., Westminster, 1901, rept. Delhi, 1984.

Vincent, W., *The Voyage of Nearchus and the Periplus of the Erythraean Sea* (Eng. trans. from the Original Greek), Oxford, 1809.

ORIENTAL WORK

Avesta, Part I, the *Vendidad*, Eng. trans. by James Darmesteter, in SBE, vol. IV, Oxford, 1887, rept. Delhi, 1974.

CHINESE WORKS

Beal, S. (tr.), *The Life of Hiuen Tsiang*, by S. Hwui-Li and Yen-Tsung, London, 1884, 1st Indian edn., Delhi, 1973.

Watters, T., *On Yuan Chwang's Travels in India*, trans. of the *Si-Yu-Ki* of Hiuen Tsang (or Yuan Chwang) with annotations, ed. by T.W. Rhys Davids and S.W. Bushell, 2 vols., RAS, London, 1904-05, 2nd Indian edn., Delhi, 1973.

ARABIC WORK

Tahqiq-i-Hind of Al-Biruni, Eng. trans. of the Arabic text by E.C. Sachau, *Alberuni's India*, 2 vols., 1st edn., Berlin, 1888, London, 1910, rept. Delhi, 1964.

Coins and Inscriptions

Barua, B.M., *Old Brāhmī Inscriptions in the Udaigiri and Khaṇḍagiri Caves*, Calcutta, 1929.

Bühler, J.G., "Sāñchi Votive Inscriptions," *EP. Ind.*, II, pp. 88 ff.

Cunningham, A., *Coins of Ancient India from the earliest times down to the seventh century* AD, London, 1891, rept. Vārāṇasī, 1971.

Fleet, J.F., *Corpus Inscriptionum Indicarum*, vol. III, *Inscriptions of the Early Gupta Kings*, Calcutta, 1888.

Hultzsch, E., *Corpus Inscriptionum Indicarum*, vol. I, Oxford, 1925.

Luders, H., "List of Brāhmī Inscriptions from the earliest times to the second century AD," *EP. Ind.*, X, 1910, App. no. 6.

Sharma, M.M., *Inscriptions of Ancient Assam*, Gauhati, 1978.

Sircar, D.C. (ed.), *Select Inscriptions Bearing on Indian History and Civilization*, vol. I (from the sixth century BC to the sixth century AD), Calcutta, 1965, vol. II, Delhi, 1983. vol. I, pp. 4-14 also for old Persian inscriptions: *Behistūn*, *Persepolis*, *Naqsh-i-Rustam and Hamadan Gold and Silve Tablet inscriptions* of Darius.

Smith, V.A., *Catalogue of the Coins in the Indian Museum*, Calcutta, vol. I, *Coins of Ancient India*, Oxford 1906, rept. Vārāṇasī, 1972.

Modern Works

Abbott, E., *History of Antiquity*, trans. from the German of Max Duncker, London, 1880.

Agrawal, D.P. and Ghosh, A. (ed.), *Radiocarbon and Indian Archaeology*, Bombay, 1973.

Agrawala, V.S., *India as known to Pāṇini* (A Study of the Cultural material in the *Aṣṭādhyāyī*), Vārāṇasī, 1963

———, *Bhārata Sāvitrī* (an indepth historical Study of the *Mahābhārata*), vols. 1 and 2, 2nd edn., Delhi, 1977, vol. 3, 1st end., Delhi, 1968.

———, *India as Described by Manu*, Vārāṇasī, 1970.

Ali, S.M., *The Geography of the Purāṇas,* Delhi, 1983.

Allchin, B. and F.R., *The Rise of Civilization in India and Pakistan*, Cambridge, 1982.

Alleyne, S.F., *History of Greece from the Earliest times to the end of the Presian War*, trans. from the German of Max Duncker, vol. I, London, 1883.

Arokiaswamy, M., "The Gupta Dynasty and the Early Pallavas of Kanchi," *JIH*, vol. LVI, pt. I, 1978, p. 108.

Bagchi, P.C., *Pre-Aryan and Pre-Dravidian in India* (Eng. trans. of original French articles by Sylvain Levi, J. Przyluski & c.), Calcatta, 1929.

Banerjee, N.V., *Studies in the Dharmaśāstra of Manu*, Delhi, 1980.

Barua, K.L., *Early History of Kāmarūpa*, Shillong, 1933, and Gauhati, 1966.

Basak, R.G., *The History of North-Eastern India extending from the foundation of the Gupta Empire to the rise of the Pāla dynasty of Bengal (c. AD 320-760)*, Calcutta, 1967.

Baveridge, H., *A Comprehensive History of India*, vol. I, 1st edn., London, 1862, rept. 4th edn., Delhi, 1982.

Bhandarkar, D.R., *Carmichael Lectures on Ancient Indian Numismatics*, Calcutta, 1921.

Bhandarkar, R.G., *Vaishnavism, Saivism and Minor Religious Systems*, Strassburg, 1913.

———, *A Peep into the Early History of India*, Vārāṇasī, 1978.

Bhargava, M.L. *The Geography of Ṛgvedic India*, Lucknow, 1964.

Bhargava, P.L., *India in the Vedic age: A History of Aryan Expansion in India*, Lucknow, 1971.

Bhattacharya, P.N., *Kāmarūpa Śāsanāvalī*, Banaras, 1931.

Bunbury, E.H., *History of Ancient Geography Among the Greeks and Romans from the Earliest Ages till the Fall of the Roman Empire*, 2 vols., 1st edn., London, 1879, 2nd edn., New York, 1959.

Bury, J.B., Cook, S.A. and Adcock, F.E., *Cambridge Ancient History*, Cambridge, 1960.

Cady, J.F., *South-East Asia: Its Historical Development*, New York, 1964.

Chakladar, H.C., *The Aryan Occupation of Eastern India*, Calcutta, 1962.

Chakravorty, B.B., *Itihāsa of Bhāratavarṣa from the Bhāratīya Viewpoint (up to Gupta Period)*, Calcutta, 1995.

Chanda, R.P., *The Indo-Aryan Races. A Study of the Origin of Indo-Aryan People and Institutions*, Rajshahi, 1916, rept. Delhi, 1978.

Chapekar, N.M., *Ancient India and Iran*, Delhi, 1982.

Chatterji, S.K., *Kirāta-Jana-Kṛti*: The Indo-Mongoloids: Their Contribution to the History and Culture of India, ASB, Calcutta, 1974.

Chattopadhyaya, S., *Racial Affinities of Early North Indian Tribes*, Delhi, 1973.

Childe, V.G., *The Aryans: A Study of Indo-European Origins*, London, 1926.

———, "Retrospect," *Antiquity*, vol. XXXII, 1958, p. 73.

———, *What Happened in History*? Harmondsworth, 1942, rept. 1985.

Choudhury, P., *The Aryans : A Modern Myth*, Delhi, 1993.

———, *The Aryan Hoax that Dupes the Indians*, Calcutta, 1995.

Cowell, E.B., "The Brahmanical Tribes and the Aborigines," rept. from M. Elphinstone's *The History of India*, ed. by Cowell, 9th edn., London, 1911, in *Ancient India* (a collection of eleven articles rept. from three different works on Indian History), Delhi, 1983, pp. 62-67.

Cunningham, A., *The Ancient Geography of India*, 1st edn. London, 1871, rept. Vārāṇasī, 1979.

Dales, G.F., "The Mythical Massacre at Mohenjodaro," in *Expedition*, Philadelphia, vol. VI, no. 3, 1964, pp. 36-43.

Das, A.C., *Ṛgvedic India — Cultural History of India as depicted in the Ṛgveda*, 2 vols., Calcutta, 1920, rept. Delhi, 1980.

Dey, N.L., *Civilisation in Ancient India*, Delhi, 1972.

Dyson, R.H., "Harappan Vedic Civilization — A continuum," in *Manthan*, JDRI, vols. XV-4-XVI-I, 1994-95, pp. 117-18.

Elphinstone, M., *The History of India*, London, 1911, rept. Allahabad, 1966.

———, "The Greek Accounts of India," rept. from his *The history of India*, App. III — "On the Greek Accounts of India" pp. 229-42, in *Ancient India (supra)*, Delhi, 1983, pp. 11-33.

———, "The Age of Manu and the Vedas," in *Ancient India (supra)*, Delhi, 1983, pp. 1-5.

Elst, K., *Indigenous Indians: Agastya to Ambedkar*, Delhi, 1993.

Frawley, D., *The Myth of the Aryan Invasion of India*, Delhi, 2001.

Fick, R., *The Social Organisation in North-East India in Buddha's time*, trans. by S.K. Maitra, Calcutta, 1920.

Geldern, R.H., "The Coming of the Aryans and the end of the Harappa Civilization," *Man*, JRAI, vol. LVI, 1956, p. 151.

Gerini, G.E., *Resarches on Ptolemy's Geography of Eastern Asia*, London, 1909, rept. 2nd edn., Delhi, 1974.

Godbole, N.N., "Rigvedic Sarasvati," *ABORI*, vol. LXII, 1963, pp. 1-40.

Gupta, P., *Geographical Names in Ancient Indian Inscriptions (up to 650 AD)*, Delhi, 1977.

Gupta, S.P., "Studies in the Indus-Saraswati Civilization: some New Developments," *Manthan*, JDRI, vols., XV-4-XVI-I, 1994-95, pp. 79-97.

———, "The Indus-Saraswati Civilization: An Overview," *Itihāsa Darpan*, A Research Journal of History, Delhi, vol. I, pt. I, 1994, pp. 46-52.

Gupta, S.P. and Ramachandran, R.S. (ed.), *Aspects of Indian History and Archaeology* (a collection of Papers of H.D. Sankalia), Delhi, 1977.

Heeren, A.H.L., *Historical Researches into the Politics, Intercourse and Trade of the Principal Nations of Antiquity*, Oxford, 1833.

Herzfeld, E., *Iran in the Ancient East*, Oxford, 1941.

Huxley, J., *Race in Europe*, OUP, London, 1939.

———, "The Myth of an Aryan Race," *Manthan*, JDRI, vol. XV, nos. 2-3, 1994, pp. 63-65.

Jain, G.C., *Yaśastilaka Kā Sāṁskṛtika Adhyayan*, Amritsar, 1967.

Jain, J.C., *Life in Ancient India as depicted in the Jaina canon and Commentaries* (6th century BC to 17th century AD), Delhi, 1984.

———, *Jain Āgama Sāhitya mein Bhāratīya Samāj*, Vārāṇasī, 1965.

———, "Trade and Commerce in Ancient India (from less known Jain Sources)," *QRHS*, vol. XVII, no. I, 1977-78, pp. 48-49.

Jain, J.P., *The Jaina Sources of the History of Ancient India (100 BC - AD 900)*, Delhi, 1964.

Jain, K.C., *Prācīna Bhāratīya Sāmājika evam Ārthika Saṁsthāyeṅ*, Bhopal, 1971.

———, *Bauddha aur Jain Āgamoṅ mein Nārī Jīvan*, Amritsar, 1967.

Jain R.C., *Ethnology of Ancient Bhārata,* Vārāṇasī, 1970.

Jayaswal, K.P., *Hindu Polity: A Constitutional History of India in Hindu Times*, pts. I & II, 5th edn., Bangalore, 1981.

Jha, Ganganath, "Aryan Invasion of India — Is it a myth?," in *Ācārya Puṣpāñjali* (D.R. Bhandarkar Commemoration Volume), ed. by B.C. Law, Calcutta, 1940, pp. 1-2.

Kaegi, A., *Life in Ancient India (Studies in Rigvedic India)*, trans. from the German by R. Arrowsmith, Calcutta, 1950.

Kak, S.C., "Vedic Studies Provide Valuable Clues," *Manthan*, JDRI, XV-4-XVI-1, 1994-95, pp. 5-36.

Kane, P.V., *Dharmaśāstra Kā Itihāsa*, Hindi trans. by Arjuna Chauve Kasyapa, vol. I, Lucknow, 1980.

Keith, A.B., *The Religion and Philosophy of the Veda and Upanishads*, HOS, vol. XXXI, pt.I, Cambridge, Mass. 1925, 2nd Indian rept. Delhi, 1976.

Kennedy, J., "The Puranic Histories of the Early Aryans," *JRAS*, 1915.

———, "The Aryan Invasion of Northern India," *JRAS*, 1919, pp. 493-529 (especially pp. 495-501, 518-19).

Kern, H., *Manual of Indian Buddhism*, Strassburg, 1899.

Kosambi, D.D., "Early Stages of the Caste System in Northern India," *JBBRAS* (new series), vol. XXII, 1946, p. 38.

———, *The Culture and Civilisation of Ancient India in Historical Outline*, Delhi, 1972.

———, *An Introduction to the Study of Indian History*, Bombay, 1975.

Krishnamachariar, M., *History of Classical Sanskrit Literature,* 3rd edn., Delhi, 1974.

Lal, B.B. and Gupta, S.P. (ed.), *Frontiers of the Indus Civilization,* Delhi, 1984.

Lassen, Chr., *Indische Alterthumskunde* (A German Work on the History and Antiquities of India), 4 vols, 1st edn., Leipzig, 1847-62, vols. I &II, 2nd edn., Leipzig, 1867-74.

Law, B.C., *India as Described in Early Texts of Buddhism and Jainism*, Delhi, 1980.

———, *Geography of Early Buddhism*, Vārāṇasī, 1973.

———, *Geographical Essays Relating to Ancient Geography of India*, Delhi, 1976.

———, *Kṣatriya Clans in Buddhist India*, Calcutta, 1922.

———, *Some Kṣatriya Tribes of Ancient India,* Calcutta, 1923, rept. Delhi, 1979.

———, *Ancient Mid-Indian Kṣatriya Tribes*, Calcutta, 1924.

———, *Tribes in Ancient India*, Bhandarkar Oriental Series, no. 4, Poona, 1943.

———, *Historical Geography of Ancient India*, Paris, 1954, rept. Delhi 1976.

———, *The Magadhas in Ancient India,* Vārāṇasī, 1976.

———, *A History of Pāli Literature*, 2 vols., Delhi, 1983.

———, "Countries and People of India (Epic and Paurāṇic Sources)," *ABORI*, vol. XVII, pt. III, 1936, pp. 236-41.

———, *Buddhistic Studies,* (ed.), Calcutta, 1931.

Levin, G.B., "Is Arctic the Original Home of Indians?," *Soviet Land*, nos. 12-13, June-July, 1968.

Levi, S., *E'tude Asiatique*, II, Paris, 1925.

Luckenbill, D.D. (ed.), *Ancient Records of Assyria and Babylon,* vol. I, New York, 1927.

Lund, S.R. and Pyasa, O.P., "Hindus in Afghanistan," in *Vivekanand Kendra Patrikā*, Madras, II, 1, 1973, p. 256.

Macdonell, A.A., and Keith, A.B., *Vedic Index of Names and Subjects*, 2 vols., 1st edn., London, 1912, rept. 3rd edn., Indian Texts Series, Delhi, 1967.

Magadh, K.N.P., *Vāgdevi Sarasvati*, Allahabad, 1995.

Majumdar, A.K., *Early Hindu India: A Dynastic Study*, 3 vols., Dhaka, 1917, rept. Delhi, 1981.

Majumdar, R.C. (ed.), *The Vedic Age*, Bombay, 1965.

———, *Ancient Indian Colonies in the Far East*, vol. II, *Suvarṇadvīpa*, Part I, Dhaka, 1936.

Martin, M.V. de St., *E'tude Sur La Geographic Grecque et Latine de l'Inde* (Geography of India as derived from the Greek and Latin Sources), Paris, 1858.

Martin, R.M., *The History of the Indian Empire*, vol. I, Delhi, 1983.

Masson-Oursel, P.&C., *Ancient India and Indian Civilization,* trans. from the French by M.R. Dobie, London, 1934, rept., 1951.

Maurice, Thomas, *Indian Antiquities or Dissertations of Hindostan*, vol. I, London, 1806, rept. Delhi, 1984.

Max Müller, F., *A History of Ancient Sanskrit Literature*, 1st edn., London, 1859, revd. and ed. by S.N. Śāstrī, Vārāṇasī, 1968.

———, *The Vedas* (collections of his lectures and writings pub. in his various works), Vārāṇasī, 1969.

———, *India — What Can it teach Us?*, London, 1899.

———, *Lectures on the Science of Language*, 2 vols., London, 1862-64.

———, *Chips from a German Workshop*, vol. I, London, 1868.

———, *Biographies of Words and the Home of the Aryas*, London, 1887, rept., 1912, new impression, Patna, 1985.

May, R. Le, *The Culture of South-East Asia*, London, 1964.

Mishra, D.P., *Studies in the Proto-History of India*, Delhi, 1971.

Misra, V.N., "Lost Saraswati: The Cradle of Harappan Civilization," *Manthan*, JDRI, XV-4-XVI-1, 1994-95, pp. 98-116.

Motichandra, *Sārthavāha*, Patna, 1966.

———, *Geographical and Economic Studies in the Mahābhārata*, Lucknow, 1945.

Muir, J., *Original Sanskrit Texts on the Origin and Hitory of the People of India, their Religion and Institutions*, vol. II, 2nd edn. London, 1871.

Munshi, K.M., *The Glory that was Gurjaradeśa*, Bombay, 1943.

Nadirshah, J.D., "Aryana Vaejo, the Cradle of the Aryans," *Proceedings and Transactions of the First Oriental Congress*, 1920, pp. 84-94.

Nath, P., *A Study of the Economic Conditions of Ancient India*, London, 1929.

Pandey, R.B., "The Purāṇic data on the Original Home of the Indo-Aryans," *IHQ*, 1948, pp. 94-103.

Pargiter, F.E., *Ancient Indian Historical Tradition*, London, 1922, rept. Delhi, 1972.

———, "Ancient Countries in Eastern India," *JASB*, LXVI, I, 1897, pp. 104-61.

———, "The Nations of India at the Battle between the Pāṇḍavas and Kauravas," *JRAS*, 1908, pp. 334 ff.

Parpola, A., "The Coming of the Aryans to Iran and India and the Cultural and ethnic identity of the Dasas," *Studia Orientalia*, Helsinki, vol. 64, 1988, pp. 208-15.

Pathi, J., "Is Indo-Aryan Invasion a Myth?," *IHQ*, 1928, pp. 678-94.

Penka, K., *Origines Ariacae,* Wien, 1883.

Phulchandra, *Varṇa, Jāti aur Dharma*, Kāśī, 1963.

Piggott, S. (ed.), *The Dawn of Civilization*, London, 1961.

———, *Prehistoric India*, Harmondsworth, 1950.

Poliakov, L., *The Aryan Myth: A History of Racist and Nationalist Ideas in Europe* (Eng. trans. from Russian by Chatto-Heinemann, New York, 1974.

Pradhan, S.N., *Chronology of Ancient India*, Vārāṇasī, 1979.

Prakash, Buddha, *Rigveda and the Indus Civilization*, Hoshiarpur, 1966.

Puri, B.N., *India in the time of Patañjali*, Bombay, 1968.

———, *India as described by Early Greek Writers*, Vārāṇasī, 1971.

Pusalker, A.D., "Aryan Expansion in India," *Purāṇa*, vol. 6, no. 2, pp. 307-32.

———, "Aryan Settlements in India," in the *Vedic Age*, ed. by R.C. Majumdar (*supra*), pp. 245-55.

Ragozin, Z.A., *History of Vedic India*, London, 1895, rept. Delhi, 1984.

Rai, R.K., *Vālmīki-Rāmāyaṇa Kośa* (Descriptive Index to the Names and Subjects of *Rāmāyaṇa*), Vārāṇasī, 1965.

———, *Mahābhārata Kośa* (A Descriptive Index to the Names and Subjects in the *Mahābhārata*), Vārāṇasī, 1982.

Rajaram, N.S., *Aryan Invasion of India: The Myth and the Truth*, Delhi, 1993.

———, *The Politics of History: Aryan Invasion Theory and the Subversion of Scholarship*, Delhi, 1995.

Rajaram, N.S. and Frawley, D., *Vedic Aryans and the Origins of Civilization: A Literary and Scientific Perspective*, Delhi, 1997.

Raman, A.K., *Āryataraṅginī — The Saga of the Indo-Aryans*, Bombay, 1969.

Raman, S.K., "Sarasvati River: Historic Legacy and Developmental Challenge," *Itihāsa Darpan*, IV, 2, 1998, pp. 37-50.

Rapson, E.J. (ed.), *The Cambridge History of India*, vol. I, *Ancient India*, Cambridge, 1922, rept. Delhi, 1962.

———, *Ancient India from the Earliest Times to the first century AD*, Cambridge, 1914, rept., Vārāṇasī, 1981.

Rawlinson, H.G., *Bactria from the Earliest Times to the Extinction of Bactrio-Greek Rule in the Punjab*, Delhi, 1978.

Ray, H.C., *The Dynastic History of Northern India*, vol. I, Calcutta, 1931.

Raychaudhuri, H.C., *Political History of Ancient India*, 6th edn., Calcutta, 1953.

Renfrew, Collin, *Archaeology and Language: The Puzzle of Indo-European Origins*, New York, 1990.

Rennell, J., *The Geographical System of Herodotus*, 2nd revd. edn., London, 1830.

Renou, L., *Vedic India*, trans. from the French by Philip Spratt, *Classical India*, vol. III, Vārāṇasī, 1971.

Renu, L.N., *Indian Ancestors of Vedic Aryans*, Bombay, 1994.

Reu, V.N., *R̥gveda Par Ek Aitihāsik Dr̥ṣṭi*, Delhi, 1967.

Rhys Davids, Mrs. C.A.F., "Economic Conditions According to Early Buddhist Literature," in *CHI*, vol. I, *Ancient India*, ed. by E.J. Rapson (*supra*), pp. 176-96

———, "Notes on Early Economic Conditions in Northern India," *JRAS*, Octob. 1901, pp. 863-72.

Rhys Davids, T.W., *Buddhist India*, Delhi, 1971.

Roberston, W., *An Historical Disquisition Concerning Ancient India*, Edinburgh, 1818, rept. Delhi, 1981.

Rockhill, W.W., *The Life of the Buddha*, London, 1907.

Sāṁkṛtya, R.D., *Ādi Mānava Kā Ādi Deśa*, Churu, vs 2021.

Sampurnananda, *Āryoṅ Kā Ādi Deśa*, 4th edn., Allahabad, vs 2022.

Sankalia, H.D., *Prehistory and Protohistory of India and Pakistan*, Poona, 1974.

———, *Prehistory of India*, Delhi, 1977.

———, *Akhaṇḍa Bhārata Mein Saṁskṛti Kā Uṣāḥ Kāla,* Vārāṇasī, 1981.

———, "Traditional Indian Chronology and C-14 dated of Excavated sites," *JIH*, vol. 42, 1964, pp. 635-50.

———, "Radio Carbon Dates in India, their Consistency and Cultural implications," in *Radio Carbon and Indian Archaeology*, ed. D.P. Agrawal and A. Ghosh, Bombay, 1973, p. 219.

Sāṅkṛtyāyana, R., *Pāli Sāhitya Kā Itihāsa*, Lucknow, 1973.

———, *Ṛgvedic Āryans*, Allahabad, 1957.

———, *Purātattva Nibandhāvalī*, Allahabad, 1939.

Sarma, D. (ed.), *Kāmarūpa Śāsanāvalī* (trans. by P.D. Choudhury, R.K. Deva Sarma and D. Sarma), Gauhati, 1981.

Śāstrī, A.M., *India as Seen in the Bṛhat Saṁhitā of Varāhamihira*, Vārāṇasī, 1969.

Śāstrī, N.C., *Ādi Purāṇa mein Pratipādita Bhārata*, Vārāṇasī, 1968.

Śāstri, S.S., "India, the Original Home of the Aryans," in *The Vedic Age*, ed. R.C. Majumdar (*supra*), App. pp. 220-21.

Sayce, A.H., *Introduction to the Science of Language*, vol. II, London, 1883.

———, *Principles of Comparative Philology,* London, 1892.

———, "The Aryan Problem Fifty — Years later," *Antiquity,* I, 1927, pp. 204-15.

Schrader, O., *Prehistoric Antiquities of the Aryan Peoples: A Manual of Comparative Philology and the Earliest Culture* (Eng. trans. of the 2nd edn. of original German Work), London, 1890.

Schwartzberg, J.E. (ed.), *Hisorical Atlas of South Asia*, Chicago, 1978.

Sen, Umapada, *The Rigvedic Era (3500-2000 BC)*, Calcutta, 1974.

Shafer, R., *Ethnography of Ancient India*, Wiesbaden, 1954.

Shaffer, J.G., "Indo-Aryan Invasions: Cultural Myth and Archaeological Reality," in *The People of South Asia: The Biological Anthropology of India, Pakistan and Nepal*, ed. J.R. Lukacs, New York, 1984, p. 88.

Sharma, R.P., *Paurāṇic Kośa*, Vārāṇasī, vs 2028.

Sharma, R.S., *Śūdras in Ancient India*, Delhi, 1958.

———, "Problems of Social Formations in Early India," General President's Address, Indian History Congress, 36th Session, Aligarh, 1975.

———, "Class Formation and its material basis in the uppper Gangetic basin (*c*. 1000-500 BC)," *IHR*, II, 1, 1975, pp. 1-13.

———, *Material Cultural and Social Formations in Ancient India*, Delhi, 1983.

Singh, G.P., *The Kirātas in Ancient India: A Historical Study of their Life, Culture and Civilization*, Delhi, 1990.

——, *Early Indian Historical Tradition and Archaeology,* Delhi, 1994.

——, "The Colonial and Cultural Expansion of the Aryans Outside India as Gleaned from the Vedic Literature," *Journal of the Deptt. of History,* Manipur University, Imphal, vol. II, 1987, pp. 17-30.

——, "The Concepts of Varṇa and Jāti in the Jain and Buddhist Traditions," *Adhyayan*, JBIAS, vol. VII, nos. 1 & 2, 1997, pp. 45-57.

——, "An Analytical and Critical study of the Classical Accounts of Foreign Expeditions of North-Western India before the time of Cyrus (BC 558-530) of Persia," *Research Journal (Humanities and Social Sciences)*, Manipur University, Imphal, vol. IV, no. 1, 1987, pp. 1-8.

——, "Trade and commerce in Ancient India in the light of Jain and Buddhist Traditions bearing on its economic and cultural contacts with the Asian countries," *Studies in History and Culture*, (Journal of the PG. Deptt. of History, Berhampur University Orissa), vol. 4, no. 1, 1996, pp. 1-13.

Singh, M.R., *A Critical Study of the Geographical Data in the Early Purāṇas*, Calcutta, 1972.

Sircar, D.C., *Studies in the Geography of Ancient and Medieval India*, Delhi, 1971.

——, *Studeis in the Society and Administration of Ancient and Medieval India*, vol. I, Calcutta, 1967.

——, *Studies in the Religious Life of Ancient and Medieval India*, Delhi, 1971.

Smith, V.A., *The Early History of India from 600 BC to the Muhammadan Conquest*, revd. by S.M. Edwards, 4th edn., London, 1967.

Srivastava, K.M., "The Myth of Aryan Invasion of Harappan Towns," in *Frontiers of the Indus Civilization*, ed. B.B. Lal and S.P. Gupta (*supra*), pp. 437-42.

Stein, M.A., *Archaeological Reconnaissances in North-Western India and South-Eastern Iran*, London, 1937.

——, "On Some River Names in the Rigveda," *JRAS*, 1917, pp. 91-99.

——, "The Indo-Iranian Borderlands: their prehistory in the light of geography and of recent explorations," *JRAI*, vol. LXIV, 1934, pp. 179-202.

——, "A Survey of Ancient Sites along the lost Sarasvati River," *Geog. Jour*, XCIX, 4, 1942, pp. 173-82.

Swarup, D., "Genesis of the Aryan Race Theory and its Application to Indian History," *Manthan*, JDRI, XV, 2-3, 1994, pp. 101-18.

Synder, L.B., *The Idea of Nationalism: Its Meaning and History,* Van Nostrand (USA), 1962.

Talagerri, S.G., *The Aryan Invasion Theory: A Reappraisal*, Delhi, 1993.

——, *Aryan Invasion Theory and Indian Nationalism,* Delhi, 1993.

Taylor, I., *The Origin of the Aryans — An Account of the Prehistoric Ethnology and Civilisation of Europe*, London, 1890, rept., Delhi, 1988.

Taylor, J., "Remarks on the sequel to the Periplus of the Erythrean sea and on the country of the Seres as described by Ammianus Marcellinus," *JASB*, vol. XVI, pt. I, 1847, pp. 29-30.

Thapar, R., *A History of India*, vol. I, Penguin Books, Baltimore, 1966.

——, *The Past and Prejudice,* Delhi, 1975.

——, *Ancient Indian Social History,* Hyderabad, 1984.

——, *From Lineage to State: Social Formations in the mid-first Millennium BC in the Gaṅgā Valley*, Bombay, 1984.

———, "Which of us are Aryans," *Seminar*, Delhi, no. 364, Dec. 1989, pp. 14-18.

———, "The Perennial Aryans," *Seminar*, 400, 12, 1992, p. 22.

———, "The Theory of Aryan Race and India: History and Politics," *Social Scientist*, XXIV, 1-3, 1996, pp. 3-29.

Thomas, E.J., "The So-called Indo-Aryan Invasion," *IHQ*, 1929, pp. 248-53.

Thomas, P., *Indian Women Through the Ages*, London, 1954.

Tilak, B.G., *The Arctic Home in the Vedas*, Poona, 1903, rept. 1925.

———, *The Orion: Researches into the Antiquity of the Vedas*, Bombay, 1893, rept. Poona, 1989.

Tripathi, R.S., *History of Ancient India*, Delhi, 1985.

Trotter, L.J and Hutton, W.H., *History of India from the Earliest Times to the Present Day*, Delhi, 1975.

Tylor, E.B., *An Introducation to the Study of Man . . .*, London, 1881.

Upādhyāya, N.M., "Kauṭilya on Social Legislation," *JIH*, LVI, II, 1978, p. 237.

Vasu, N.N., *Social History of Kāmarūpa*, vol. I, Calcutta, 1922.

Vaidya, C.V., "Aryan Invasion of India — not a myth," *IHQ*, 1929, pp. 253-60.

Vogel, J., *Catalogue of the Mathura Museum*, Allahabad, 1910.

Wagle, N., *Society in the time of the Buddha*, Bombay, 1966.

Wales, H.G.Q., *The Making of Greater India: A Study in South-East Asian Cultural Change*, London, 1951.

———, "Archaeological Researches on Ancient Indian Colonization in Malaya," *JRASMB*, vol. XXVIII, 1940, pp. 5-40.

Waradpande, N.R., *The Aryan Invasion: A Myth*, Nagpur, 1989.

Weber, A., *History of Indian Literature*, Eng. trans. from the second German edn. by J. Mann and Th. Zachariae, London, 1882, rept. Delhi, 1981.

Weber, Max, *Religion of India: The Sociology of Hinduism and Buddhism,* New York, 1968.

Wheeler, J.T., *India from the Earliest Ages (Hindu, Buddhist and Brahmanical Revival)*, vol. III of *The History of India*, Delhi, 1973.

Wheeler, M., *Early India and Pakistan to Ashoka*, revd. edn., London, 1968.

———, *Civilization of the Indus Valley and Beyond*, London, 1966.

———, *The Indus Civilization*, Cambridge, 1968.

———, "Archaeology and the Transmission of Ideas," *Antiquity,* vol. XXVI, 1952, pp. 180-92.

———, "Ancient India: The Civilization of a Subcontinent," in *The Dawn of Civilization*, ed. S. Piggott, London, 1961, p. 249.

Wilson. H.H., *Ariana Antiqua: A Descriptive Account of the Antiquities and Coins of Afghanistan*, London, 1841, rept. Delhi, 1971.

Wilson, J., *India Three Thousand Years Ago: The Social State of the Aryas on the banks of the Indus in the Times of the Vedas*, Bombay, 1858.

Williams, H.S. (ed.), *The Historians' History of the World (A Comprehensive Narrative of the Rise and Development of Nations as Recorded by the Great Writers of all Ages)*, vol. I, Oxford 1907.

Woolner, A.C., "The Rigveda and the Punjab," *BSOAS*, vol. VI, pp. 549-54.

Journals and Periodicals

Annals of the Bhandarkar Oriental Research Institute, Poona.

Antiquity — A Quarterly Review of Archaeology, Cambridge.

Asiatic Researches.

Bulletin of the School of Oriental and African Studies, London.

The East and the West, Calcutta.

Epigraphia Indica, Delhi.

Geographical Journal, London.

Indian Culture — Journal of the Indian Research Institute, Calcutta.

Indian Historical Quarterly, Calcutta, new reprint, Delhi.

Indian Historical Review, Journal of the Indian Council of Historical Research, Delhi.

Indian Antiquary, Journal of Oriental Research, Bombay.

Itihāsa Darpan (Research Journal of History), Delhi.

Journal of the American Oriental Society.

Journal of the Asiatic Society of Bengal, Calcutta.

Journal Asiatique, Paris.

Journal of the Assam Research Society, Gauhati.

Journal of the Bhāratiya Itihāsa Adhyayan Saṁsthān, Allahabad.

Journal of the Bihar and Orissa Research Society, Patna.

Journal of the Bombay Branch of the Royal Asiatic Society, Bombay.

Journal of Deendayal Research Institute, Delhi.

Journal of the Ganganath Jha Research Institute, Allahabad.

Journal of the Greater India Society, Calcutta.

Journal of Indian History, Trivandrum.

Journal of the Indian Society of Oriental Art, Calcutta.

Journal of Oriental Research, Madras.

Journal and Proceedings of the Asiatic Society of Bengal, Calcutta.

Journal of the Royal Anthropological Institute of Great Britain and Ireland, London.

Journal of the Royal Asiatic Society of Great Britain and Ireland, London.

Journal of the Royal Asiatic Society, Malayan Branch, Singapore.

Journal of the Royal Geographical Society, London.

Memoirs of the Archaeological Survey of India, Calcutta.

Nāgarī Pracāriṇī Patrikā, Kāśī.

Purāṇa, Half-Yearly Bulletin of the Purāṇa Department, All India Kāśīrāj Trust, Rāmnagar, Vārāṇasī.

Quarterly Review of Historical Studies, Calcutta.

Science Age.

Seminar (monthly), Delhi.

Social Scientist, New Delhi.

Vivekananda Kendra Patrikā, Madras.

Proceedings and Report

Proceedings of the Asiatic Society of Bengal, Calcutta.

Proceedings of the Indian Oriental Conferences.

Proceedings of the International Oriental Congress.

A Quest After the Lost Vedic Sarasvati River — An Expedition Report, trans. into Eng. by V. Dhundiraj Bapat and K.R. Umapathy from Original in Marathi by L.S. Wakankar and C.N. Parchure, Mysore, 1994.

Dictionaries, Encyclopaedia and Gazetteer

Dictionary of Pāli Proper Names, by G.P. Malalasekera, 2 vols., London, 1937-38, rept. Delhi, 1983.

Encyclopaedia Britannica.

Geographical Dictionary of Ancient and Medieval India, by N.L. Dey, Delhi, 1971.

The Imperial Gazetteer of India.

Index

Index

Indo-Aryans, 7, 18-19, 22
Indo-Iranians, 8, 16-17
Indo-European Family of Languages, 4, 7, 11, 18
Indus-Sarasvati Civilization, 26